"All his life he tried to be a good person.
Many times, however, he failed.
For after all, he was only human. He wasn't a dog."

—Charles M. Schulz

Under the Apple Tree
As Time Goes By

As Time Goes By

RUTH LOGAN HERNE

Whistle Stop Café Mysteries is a trademark of Guideposts.

Published by Guideposts Books & Inspirational Media
100 Reserve Road, Suite E200
Danbury, CT 06810
Guideposts.org

Cover and interior design by Müllerhaus
Cover illustration by Greg Copeland at Illustration Online LLC.
Typeset by Aptara, Inc.

ISBN 978-1-959634-12-6 (hardcover)
ISBN 978-1-959634-15-7 (epub)
ISBN 978-1-959634-17-1 (epdf)

Printed and bound in the United States of America
10 9 8 7 6 5 4 3 2 1

AS TIME
GOES BY

Dennison, Ohio
September 1947

The walk seemed longer than usual today.

Buddy plodded down the short gravel path. He'd gotten used to the feel of the little stones a long time ago. It was different from the main roads. More normal for a dog's feet, that feel of this and that beneath thick paw pads, but the pads weren't so thick anymore. Not as resilient. They cracked sometimes. Used to be just in the cold, but now it was in the heat too, and still he walked.

It's what he did then and what he'd do now. That was all there was to it.

He turned the corner and then turned again onto the main road a few blocks away.

It wasn't busy this early. Busier than it used to be. But not too bad.

He didn't look forward. He kept his gaze trained down, at the road. Step by step, section by section. Looking forward made it seem too long, so he'd stopped looking forward awhile back, when the trees were still bare.

They weren't bare now.

They were leafy and shady and nice, and when the wind blew through them, he'd lift his snout and breathe deep, just like he used to when The Boy was home. But The Boy had been gone a long time. Most all the boys had been gone, but some had come back.

They'd come back different, yes.

But they'd come back.

They smelled pretty much the same—boys were like that—but even with his eyesight fading a bit—just a bit—he read the lost look in some eyes. The shadows behind the smiles.

He smiled when they smiled at him as he hung out at the station. Folks thought that was funny, a smiling dog, hanging around the depot day after day. He smiled on purpose because it made them happy. He liked making people happy. It was what he did. What he'd always done.

He wagged his tail and smiled at the folks around him. The ones who threw him scraps and the ones who stopped to offer a nice scratch behind the ears. He smiled at the ones who didn't quite dare touch a dog, even if they wanted to. He understood their hesitancy. It was like that in some people. Some dogs too.

Not him.

The blast of a train whistle broke the morning quiet.

His ears perked of their own accord. His pace picked up, but when he heard the rumbling of the wheels, he knew the train was coming the wrong way.

The Boy had gone toward the rising sun. That meant he'd come back from the rising sun, and so, each day, Buddy made his way to the station, looking and waiting for the right train to come. The right soldier to step off. The right hand to reach for his head to give him a rub in just the right spot.

And each day he went home alone.

Slower now. The days seemed longer than they'd been before. And the walks harder. The nights colder. Some days it seemed like he heard The Boy's voice, calling him, laughing with him.

But he'd wake up from the sound and realize it was just a dream.

He'd stretch. He'd yawn. And then he'd go to sleep again, wishing for the one thing he couldn't have.

The kind touch of The Boy's hand just one more time.

CHAPTER ONE

Dirt flew into the air as Janet Shaw pulled her car up to the curb to drop off some much-needed baking supplies for the café's commemorative "Lassies for Love" doughnut day.

Back in the 1940s, Salvation Army volunteers created delicious fried doughnuts drizzled with glaze or dusted with sugar to treat the troops going off to war. Their contributions of time and talent had put Dennison, Ohio, on the map during a rough time, and this year she and her business partner and best friend, Debbie Albright, planned to celebrate that effort on the Fourth of July, which also happened to be her birthday.

In five days!

There was so much to do, but as she exited the car, she saw that their resident pooch had digging on his mind.

The fine loamy soil flew up, across, sideways, and even forward somehow, possibly defying laws of physics.

Crosby...at it again.

She spotted the soil-based storm just as Debbie dashed out the back door of the Whistle Stop Café. Some might call her friend's plunge into a whole new life as a café owner a midlife crisis.

Not Janet.

She preferred to think of their new partnership as an absolute blessing.

A blessing replete with a digging dog, flying dirt, and doughnuts.

"Hey, pup!" Debbie scolded. "We can't have miniature potholes tripping people every time they come this way. The insurance company is going to hike our rates due to hazardous conditions."

Crosby sat back, delighted with her attention and clearly proud of his efforts.

"Don't play innocent with me or even pretend you're following orders, because I know for a fact that you and Janet reached an agreement just a few days ago," she went on as Janet approached. "You, sir, are breaching that contract."

"Technically, he's not." Janet dusted her hands on her navy blue capris. They went well with her patriotic T-shirt, fitting for the coming holiday week. "Our agreement was of a more geographic variety," she explained. "He's close enough to the prescribed area to be on the right side of the border clause. Smart dog."

Debbie rolled her eyes. "It was more of the location, location, location-type contract, I presume?"

"Exactly." Janet opened the back door of her car, where the supplies sat. "I figured old habits die hard, and he and Harry are pretty set in their ways—"

"A ninety-plus-year-old retired conductor and a seven-year-old dog."

Janet nodded. "Yes. So I gave Crosby explicit instructions to dig here. Not out front or on the side. I figured there's not much he can hurt over here under the tree. It's just enough off the beaten path."

"We got us some trouble, ladies?" Harry Franklin interrupted them. The elderly railroad man came their way from the side of the restored vintage depot. "My boy's a digger, sure enough, and I probably should have made him toe the line way back when, but nobody much cared about his digging before this place got so busy."

Janet reassured him quickly. "He's fine, Harry. I was just explaining to Debbie that Crosby and I renegotiated terms of use, and he's agreed to keep the majority of his digging on this side of the depot."

"A shady spot and a soft turn of earth, the stuff a dog's dreams are made of." Approval laced the old man's voice. "I sure am grateful you ladies don't mind a pair of old-timers hangin' around."

"Mind it?" Debbie crossed over and looped her arm through his. "Harry Franklin, you and Crosby are always welcome here."

The elderly Black gentleman grinned at her. He'd lost some teeth along the way and he walked much slower these days, but Harry Franklin did all right for being a few years shy of a hundred. And he remembered more than most people forgot in a lifetime.

"Coffee, Harry?" asked Debbie. "And maybe some toast and eggs for our two favorite customers?"

Gracious as ever, Harry dipped his chin slightly. "We'd be most obliged, thank you."

He followed her inside.

Crosby started after them then paused. He gave the café a searching look. Almost longing.

But then he did a quick whirl-around and headed right back to the base of the tree. That oak had seemed old when Janet was a little girl. If it had survived all these years, a spot of digging here and there shouldn't disturb much. The thick roots were no longer completely buried. They pressed up, out of the earth, before stretching downward again.

She took a breath and gazed around, content. Content for the first time in a long time. She'd enjoyed working at the Third Street Bakery over in Uhrichsville for nearly twenty years. The Whipple family had been good to her and her family. And Charla Whipple had taught her so much. Janet had become the protégé, entrusted with many tricks of the trade, but the Whipples were retiring. The bakery was closing. So when Debbie had broached the idea of opening a café and bakery right here in the historic depot, Janet saw it as perfect timing. Her daughter would be leaving for her freshman year at Case Western Reserve University in Cleveland in less than two months. Tiffany was a delightful young woman and a wonderful student, and—

Her only child.

Knowing she was moving away had opened a hole in Janet's chest.

Focusing on this new venture with her best friend was a good way to suture that gap. Was it a coincidence to have it all fall into place like that? Or God's perfect timing? Janet sided with the latter, and she was grateful for it.

She turned to gather her purchases as dirt began flying again.

Then she paused when she heard a different sound.

The dog pummeled the soil like a champ, something he did at least twice a day, but this time was different. Sounded different. Instead of the steady drum of Crosby's paws and the rain-down of rich topsoil against the tree, there was a new noise. Metallic and dull.

She edged in. "Crosby. Stop."

He looked puzzled and a trifle indignant, but she didn't blame him. She was messing with their agreed-upon contract. "What have you found, fella?"

He wagged his tail, now clearly pleased that she'd noticed his success.

She bent toward the hole. Something rusty and dirty lay beneath Crosby's excavating efforts. "What is this, boy?"

She reached in. Whatever it was wouldn't budge, and she couldn't pry it loose. On top of that, a good cook didn't work a busy public kitchen with dirt-stained hands. She stood up and crossed to the maintenance shed just up the tracks. There were a few tools in there, including gardening gloves and a small trowel for replacing the annual flowers they had put in pots and borders around the vintage building.

She donned the gloves and grabbed the trowel.

Crosby seemed unperturbed by her intrusion into his find. He sat back on his haunches and watched as she dug a narrow band around the item.

The dog crooned softly. Urging her on? Or just offering approval?

The trowel caught an edge. She gave it an extra thrust then pushed the handle down, using the small spade as a lever.

The hole was deep enough that the dark, moist soil and thick shade made it hard to see inside.

The maneuver eventually worked, and the edge of the item lifted up. With a few more twists and turns, she was able to lift it out, tilting it to squeeze through the gaps made by the thick, branching roots.

It was a rectangular can of some sort, an old tin, like a metal cigar box. It slid up and out of the hole, dirty and rusted, a real mess.

She gave it a gentle shake. Nothing much moved, but it contained something. The weight indicated that.

Crosby leaned forward.

"It's your find, boy. I'm not claiming it," she assured him. "But I *am* going to wipe it down before I pry off the lid to see what's in it."

The dog seemed okay with that decision. When she stood, he reexamined the hole as if to make sure she'd done a good job. Content with her efforts, he yawned, moved aside, and did a three-circle spin before collapsing on a patch of soft green grass for his first morning nap.

She retrieved the bags from her back seat, carried everything inside, and, after putting the bags on the counter, moved to the service sink. Using wet paper towels, she washed down the top, bottom, and sides of the container, gradually revealing a vintage candy tin decorated with flowers painted to look like needlework. The name of the company started with an *S*, but that was about all she could make out.

"What's this? Buried treasure?" Debbie kept watch on the eggs while spreading soft butter—never margarine—on three pieces of white toast. Two for Harry. One for Crosby. The funny dog enjoyed his one-egg-on-toast morning meal on a regular basis.

"Buried, anyway. I'm not holding out hope for treasure," replied Janet as Harry leaned in to peek over the counter. "Crosby unearthed it. Well"—she made a face—"I helped. Let's dry it off…"

"And wedge it open?" suggested Debbie. "Away from your cooling cakes, of course."

"Far away," agreed Janet. She spread a dish towel on the counter and set the box on top. After applying a sturdy butter knife, she was able to loosen the top.

Miniscule debris sprinkled onto the towel as the lid came loose. It wasn't an easy process. When one side inched up, the other pitched down, but then, with one final nudge, the rusted old cover came free.

Harry reached over to lift it off.

A cluster of medals sat inside, nestled in a worn clutch of red velvet. The velvet was bunched around each one, creating individual pockets.

"That's why it didn't rattle when I shook it," Janet said. "I don't know what all these are, but I recognize that one right off." She pointed to the upper left corner.

"A Purple Heart." Harry's voice cracked. He stared at the medals. "I've seen more than a few of those in my time," he said. "Some for boys who came back. Some who didn't. But I've never seen a collection of medals like this."

"All one person?" Janet wondered aloud.

Harry frowned. "I don't know anyone who gathered brass like that."

"Stolen?" asked Debbie, but then she dismissed that idea. "If they were stolen, wouldn't the thief have returned for them at some time?"

"You'd think so. But maybe they couldn't," Janet said. "Maybe they got put in jail for something else and couldn't get back here and these medals have been hidden away for all these years. And if that's the case…" She straightened her shoulders and lifted her gaze. "There's only one thing we can do."

Debbie nodded understanding. She knew Janet's family history. "Find the rightful owners. But how?"

Harry shook his head. "I can't rightly say. I know there were plenty of medals given out during the war. A righteous number, well deserved, but how do you find out who each one belongs to in a box of eleven? No, twelve," he corrected himself as he pointed out a much smaller lapel pin that had fallen into the corner between the velvet and the box. "It's not like they're marked or anything. How do we do this?"

Debbie drew a deep breath and exchanged a look with Janet. Janet's great-grandfather had served in World War II. Her grandfather and two great-uncles had served in Korea. Grandpa had been the only one to come home, and he'd spent a lifetime missing his two little brothers, so Janet knew exactly what they needed to do. She smiled at Debbie then faced the thoughtful man who'd grown old doing so much for so many. "Harry, my friend, we do whatever it takes."

CHAPTER TWO

T he bell above the front door jangled.

Janet slipped the vintage can off the counter, but there wasn't much that got past local attorney Patricia Franklin. Harry's lovely and accomplished granddaughter arched a sculpted brow that said plenty without uttering a word. Then she noted Janet's tucked hands with a glance. "Something I'm not supposed to see?"

"Something I didn't want random strangers seeing," whispered Janet. The back door was open, and voices tended to carry in the early morning quiet. She wasn't ready to have everyone know what they'd discovered. Not yet. But Patricia was different. She knew how to keep things quiet. "Crosby just unearthed this," she said in a more normal voice, and brought the rusty box into sight again.

"Wow." Patricia gazed at the medals then her great-grandfather before moving to get a closer look. "This is a marvelous find, isn't it, Pop Pop?"

"I've never seen the like," said Harry. "That's a lot of honor to find buried under a bunch of tree roots."

"Who buries medals of honor?" asked Debbie. She slipped Harry's complimentary breakfast onto the counter then crossed to the coffee corner to make Patricia signature coffee. Patricia had started each day with a stop at the café since they opened,

As Time Goes By

purportedly for a delicious beverage and a fresh pastry, but Janet was pretty sure it was to check on her aging grandfather without appearing to check on him. Harry was a good old soul with a heart of gold, but while he loved his granddaughter, he clung to well-earned independence.

"I can't imagine it," said Harry as he cut up his eggs. "If it's been there right along, why's Crosby finding it now? He's been digging here and there for years, as naughty as that is. What drew him to it today, do you suppose? Is there a reason behind it, or did he just get lucky?"

He made a good point. Janet moved the medals to the back corner of the cooking area. Out of sight but not out of mind. "One of the advantages of being married to Dennison's chief of police is being able to pull him in on things like this," she said as she typed a short text to her husband. "I think we should keep this on the quiet side, but I'm going to have Ian come take a look. If they've been reported stolen, his office might have a record of it. Although I don't know how far back records go or what's been computerized versus really old paper trails." She turned as Debbie delivered Patricia's peppermint mocha. "Our new fryer is supposed to be delivered today."

"I saw the jugs of oil in your car," Debbie replied. "You're okay with practicing doughnut production ahead of time?"

"Yes, ma'am."

"I love that you're recreating the doughnuts the Salvation Army volunteers passed out to service men and women," said Patricia. "The romantic in me wonders just how many of those chance meetings ended up becoming love stories. You know the kind," she added as she inhaled deeply. "Hmm. Pen pals to sweethearts? And Debbie, I would love one of those bear claws to go along with my coffee. Nobody makes them like Janet does."

"They're the real deal," Harry confirmed. "Our Janet has got herself a calling when it comes to baking."

"We got the idea to do this on National Doughnut Day a few weeks ago," said Debbie. She put the bear claw into a little white wax paper bag and handed it to Patricia. "Janet used to make doughnuts for the bakery in Uhrichsville every fall. We don't have the space for a full-on operation, but we thought it would be the nostalgic touch we wanted for the café."

"I love it," Patricia declared. "The beginning of a new tradition, and nothing wrong with that. Moving forward by appreciating what's gone before is old-time wisdom in my book. I'll see you all later," she said as she moved toward the front door. "I won't say anything to anyone about the medals, but it's a puzzle, isn't it?" She posed the question as Ian came through the front door. He held it open for her and then crossed the small dining area once she'd gone through.

"Secret stash found?" He waved his phone in the air and offered Janet the cute, crooked smile he'd passed on to their daughter. "Could you be more cryptic, darlin'?"

Janet grinned. "It got you over here, didn't it?"

"Well, my office is three minutes away, and you did make lemon poppy seed cake this morning, so my presence was a given. I was planning a walkabout in any case. What've you found, lassies?"

Ian's family had immigrated to the US when he was a boy, but no one in the Shaw family had lost their Scottish burr. It was one of the first things Janet had liked about him over twenty years before, and she loved it just as much now.

Debbie brought the box of medals his way while Janet washed her hands. They'd be getting busy soon, and she had a lot of work to do before the fryer was slated to arrive. Once it did, she wanted to assemble it and get it filled and operational before she made the dough they'd use for their first practice session.

"Whoa." Ian examined the tin carefully. "This was under the big oak tree?"

Janet nodded as she measured out dry ingredients. "Crosby was digging, and I could tell he'd found something. So I checked it out, and that's what we found."

Ian let out a low, soft whistle. "This is a lot of brass. And it might be important brass. I'm no expert on World War II awards, but I've been to enough ceremonies to know we're looking at considerable recognition of effort. And the way each one is nestled in the red velvet means someone took care to tuck them away. They didn't just toss them into the can."

"Which means they cared about the medals," noted Janet.

"So why bury them?" Debbie started a fresh pot of coffee as she mused. "Did they place them carefully because they meant something, or because it keeps their monetary value intact?"

It was a good question. "Either way, someone didn't want the medals found, but now that they're here, we need to figure this out," Janet said. "Stolen or hidden, someone, somewhere, would probably like these back. The question is, how do we go about finding them?"

"I'd take a trip to chat with Winifred Gayle," Harry advised them. "For well over a decade, maybe two, that lady would come and take a seat on the bench that used to be right under that oak tree. Not doing anything much but sitting there, watching folks come and go. Eventually, the bench got unstable, falling apart, and they got rid of it. Come to think of it, they were supposed to replace it and never did. Funds got tight, I guess. But there had to be a reason for a gal like that to sit on a lonely bench several times a week, year after year."

Debbie frowned. "I've never met her."

"The Gayles kept to themselves most times. Her niece has a farm about fifteen minutes outside of town, and Winifred's been living there a few years. She's a character." Harry had finished his breakfast and sat back, smiling. "But aren't we all?"

"Can we get out there today?" asked Debbie, but Janet shook her head.

"No. By the time I put the fryer together, get it ready, and make the dough for practice round one, it'll be suppertime. And I've only got Tiffany home for seven more weeks before she heads off to college, so I'm trying to make her as many suppers as I can."

Ian put an arm around her shoulders and kissed her head. "You might as well head out to the Gayle place," he told her. "Tiffany is going to the movies with friends this afternoon and won't be home for supper. I think she's handling the idea of this bend in the road better than we are. I'm good with a couple of fried bologna sandwiches, and I promise I won't leave the frying pan in the sink."

"And we'll have taste-testing doughnuts for lunch. Glazed, right?" asked Debbie. "Because I'm already happy at the thought."

"Glazed, yes, and Ian Shaw, you know I hate it when you're right. Tiffany is understandably excited about moving on, and I've been half-dreading this day for a good year. Yet I'm so proud of her, I could burst. Still, being right and boasting about it is terribly unbecoming."

Ian laughed and gave her shoulder a little squeeze. "You live your life with laughter through tears, love, and it's a smart man who learns to go along with the ride. And I wouldn't have it any other way."

His words made everyone smile. Ian's reasonable responses to everything had gotten him appointed to chief of police years before. The town loved him. He handled things with the same calm assurance that worked with his family. He and Janet had been blessed with Tiffany, and although they'd wanted more children, that hadn't happened.

God's will.

But she'd be lying to say the thought of Tiffany leaving didn't carve an aching hole in her heart. And yet her daughter's growth and joy were the most important things of all. Besides, Cleveland was only ninety minutes away. "I'll drive treats up to her once she's gone. What freshman isn't happy to share fresh-baked goods from home?"

"We can stop at that little barbecue place when we go through Canton," Ian suggested. He moved toward the door. "A diner alongside a railroad track? Who'd have guessed that would be a Janet favorite?" he teased as he went through the door.

It was. She loved everything about the tiny diner in Canton. The setting, the service, the food. Was she really that predictable?

"I love Kennedy's too," Debbie said as two couples approached the front door. "No better barbecue around. The way I see it, Janet?" She lifted both brows and grinned. "You and I have managed to surround ourselves with things we love, and if we're lucky, we'll get to do this as long as we want. That's a pretty solid take-home right there."

Janet winked at her. "I agree 100 percent. And there's the delivery truck pulling up outside, which means our afternoon schedule is on target, and tonight?" She broke some eggs into the big mixing bowl and hit the power button to get them properly foamed. "We meet the Gayle family."

CHAPTER THREE

Debbie held a box of twelve glazed doughnuts as Janet parked the car at Hummingbird Acres. The quaint farm came up as "open for business" on the internet, but there were no other cars on the gravel drive and none by the historic barn that was in need of TLC. The lack of fresh paint hadn't dissuaded the owner from hanging inviting signs beneath the barn's metal-roofed overhang. Once the car was parked, the friends climbed out and moved toward the twin open doors.

The house was set well away from the road. Far enough back that Janet couldn't see details, but it looked better kept than the barn.

They walked inside the barn, and Janet stopped abruptly.

The outside hadn't offered any preparation for what the sprawling structure contained. Inside the doors, the aged building was set up with booth after booth of inviting warmth. Americana. Farmhouse chic. Country. Even a booth filled with Victorian-esque home decor, complete with ruffles and frills. The worn barn housed a group of shops, situated between old stalls and the hayloft.

"I'm in love," Debbie declared. "This is adorable, and why have I never heard of it?"

"Because you've only been back in town for a few months," Janet suggested. "Although I didn't know it existed either," she admitted.

A woman about their age and a teenage girl approached them. "First time here?" the woman asked.

"First but not the last," Janet assured her. "How long has this been in business?"

"Three months. Almost," answered the girl.

The woman extended her hand. "I'm Marcy Gayle. This is our first year, and we're struggling to get the word out on social media. It seems we should have started that a year or two ago, because we're just enough off the beaten path that if you don't know about us, well"—she made a rueful face—"you don't know about us. This is my daughter, Claire. And yes, I resisted all temptation to name her Dorothy," she quipped. "Doing so would have just tempted some rogue tornado to come our way."

Janet and Debbie both laughed while Claire rolled her eyes. Janet shook Marcy's hand. "I'm Janet Shaw."

Marcy flashed a look of recognition. "The police chief's wife?"

Claire made the other obvious connection. "Tiffany's mom? She's a year ahead of me in school."

Janet nodded yes to both. "And local baker. This is my partner, Debbie Albright. We've recently opened the café and bakery at the depot. In fact, we brought you a treat. A bribe of sorts but not in a bad way."

Marcy lifted the top of the proffered box and sniffed. "Fried doughnuts?"

"We're doing a nostalgia event on the third and fourth of July at the Whistle Stop Café," Debbie explained. "Janet was practicing her skills with our new fryer."

Janet shrugged. "I like to be familiar with what I'm doing. Saves me piles of embarrassment."

Marcy laughed, and Janet was about to launch into the reason for their visit when the back door of the barn flew open and a vision burst through. Not the apparition sort, but the dressed-for-another-century sort. The woman marched forward with a take-charge attitude.

High spots of color appeared on Claire's cheeks. "Auntie."

Marcy seemed to take it all in stride. "Aunt Winnie, come and meet these women."

Winifred Gayle. The woman who liked to sit on the long-gone bench. And by her mode of dress, a woman with her own set of parameters.

"I'll not be seeing a soul today, Marceline." Winifred Gayle offered the pronouncement as she wrapped her arms around herself. When she did, the odd cape-like cloak she wore—in eighty-two-degree weather—wrapped around her too. "I'm not in my receiving clothes, and those who come unannounced are most unwelcome. See them out."

The woman's speech gave Claire time to recover. She moved closer to her great-aunt. "Auntie, we're running shops here, remember? People are supposed to drop by unannounced. To buy things. We want them to come."

"Commoners take to such avenues of life, dear. Not those committed to heightened expectation."

"I agree, Miss Gayle." Janet's respectful tone caught the older woman's attention, and she seized the moment to take a step closer. "And yet when we meet with the common, we realize we're not that dissimilar beneath the skin. 'I think the king is but a man, as I am: the violet smells to him as it doth to me.'"

"William Shakespeare," Miss Gayle said. She raised her brows as she perused Janet more closely. "The man was a sage. A playwright and poet. The world's greatest writer in the English language."

"He was a keen observer of the human condition," said Janet.

Winifred studied her. She swept Debbie a dismissive look, sniffed, and faced Janet once more. "I shall entertain speech from you as needed."

Debbie nearly choked, and it took all Janet's willpower not to laugh, but she managed. "It is my pleasure to share time with you, Miss Gayle." As she suspected, the formality of the gesture seemed to ease Winifred's reserve. "I have brought doughnuts, freshly made at the depot café."

"You work at the depot?" The mention of the train station clearly hit a nerve with Miss Gayle.

"We both do," said Janet. "We've opened a café there. We love the history of the depot. The history of the railroad. The—"

"There is nothing to love there." The cold, slow speed of the words hit the air with a solemn force.

Janet froze.

So did Debbie. For that matter, Marcy and her daughter looked pretty uncomfortable too.

"A place rife with sorrow, soaked in grief, sabotaged by separation. No. I will not speak of it, of the travesties that have gone before. I will bury those notions in every way and continue to live a life unbound by traumas of the past."

She didn't just turn and walk away. She whirled about, the cloak swirling right along with her. Then she marched her way out the way she'd come in. Quickly, firmly, and clearly angered.

Janet stared after her. "Oh my." As the door slammed shut, she turned to Marcy and Claire, dismayed. "I'm so sorry. I had no idea that would happen. I can't imagine what you must think of me."

Marcy shook her head. "It's Aunt Winnie," she told them. "My husband is her nephew. Before she came to live with us, she was alone in the world. And her grasp of reality wears thinner as the years go on. We never know if she's actually dealing with fallout from a difficult past or being rude because she thinks she's some sort of English royalty, stolen from her crib in post-war Europe."

Janet's mouth dropped open. "She believes that?"

"She's believed it for years and years, so my husband tells me," said Marcy. "But she was born in Cleveland."

"It would be fun to have a princess in the family," Claire teased. "And princess or not, can I try a doughnut? I'm starving."

Her mother handed her the box.

"We drove out here to see your aunt and ask about her relationship to the depot," Debbie said.

Marcy spread her hands. "Well, you saw how far that went."

"We did." Janet grimaced. She hated the thought that they'd upset the old woman. "We came because Harry Franklin told us how she used to come and sit on a bench there, several times a week. Just sitting and waiting."

"I don't know anything about that," Marcy said.

"So she's never mentioned it or said why she went to the depot all those times?" asked Janet.

Marcy shook her head. "That was long before my time. She lived right along the village limits for decades. Some days she preferred being considered a Uhrichsville resident. Other days she spurned that and thought of herself as a small-town girl."

"Like Uhrichsville is some sprawling metropolis?" Debbie quipped, and Marcy nodded.

"Borders matter to her. Demarcation. Lines in the sand. People knowing their place. She was a great reader and writer in her day, and it's hard to know where reality leaves off and fiction sets in. I'd come see her again," she advised them.

"I'd hate to upset her—" Janet began, but Marcy interrupted her.

"No worries on that. Her mind does a good enough job on its own. She's clearer in the morning, although I'm sure that's a hard time to get away from a bakery."

"It is." Janet and Debbie had open time in the late afternoon, but mornings were busy. "We'll see what we can do. And thank you for extending the invitation. It's greatly appreciated."

"I've found that coincidences in life are often God moments in disguise," Marcy replied.

Janet wholeheartedly agreed. "We'll look forward to coming back at some point, early in the day. You're sure it won't upset her?"

Marcy weighed that for a moment and then sighed. "It might. It might not. And it might unlock a door that's been slammed shut for a lot of years. I've found that if I let her lead the conversation, I learn more than if I pepper her with questions. Did something happen at the depot?" she asked. "Something that led you here?"

Janet decided the truth was more important than the secret. "We found a box of World War II artifacts, and we don't know why they were left at the station all this time."

"Hmm." Marcy frowned. "She was born in late 1948, so post-war, but who knows? A lot of things went on back then. I'm not a history buff, although I do love old houses and farms. But I'm curious." Her phone rang in her pocket. She excused herself to answer it, and Janet turned to Claire.

"I need four of those old glass insulators, please." She indicated a vintage glassware display close by. "The pale green ones. I'm going to use them as candleholders for an Advent wreath come December."

"Clever idea," Debbie said. "I wouldn't have thought of that, but I know I'll love it. Can we get eight instead of four, and we'll put a wreath on the café's shelf?"

"Yes, absolutely. That shade of green will be pretty against a fresh wreath." Janet wasn't a crafter by trade, but she loved doing fun things for the house, and this would be lovely. "Not enough color to mess with the purple and rose candles but old-fashioned enough to fit a house like mine."

"My mother says old houses have a certain charm," Claire said as she wrapped each insulator in white tissue. "She says a new house just *is*, while an old place has decades of stories in its walls. Although I think the most storied things we've found in the walls have been mouse skeletons and really ugly old plumbing."

Janet laughed. "You handle yourself well out here, Claire. You make it inviting to come back."

"This was my mom's dream ever since I was small." She smiled and glanced around. "I like seeing her dreams come true."

"And it's nice that you notice," said Debbie.

Claire handed Janet the bagged glass globes. "Best of luck with Auntie next time. On a good day, the stories are amazing."

"And on a bad day?"

"Even better." She grinned. "The trick is finding the line between fact and fiction. Have a nice afternoon."

"You too."

"Nice meeting you, Claire." Debbie led the way to the car and didn't say anything until they got out onto the road. Then she let out a long breath of air. "Well, that's a tilt I didn't see coming."

"Winnifred's reaction?"

"Yup." Debbie silenced the radio station and angled toward Janet. "'I will bury those notions,'" she quoted from Winnie's little speech.

"'A place rife with sorrow and soaked in grief,'" Janet repeated. "It certainly sounds like Winnie has a link to the depot. And buried notions?" She exchanged a quick look with Debbie as they came to a stop sign. "Could that be a reference to the buried box? Or do you think it's a more ethereal burial?"

"I don't know," Debbie said. "What brings a woman to a lonely bench day after day, just sitting, doing nothing? Unrequited love, maybe?"

"That's my thought as well. Let's go visit her again right after the Fourth of July. We could either go separately or get someone to watch the café for an hour or two."

"She took a shine to you. You go see her on your own, and then you can tell me all about it once you get back. I'll be honest, I'm not comfortable leaving a fledgling business in anyone else's hands when we're this new. I like knowing one of us is in charge."

"I agree. So I'll head out there next week. And, hey—" She paused dramatically.

Debbie raised a brow.

"Isn't that Greg Connor heading toward the depot with his boys?"

Janet didn't miss Debbie's quick smile or the rise of color to her cheeks.

"I told them you were making doughnuts when they stopped in for coffee this morning," Debbie said.

"I love a good test audience," Janet declared. "We've got cinnamon-sugar and glazed inside. And maybe Greg can help us roll the fryer into the shed. I don't expect anything would happen if we left it outside overnight, but why tempt fate?"

"You get the doughnuts. I'll get the fryer."

"With Greg."

Debbie rolled her eyes, but Janet noticed an uptick in her smile. An uptick she was really happy to see.

CHAPTER FOUR

*J*anet realized she wasn't doing a great job of hiding her emotions when Ian approached her a few hours later. "Wanna take a walk, lass?"

Ian often called her "lass" when she was upset, and she wasn't really upset, she was—

Janet sighed, set her book down, and looked up at him. "No."

"Ice cream shop?"

That was an actual temptation, except that usually when they went to the ice cream shop, there were at least three of them. Ian. Her. Tiffany. And whatever friends Tiffany might like to—

She had no idea where the storm of tears came from.

It engulfed her, like a winter squall. Blinding and overwhelming.

There was no reason to cry right now, for goodness' sake, but that was how squalls were. They caught a person unaware and left as quickly as they came.

"Hey. What's going on? Problems at the café? The bakery? Was someone mean to you, darlin'? Because you know that's not allowed."

She half laughed, half sobbed, and leaned her head against his chest. "I hate that she's leaving."

"Oh." He sighed too, and his arm tightened around her shoulders. "I do too. Mostly because some very sizable checks will be exiting the premises at the same time. I may miss that even more than the kid in question," he teased.

She jabbed him with her elbow. "Ian Shaw."

He laughed and pulled her close. "We gave her roots and encouraged her wings. Now that she's threatening to use those wings, it's a whole new world, isn't it?"

"It is. And I don't like it. I pretend to like it for her sake, but I keep wondering if that's all there is. I get eighteen years and then she's gone? Pretty much off on her own?"

"Well, there's laundry."

He made her smile.

"I know she can do her own," he went on, "but I hear from others that they frequently come home to do laundry and see their friends."

"Not good old Mom and Dad?"

"Not till senior year."

"Ian. You are not helping the situation." She pretended to glare at him, but he just handed her some tissues and ignored the glare. "I'm at a juncture here and don't know how to handle it."

"You already have, lass. You just don't know it. You raised her. Taught her to be independent. Taught her to be honest and have integrity and to love God. Taught her to be giving and kind. It's not the handling that's hard. It's the saying goodbye. You've never liked them, Janet. Even when we were young and had to go off to school, you hated goodbyes."

He was right. She did hate goodbyes.

"Then once it's done, you move forward like the successful, industrious woman you are and carry on. And now with a new business, a new place, a whole new career."

"You mean I bury myself in work."

He grinned. "That's a less romantic way of putting it, but yes. And once you've gotten through, you get normal again."

"I'm normal all the time," she told him. "My normal."

"Every woman is." He laughed when he said it, and then he kissed her. "They've got that new little ice cream place over by the water park. It's only open through Labor Day. I say we go mask our sorrows—"

"You're not looking all that sorrowful," she said, but she softened the scolding with a smile.

"I will when that first tuition check comes due," he promised. "Although, we raised a smart kid, so the scholarship and the Wainwright grant will help. And Grandmother's bequest."

Ian's grandmother had passed away several years before. Grandma MacIntyre had left each of her grandchildren a generous college fund. Between the scholarship that paid half of Tiffany's tuition, a renewable grant, the legacy, and their savings, Tiffany could complete her undergrad degree with few student loans. After that it was up to her.

They'd done all right.

And if Tiffany found that college wasn't her forte, they'd handle that too. Ian was right. They'd raised their daughter to be smart, curious, and frugal.

And—

Case Western was only ninety minutes away.

Ian stood and stretched out his hand.

She accepted the gesture and stood too. Then she stretched up to kiss him. "I've changed my mind."

He raised one brow.

"About ice cream."

He grinned.

"And let's take a walk with it, like we used to."

"A pair of sweethearts."

It was her turn to smile because that was exactly what they were. "Yes."

"I'll get the keys."

She didn't bother grabbing a sweater. It was eighty degrees with an expected overnight low of seventy.

But it would be dark by the time they got home, so she switched on the front porch lights. Ian teased her about it, but she'd decided a long time ago that Tiffany would never come home to a dark house. No matter what happened or where she'd been, the light would always be on. And that was a promise she meant to keep.

She texted Tiffany about what they were doing as Ian drove the car out of the driveway.

Tiffany replied with a thumbs-up.

Janet sent back a hugging emoji and put the phone away. She looked up as they approached the depot.

Someone was walking, head down, behind the building.

Moseying? Checking out the classic structure? Cutting through?

She dismissed that quickly. There was no reason to cut through when there was a perfectly good sidewalk. Unless one didn't want to be seen. The person moved cagily, head tucked, hood up—in a heat wave.

She put a hand on Ian's arm. "Ian, stop. I saw someone on the far side of the building."

God bless her sweet husband, he didn't ask questions.

He pulled into a small commercial lot on the opposite side of the street and got out. "Stay here."

She made a face as she reached for the door handle. "You can't be serious."

"Quite serious," he said. "People that lurk behind closed buildings aren't always friendly or honest."

"It's probably someone walking a dog."

"Then there's no need to worry," he replied. "I'll be right back."

Major crime wasn't a big concern in their area. It was barely a minor concern, which meant waiting in the car was silly. She climbed out and headed the other way so that Ian would cover the depot on one side and she'd come in from the other.

She'd just passed the museum doors when she heard Ian talking.

No one came her way and, after waiting a moment, she rounded the corner of the museum side of the depot.

Ian stood with his phone in hand. Behind one of the big potted flowers that flanked the old-world-style benches, something lay at his feet.

Her heart jumped.

Ian spotted her. He put up a hand, disconnected the call, and came her way. "Dead raccoon," he said. "Looks like it was real sick, so I called Tom."

Tom Baxter oversaw animal control in the area.

"He'll take care of it and sanitize the area," Ian continued. "It could be rabid."

"That's all there was?" she asked. "No person wearing a hood?"

He frowned. "I didn't see anything like that."

She'd seen a person, that much she knew. But they may have darted back the other way when Ian came around the corner. Or maybe the dead animal scared them off. "Well, it wasn't a raccoon, but I'm glad the poor thing is out of his misery."

"Me too. Tom will inform the health department."

Tom's car pulled up right then. He chatted with them briefly before getting to work.

"You still good for ice cream?" asked Ian as they walked to the car. "I know it's never fun to see an animal that's passed."

"I'm glad we found it now. This spares visitors from stumbling on it in the morning."

He smiled in response. "Then let's go."

While he drove the short distance to the ice cream shop, Janet made a couple of quick notes in her phone.

One was about Winnie Gayle and her strange replies.

The other was about a figure, not too tall, slipping through the shadows behind the depot.

Whoever it was, their movement had brought attention by trying to avoid attention.

There was nothing behind the depot to steal. No money was kept on the premises. But the museum did house a solid collection of memorabilia, some of which was deemed valuable.

She didn't know why they were there, but that wasn't the question. The question was, where did that person go? A black wrought iron fence separated the depot and vintage train car display from the active side of the tracks. But if they'd crossed the broad tracks,

Ian would have noticed. And if they were behind the depot, he would have seen them.

So did they hop the fence? Duck behind one of the restored train cars?

Possibly. The vintage cars were plenty big enough to provide cover for someone. She sent Debbie a quick text. POSSIBLE RABID RACCOON BEHIND DEPOT. IT'S BEEN REMOVED. AND ODDLY ACTING PERSON ALSO BEHIND DEPOT. THEN DISAPPEARED. WHY?

Debbie texted back quickly. SOMEONE HOPING YOU LEFT DOUGH-NUTS OUTSIDE. She added a laughing emoji then got serious. ANYONE WE KNOW?

COULDN'T TELL. CHIN DOWN, HOOD UP.

IT'S SEVENTY-EIGHT DEGREES.

YEP. AND WASN'T WALKING NORMAL. SCUTTLING.

LIKE A SPIDER?

NO. JUST... FURTIVE.

YOUNG LOVE?

Janet hadn't thought of that, but the disappearing act made that seem less likely. ONLY IF WE'RE TALKING CAPULETS AND MONTAGUES. SECRET RENDEZVOUS. BUT NO ROMANTIC OVERTONES.

A few moments passed before Debbie's next text. DID YOU TAKE THE MEDALS HOME?

YES. THEY'RE IN MY SAFE.

OKAY. PROBABLY UNRELATED, BUT...

Janet understood. BETTER SAFE THAN SORRY. SEE YOU IN THE MORNING.

I'LL BE THERE.

Ian parked at the ice cream shop.

She put the phone away and met him around his side of the car. She took his hand and smiled at him. And when he smiled back, she gave his hand a squeeze. Nothing major. Just enough to tell him she was all right.

They'd been alone and just fine for six years before Tiffany was born.

They'd be just fine again.

Jackson County, Wisconsin
June 1946

Who would have guessed that a train seat would change a life?

Not Jerome Flaherty, but that was exactly what had happened the year before. He'd come home from the war with no place to go.

The lack of direction hadn't worried him. Not having a spot just meant he had limitless options. Choosing one would be tough, but then he happened to take a seat alongside Gordon Chilson on the train.

Three states and a lot of stops later, Gordon had offered him a job at his family business in central Wisconsin, and the rest was history.

Chance? Or a higher power?

Jerome went with the latter. His mama would skin him alive if she knew he'd thought anything else, and he respected his mother. She was in the deep South now, away from long, cold winters and hardscrabble soil, but winter never bothered him. It challenged him, sure. It challenged lots of folks. It was winter, after all.

But bother? No. He had food and a warm room. He was good.

He steered the giant earthmover toward the newest rise of a mammoth road project. This road would take the place of a narrow gravel trail that stretched west to Minnesota. A trail that turned to mud every spring and fall. A trail that had challenged wagons years ago and, more recently, bogged down cars in the wet months. The sharp north wind guaranteed drenching rains on both sides of winter. An asphalt road would make the link to the neighboring state sturdier, safer, and nicer.

Chilson Construction had landed the contract for this new road. It was a beaut, but as his rig crested the rise, Jerome got the first good view of the roughed-in descending grade.

It looked wrong.

Not bad in a general way, but he hadn't spent four years building roads with the corps and come away stupid.

Runoff would wreak havoc with this road in a few years' time.

He'd seen washouts along the Alaskan Highway. Some because it was built so fast. Some because not everyone saw what he saw. It wasn't hard for engineers to recognize and combat the influences of raging water. Rivers, streams, and lakes. Those were measurable tangibles. His knack was more in tune with nature. Rain and snow were a given. Depending on circumstances, runoff from them could spell calm or disaster. Everything drained eventually, but it was how moisture was shed that made a difference. He could tell from here that this project needed bigger, broader culverts, rock beds, and drains.

A few hours later he finished his assignment, parked his rig, and headed back to town.

Black River Falls was growing. Construction sounds surrounded him, but it wasn't today's sounds that spurred Jerome to find Allen Chilson, Gordon's father. It was tomorrow's potential.

Allen was just pulling up to the office in his old pickup truck when Jerome rounded the corner. "Hey, boss. A word?"

"Yeah." Allen headed his way. "You didn't break another rig did you, Flaherty? Because that's getting to be a habit out there." He grinned, and Jerome grinned back. Old equipment could break when least expected and most needed, and it seemed to happen with Jerome in the driver's seat more often than not.

"Those new machines don't break easy. That's a marvel in itself."

"Says you," Allen shot back. "What's got your face looking like you just scarfed down one of Reesie's lemon bars when she goes frugal on the sugar? Even the hounds turn their noses up at them."

Reesie was Allen's niece, the middle daughter of his brother Lyle. She flirted with Jerome shamelessly while her older sister spent way too much time reading and wouldn't give him a second look, when he'd do about anything to get Frances to look his way. Wasn't that the way of things, most times? Didn't mean he'd given up the thought of raising her chin out of those books. Just hadn't quite figured out how yet. But that was a problem for a different day. He motioned west. "Drainage on the downslope. Not enough. Ineffective. Or will be, in any case."

Allen frowned then motioned to the door. "Show me."

"Hey, Jerome." Allen's wife, Jane, ran the office and the firm. She waved to him from across the floor.

"Mrs. C." He tugged off his cap and nodded her way.

They'd tacked plans to the side wall. The Chilsons had built a business hauling dirt, sand, timber, wood, and supplies to farms, settlements, communities. Whatever folks needed. But their core business now was roads. And with the war over, roads were big business. Jerome crossed the room and pointed to the lower juncture on the engineering map. "Here."

Allen brought a hand to his chin and frowned. "You know that's all been laid out by professionals."

Jerome shrugged. "I know half of them graduated at the bottom of their class and haven't spent the last four years building roads." He'd been assigned to the Alaskan Highway project when the commander realized he'd worked for a roadbuilding crew before enlisting. He'd half froze running grade up north, but he'd learned what worked and what didn't, and he took that knowledge to Europe once the Alaskan road was complete.

"Now, I've got no way of knowing where this particular fellow stood in his class, but he should have given more thought to the angle of descent, the prevailing winds, and the swale that comes in from the right in the spring and fall. All we need is a real hard rain or a stalled storm system, and this tuck here is going to be overwhelmed. It'll swamp this section of road." He pointed to an area on the map. "The water will eat away the soil and undermine the pricey culvert you're *about to install. It'll find its way through whatever we put in its path to get to Hard Bend Creek and then on to the river. Nothing in this plan is going to hold that back when conditions combine. You get a record rainfall combined with fast snowmelt, and we're in trouble. Big trouble."*

"You can tell this by looking?" Allen didn't sound doubtful. He sounded impressed.

"Looking and working nonstop for four years," said Jerome. "I learned a lot by fixing things the Germans blew up in Europe, but some of the best learning was seeing how things were done in Germany. Hitler was evil ten ways to Sunday, but their German roads glimpsed the future. I did my share of studying and sketching. Then I brought that knowledge home."

Gordon had come in while they were talking. He overheard Jerome's last statement and came closer. "I never got to Germany."

"It was different from other parts of Europe," said Jerome. "I read some of what Eisenhower thought about their roads, and he's not wrong. The calculations of earth, wind, water, runoff, speed, and precipitation are like a dance, but it's a dance that goes off the deep end—pun intended—if it's not done right. I can run the numbers tonight, if you want to see them."

"I do, but I also want to know how a guy who never went to engineering school knows how to formulate equations for building?"

Jerome shrugged. "It's clear enough if you know what to look for. Read the signs. And work with the land, not against it. As much as you're able to, anyway."

"Allen, your daddy was like that." Mrs. C jutted her chin toward Richard Chilson's picture on the wall. "He saw the problem before folks even knew there could be one."

"Assessing all angles. Which is what the engineers are supposed to do," observed Allen in a dry tone. "It's certainly what we pay them for."

"To be fair, if they saw the trajectory now, they'd probably see what I'm seeing," Jerome replied. "A picture's worth more than words, any day. A washout that requires major road repair doesn't have to happen. And remember how I reached out to a couple of the guys I worked with in Alaska?"

They'd had that conversation a few weeks before, and Allen nodded. "They get back to you?"

"Four of them," Jerome replied. "Good men. Hard workers, and they know the equipment."

"I could use half a dozen more men to keep all the plates spinning, that's certain."

"I'll send word to them."

"And you'll work those figures for me?"

"You'll have them by morning," Jerome promised. He headed home. It was a one-room rental in a boardinghouse where Mrs. Ingerson kept a nice house and fixed a solid supper. He'd spent the extra fifty cents for a bigger room so he could work on his maps, but then she'd reduced his rent because he was handy with fixing things around the house for her.

It worked. He banked a good share of his money, she got free repairs, and he got a square meal that made him think back to when such things were scarce. Thin suppers. Pale soups. Little solid food.

They'd scraped by when he was growing up. It had been a spare existence. Then war came and changed everything. They'd all moved on. Him. His sisters. His mother. And his dog.

His heart sank, thinking about Buddy. His older sisters were all right. Not happy. Not yet, anyway, but he hoped that would change for them. Hope filled America now. It oozed from the cracks in the walls, from the seams in the streets, and rang from the belltowers of churches and the sound of ongoing construction. Not just here but everywhere. It made the cover of magazines and headlines in papers.

That was his one indulgence. He liked to read newspapers. He liked to keep his finger on the pulse of things. *Not because it sounded smart to the ladies, like Allen teased. But because a fellow could get more education out of newspapers, periodicals, and the library than any college could offer, and a man didn't need a piece of paper to prove his knowledge. Not if he had the right boss. And Jerome did.*

CHAPTER FIVE

*E*arly the next morning, a knock on the café's back door almost sent Janet out of her skin.

Darkness surrounded the historic depot, but outdoor lights kept the area bright throughout the night. Plenty light enough to feel secure in a low-crime town like theirs. And still her heart did a slam dunk in her chest that would have made a professional basketball player proud.

She hadn't locked the door. She'd never locked the door, hadn't thought of it until this moment, and right now she wished she had.

She whirled around and looked out the window. No one was there. No person. No shadow. Nothing. The area was well lit, and the black wrought iron fence wasn't an easy vault or climb, so whoever it was couldn't have gone that way. Truth be told, there was no time for anyone to run away and not be seen through the rear window or the door. So who was it? And where did they go?

Memories of the night before flooded back. The person wearing a hood. She moved toward the door and reached for the handle. Should she open it and look outside?

The birds were chirping up a storm. They didn't care that dawn was a solid thirty minutes off. They had no time to waste.

She didn't open the door. She locked it instead, and then a sudden thought occurred. A comforting thought.

Birds.

Every year random twitterpated birds managed to fly into one or more of her windows, and the sudden, unexpected *thunk* always startled her.

Of course.

Her heart slowed to a more normal rhythm, which calmed her pulse and her breathing.

She had four pies in the lower oven and cookies in the upper one, as well as three piecrusts ready to bake at the higher temperature of the low oven and a tray of lemon bars waiting for the cookies to finish.

She loved predawn baking. The quiet soothed her. Just her and the frogs and the birds. It had been the same at the bakery. Charla Whipple was more than happy to let her take the dark-of-night shift.

No one was outside.

That fact strengthened her twitterpated bird theory. Nesting birds were often distracted by love, so she chalked the sudden noise up to avian romance and returned to work.

But she didn't unlock the door until Debbie arrived forty-five minutes later.

Debbie didn't come straight in though. Janet saw her set her bag on one of the benches facing the railroad tracks, and then she moseyed around for a few minutes. By the time she came to the back door, it was unlocked and Janet had set the last tray of ginger cookies to cool on one counter while picture-perfect pies rested on another.

"The mix of aromas in this place is intoxicating," Debbie said as she stowed her bag beneath a kitchen counter. She took a deep breath and smiled. "Is that strawberry-rhubarb pie I smell?"

"A crowd-pleasing favorite," Janet replied. "I'll make another if this one goes quickly. There's something about early summer that says berries. The more the merrier."

"I can't disagree. I took a quick look around the train cars before I came in." Debbie grabbed a train-themed apron. "I wanted to see if I spotted anything out of place now that it's light out."

"Anything of note?"

"Three cigarette butts."

It would be the perfect spot for kids who weren't supposed to smoke to light up. Customers used the sand-filled cans up the way because the depot didn't want stale smoke driving nonsmokers away. But those cans were in the open. People who didn't want anyone to see them smoke could duck between the train cars.

"And this." Debbie stuck her hand into her pocket and withdrew a button.

Tiffany's button.

Janet recognized it instantly. They'd joked about the vintage-looking heart-shaped button on one of Tiffany's favorite shirts because Janet's mother had sewn similar buttons on a shirt nearly forty years before.

Debbie spotted her expression right off. "What is it? What's wrong?"

Janet had to swallow hard to get the words out. "Tiffany has buttons like that. Exactly like that. On that cute ruffled top she loves to wear. Although I haven't seen her wear it lately."

Debbie waved that off. "We live in small-town USA," she reminded Janet. "Moms all shop at the same stores. Order from the same sites online. I'm going to guess that whatever company made that shirt made more than one. Let's not borrow trouble."

She had a good point. Janet used to joke with parents when kids would show up at school or functions wearing the same outfits or jackets or boots or gloves, especially before online shopping was a big thing. Limited local options meant they all drove to the mall in New Philadelphia and bought clothes there.

Janet went back to slipping cookies from parchment-paper-lined trays. "Not to borrow any more trouble, I'm going to say that I'm 100 percent sure that the predawn knock on the back door was a bird. Not a murderer."

"Wait. What?" Debbie had been wrapping silverware in napkins. "Someone was here this morning?"

"That's just it, no one was there. There was only one knock on the door and then nothing. No one. Hence my bird theory."

Debbie frowned and stopped the silverware prep. "I've never had a bird knock at my door. Perhaps Cleveland birds are antisocial?"

"You were in an apartment on the fourth floor," Janet pointed out.

"True. And yet birds can fly that high, I believe."

"I think this was more of a gathering-nesting-material-type deal," Janet reasoned. "Or a male bird wanting to fight off his reflection to earn the attention of a mate."

"It's July." Debbie lifted a doubting eyebrow. "Birds nest in spring. But nice try."

Janet laughed but stuck to her theory. "Second nesters. Some of the migratory birds do a second nest. The ones that come back early anyway."

"And you're sure it wasn't someone pranking you?" asked Debbie. "Playing Ding-Dong Ditch?"

Ding-Dong Ditch was a silly, childish game. Kids would ring the doorbell for no other reason than to see someone come to answer the door and find no one there. Preadolescents had found this nonsense particularly amusing thirty-five years ago. "I would have caught a glimpse through the door or the windows. My vote is bird."

Harry and Crosby sauntered along the backside of the depot right then. They moved at a measured, normal pace until Crosby made a mad dash for the door. Nose down, he did a thorough sniffing around the entrance then along the entire length of the depot, as if tracking something.

Or *someone.*

A shiver set the hairs along Janet's neck on edge.

Debbie followed the dog's movements.

When Crosby came loping back as if to share the results of his excursion with Harry, she looked over at Janet. "Do birds generally walk the full length of the depot?"

"Hop. Or fly," Janet said. "Crosby probably smells that raccoon from last night. Of course he'd be sniffing along the building. Ian found it toward the other end."

Debbie acknowledged that with a nod. "Maybe. I think I'm looking in the shadows for something that doesn't exist. Not that I'm spooked." She frowned. "More like mystified. For today, however,

Mom sent you this recipe for fried doughnuts." She handed over a printed sheet. "She says it's what Aunt Lucy used when she worked with the Salvation Army women in the sixties. Mom thought it was better than the original recipe."

"I'll give it a go this afternoon." Janet scanned the recipe before tacking it to the corkboard above her mixing area. "Good balance of ingredients here. Nothing says I have to use the original if we have a better one." Janet hadn't gotten to be a prizewinning baker by marrying herself to subpar recipes. "I want to honor military and customers of old by creating the best possible fried doughnut we can today. I'm open to all ideas. Text your mom that we'll drop some off later this afternoon."

Debbie lifted her hand for a high five. "She'll be happy. And if she's happy, I'm happy, because she might stop talking about new beginnings, men, and fresh starts. If I'm lucky."

Janet burst out laughing. That was the one thing Debbie had feared would happen if she moved back to her hometown. "Your mom just wants what's best for you," she teased.

Debbie had been away for a long time. She'd lost her fiancé the year after she graduated from college. The tragedy of that broke her heart. She had poured herself into her ladder-climbing job in Cleveland until she realized she wanted something different for her life. Less intense. More hometown. More people-oriented. When the opportunity to open the café came along, she'd called Janet right away.

God's timing.

"Not one person in Cleveland cared about my love life," Debbie said as Harry approached the door. "Except me. But that's not true here. My mom wants me happy, and that isn't a bad thing. Annoying, on occasion..."

"The beauty of nearby family," quipped Janet as Harry came through the door.

Crosby didn't settle down as he usually did. He made a full-on show of sniffing the doorframe again. He looked worried. Just a little. Finally, he took up his spot under Harry's stool.

Janet got out the egg-frying pan to prepare Harry and Crosby's breakfast. When Debbie gave the back door a questioning look, Janet knew she wasn't buying the bird theory completely.

But what other options were there? None she could think of. Not even a comic book superhero could have sped off that quickly, so a bird was the only logical explanation she could think of right now. She posed the question to Ian when he came by for coffee a few minutes later.

His grimace surprised her. "I'm not saying it wasn't a bird," he told her. "But here's what I've found over the years. Sounds are funny."

They'd just opened. No one had trickled through the door yet, so Debbie and Harry leaned in on the conversation. "Funny how?" Janet asked.

"When you first hear an unexpected sound, you're pretty sure you know where it came from, but people are wrong about that fairly often," Ian explained. "Hearing plays tricks on us. Sometimes your ears have to home in on the noise. You think it came from one place, but if you hear it a second time, you realize it came from another. Like around the corner of the building."

Janet crossed her arms. "I was here. Noise was there." She pointed to the back door. "End of discussion."

He accepted that and straightened up as a customer came through the front door. "You're probably right. I'm just saying it's not uncommon to misconstrue the location the first time. By the second noise, our ears and brain are wired to locate the sound." Ian gave Janet's hand a quick squeeze. "Gotta go. Meeting at nine. Great coffee, ladies."

Working cops got free coffee throughout the day. The Whipples had done that in Uhrichsville, and she and Debbie wanted to continue the tradition. They'd also kicked off their new venture with a Bottomless Cup Club. For twenty dollars a month, people could get free coffee all month long, no matter how often they came by to fill their cups. Some stopped by twice a day. Most swung by in the morning, on their way to work, but there were some old-timers who liked to gather at the corner table and chat. Older men. A few were widowed, and a couple were still married. A nice crew who enjoyed the endless refills and the café's nearby location. Janet was pretty sure they would become cold-weather regulars, and she liked that idea. Jim Watson liked to mosey in fairly often. He edited and published the *Gazette,* the widely read local newspaper.

Janet had no idea what kind of business to expect on a holiday weekend, but the depot museum was a popular spot for vacationers. The nostalgic themes of sacrifice and service drew people, and a surprising number of homeschooling parents and cooperatives made the museum a summer and fall field-trip stop, according to Kim Smith, who ran the museum.

Carloads of people meant sales, which was never a bad thing. By one thirty, they were low on bread, out of rolls, and had two pieces of pie and two dozen cookies left.

The last patron didn't leave until two thirty, which meant they cleaned and polished until nearly three thirty. But when Debbie reviewed the day's receipts, she whistled. "This was an amazing day." She spoke softly so the people who were wandering the track side of the depot checking out the vintage trains and posters wouldn't hear her through the open back door. "I'm not sure how to prep for the weekend—"

"We need to go shopping. We have limited deliveries coming in on Monday because the Fourth is Tuesday." Janet had turned on the fryer to do a trial run of Becca Albright's doughnut recipe. "I'm well-stocked on baking supplies, except for strawberries and blueberries. I want to do some of those whipped-cream-topped patriotic cakes. They're easy to frost and decorate, and they keep well." She pointed to the refrigerated bakery section. "I want that whole section to say 'I love my country' by Monday morning. If today's traffic was any indication, we're going to be busy. Dennison may not be a destination place, but it is a great stop on your way."

Debbie added Janet's items to the grocery list just as Janet's dad came around the back. "Hey, girls." He opened the door and stepped inside. "Ready to close it up for the day? Janet, your mom was hoping you'd both come by for hamburgers on the grill."

"Dad." Janet exchanged a look with Debbie. "Do you have time to do some shopping for us? We got slammed today…"

Her dad cut her off quickly. "Say no more. Your mother would be relieved to have me out of the house for a few hours. Groceries? Got a list?"

Debbie wasted no time in handing him the list they'd just completed along with the café's credit card. He tucked both into his back pocket. "On it. I'll call if I'm confused about anything. I'm not savvy enough to know what to substitute if something's out of stock."

"You're a lifesaver, Dad. And we're an absolute yes to food tonight, no matter what it is. If I don't have to cook it, I'm totally in."

He waved as he headed out. "Glad to do it. I'd rather keep busy than sit around getting older by the day. I don't mind being retired," he told them as he reached the door. "But I'm not quite used to it either. There's a lot of hours to fill with not much business this time of year. Doing accounts will keep me busy from October through spring, but no one cares about that in the summer. I'm happy to help you girls get this place up and running."

He left as a familiar figure floated across the brick-lined patio area between the depot and the wrought iron fence.

Winnie Gayle had come to the depot.

She wore some sort of old-fashioned dress, much like she had the day before. It wasn't belted but flowed freely, Woodstock-friendly, and a sheer sleeveless outer garment completed the hippie look. The only thing missing was a flower crown. Janet wasn't a fabric guru, but she thought Winnie's dress was coarsely woven cotton and the outer garment was something like gauze.

Janet looked at Debbie, and Debbie looked at her. Then they walked out the back door together.

If Winnie Gayle had left the sanctity of her house to pay the depot a visit, Janet wanted to know why.

CHAPTER SIX

Marcy came their way as Winnie headed straight for the thick-trunked oak. "I had to bring her by," she told them, her voice low. "She was in such a state, there was little choice in the matter."

"I'm so sorry," whispered Janet.

Debbie echoed that sentiment. "We never meant to upset her."

Marcy brushed off their apologies. "This isn't about you ladies. Auntie's harmless, but her mental state is fragile. We converted the carriage house into an apartment about seven years ago so she could live with us. That way she can be independent but close enough for us to jump in if we're needed. Your visit didn't cause this. She was on the edge already. And maybe it's good for her to visit old haunts. To think back. There's a restlessness to her soul. Maybe she needs some kind of closure."

Janet glanced at the fryer. It wasn't at the right temperature yet, so she moseyed Winnie's way. "Isn't that a beautiful old tree? And such wonderful shade."

"The shade helped, you know."

Winnie wasn't looking at Janet. She was looking at the tree. She squinted then rounded the tree before coming back to Janet's side. "It's a comfort when the harshness of the sun cannot be borne. Not with any sort of grace, that is."

"And yet it's hot out today and you're wearing nothing on your head," noted Janet.

Winnie smiled. "The sun brightens my hair. He said it gave me hints of silver, and I'd laugh because it would be a long time before silver marked the passage of years." She sighed. Then she crossed to the wrought iron fence and grasped it with both hands. "This wasn't here."

She was right. The fencing was installed to keep museum visitors away from the active tracks. "No." Janet waited.

"Nor these railcars." She indicated the array of vintage cars that now flanked the depot. Janet nodded in agreement.

"And the bench is gone."

Janet recalled the particular bench she referred to, the one Harry had mentioned as the one Winnie sat on under the tree. She followed Winnie's line of thought. "The wood rotted, and the bench gave out after a while. They haven't replaced it. Although there are a number of nice benches along the wall there. People like to sit there and remember."

"A prosaic setting with little to foster dreams and imagination." Winnie cast a dismissive look toward the very nice benches lining the depot's outside waiting area. "What would be the point of sitting there when it's busy? You can't see anything. Nothing of note, anyway. You can't see the trains roll in, day after day. And a tree offers repose of its own sort."

Janet sensed the poet in the woman and offered a childhood memory. "'I think that I shall never see—'"

Winnie took up the poem with almost childlike glee. "'A poem lovely as a tree!'" She laughed. "Oh, I do love a good recitation, and

I despised those who criticized Kilmer as simplistic. Some of the very best things in life are simple. A walk, regardless of weather. A picnic. An afternoon of quietude, letting peace soak in. I enjoyed lyricism ever so much. I was skilled, you know. At writing. And recitation. At so many things. Back then." She eyed the spot where the bench used to be. "Before."

"Before...?" Janet led with the single word, but Winifred Gayle wasn't buying it.

She turned away from the tracks and the tree. "Change." Her voice shifted down, and her expression soured. "I can't abide it. I prefer things as they are, although I am rarely consulted. That's how I would do it if I could." Her voice wasn't tepid now. It was hot. "I would like for things to stay the same."

Marcy had started moving their way the moment Winnie grew agitated. The younger woman's gentle smile and tone seemed inherent. A part of her. "And yet without change, we'd have no butterflies, Auntie." Her manner softened the moment. "No baby chicks. No snow for Christmas and no daffodils in spring. Not all change is bad. Some simply happens. 'To everything there is a season,'" she said, quoting Ecclesiastes.

The gentle common sense helped, and Winnie calmed down. "I know." She wrung her hands, glanced toward the tree once more, and sighed. "They should have replaced it."

Janet wanted to lead her on, but she bit her tongue.

"The bench, I mean. It was there for a reason."

Marcy raised her eyebrows. "What reason, Auntie?"

Winnie rolled her eyes. "It was right there on the plaque," she announced, as if they should know about it. "And I've always believed one should follow the examples set by the best among us."

Marcy shared a puzzled look with Janet. "I can't argue with that."

Nor could Janet, but her oil was hot, and her dough was ready, and nothing Winnie said made real sense. "Ladies, if you hang around for a little bit, I'm about to drop some fresh doughnuts from a different recipe. I'd value your opinions, since you sampled the first ones. If you don't mind waiting."

"Auntie?"

Winnie glanced around then shook her head. "Home, please. We can come another time. Thank you very much for the invitation, but we regret to inform you that we must decline at this time." She rambled the words, a little lost.

"Another time, then," said Debbie.

Winnie ignored her and started walking the wrong way.

Marcy reached out and touched her arm gently. "Our car is this way, Auntie. In the little lot across the way."

"Our car."

She looked surprised. Confusion filled her gaze, and then she zeroed in on Marcy, and it was like a light bulb blinked on. "Of course it's there. Right where it should be. Would be, under any circumstances. Good day." She didn't look back at Janet or Debbie, or even Marcy. With a firm stride she moved across the brick surface and around the building, and Marcy followed.

Janet hurried inside to gather her equipment. She put the dough, the rolling pin, the doughnut cutter, the spatula, and tongs on a tray, which she took out to the frying station.

Debbie had set up a glazing area on a table alongside the fryer. Janet cut the dough and fried the doughnuts, eight at a time. As each doughnut cooled, Debbie dipped its top into the glaze then set it aside. The warm scent of nutmeg filled the air. It was warm but not muggy, and the soft breeze carried the delicious smells.

People followed the scent. By the time they'd given out all but a couple dozen, they'd made new friends and new customers. Debbie's mother was right—this recipe was top-notch, and the happy smiles on people's faces proved that. This was the recipe she'd use for their Independence Day Salute. All gave some, and some gave all, and a lot of those brave men and women had passed right through this station eighty years ago. They'd gotten the best the volunteers had back then.

She intended to give their descendants and all the travelers the very best again.

Janet dropped off doughnuts for the police department's evening shift and took the last few home for her parents and Ian to try. She took a quick shower and hurried to her parents' house.

Tiffany was already there. "Mom, hey. Doughnuts? For real?" She sniffed the plastic-wrapped plate and sighed. "I don't have to wait until after supper, do I? Because I'm starving, and in a few short weeks I won't even be here to test recipes for you."

"And just like that, the kid goes straight for the jugular," Janet quipped as she handed the plate over. "Save some for your dad and Grandma and Grandpa. I want their opinions to compare with the last batch I made."

Tiffany didn't hesitate to bite into one. "Better," she assured her mother. "Definitely better. These melt in your mouth."

The exact response Janet wanted. "Agreed. And I'm so glad you're with us tonight."

"Well, there's food," joked Tiffany.

"The perfect enticement," agreed Janet's mom as she came into the kitchen. She gave Janet a hug then tasted a piece of doughnut. "This is it." She proclaimed the words like a full-on declaration. "I've never had better."

"Then I'll stop testing," said Janet. "What can I do to help?"

"You can get the tea out of the fridge," said her mom. "Other than that, we're done. Debbie just pulled in. Who's that?"

Janet reached for the tall glass pitcher as her mother posed the question. "Someone is with Debbie?"

Mom shook her head. "I don't know if he's with her. Drove over separate, but he's following her up the driveway. I wonder what that's all about." Janet's mother had retired shortly before her father. She'd been an editor for a Christian publishing house in nearby Uhrichsville, and she loved people. She also loved a good story.

Janet handed Tiffany the pitcher and looked out the window. "It's the loan officer from Third Street Bank," she told them. "The Whipples worked with him when they did that expansion a decade ago. He arranged their loan so they could incorporate the dry cleaner spot next door to the bakery." She turned to her mom. "Did you guys apply for a loan?" she asked.

"Nope. And you're right, I recognize him now," her mother replied. "It's been a long time since I had to go into the bank. I do everything online now."

"We use the one here in town," Janet said. "I like the small-town feel. And they serve a lot of first responders and medical staff." She watched the banker cross the drive toward Debbie. "This guy's name is Karl. He ordered white cake layered with custard cream and pineapple filling for his wife's birthday every year, and for every Thanksgiving. We always tagged the order with 'Karl from the bank.'"

"Sounds amazing." Her mother grinned. "The cake, I mean. We might have to give that one a try."

"It's a great combo. I'll whip one up next week," Janet promised as Debbie sent a quick, pleading look toward the window. Janet crossed to the door.

"I'm in if you substitute lemon," Tiffany called after her. "I vote no to pineapple."

"Your wish is my command. At least for the next few weeks." She winked and headed outside. Her lifelong friend wasn't the type to need intervention under normal circumstances, but Janet hadn't missed the silent plea Debbie directed at the house.

She put on a placid face and walked their way, noting Karl's new-model luxury car. Clearly, the banker was doing well for himself.

"Janet, I'm so glad you're here." Debbie wasn't prone to excitement, but her tone indicated that something was up.

"Yes, ma'am. My mom made a pitcher of sweet tea, and I wondered if you would like some. Either of you," she added, including Karl in the look.

He stuck out a hand so quickly that she didn't think twice about taking it.

"Karl Kurtz," he announced. "You used to make my wife's birthday cake for me."

She nodded and smiled. "White cake, filled with custard cream, split layers filled with pineapple glacé."

He looked pleased that she remembered. "Her favorite. I'm hoping you might consider making it for us at your new place at the depot. Now that the Third Street Bakery has closed its doors."

"I'd be happy to do that, Mr. Kurtz."

"Karl." He said the first name quickly, as if wanting to make friends. "Her birthday isn't until spring."

"April, right?"

He nodded. "Yes. Great memory."

She accepted the compliment with a smile. "Just let me know when you want it, okay? We're happy to oblige."

"Wonderful." Why would someone drive across town in July to order a cake for April? That made no sense, but his next question cleared the cobwebs from the air. "I understand you ladies may have found my medals."

Janet exchanged a quick frown with Debbie. She hadn't told anyone except Ian about the medals.

Debbie hiked her brows in response, clearly just as surprised.

Janet stayed intentionally nonchalant. "I'm not sure I understand."

"You found a cache of medals, correct?"

"Define *cache*," Debbie said.

Karl waved a hand. "I lost an old tin filled with World War II memorabilia about twenty years ago. You can just imagine my dismay when they disappeared. I was in the depot recently, but try as I might, I couldn't find them. The metal box was old. Faded flowers on the top. It had a candymaker's name on it, but I don't remember what it was. Started with an *S*."

"Family medals?" Debbie asked, and Karl's slight hesitation strengthened Janet's doubts.

"Which Kurtz served in the war?" she asked.

"My uncle Jack," he said. "Jack Logan. On my mother's side. He and his brother Lawrence both served."

"That's what makes our depot so special, isn't it?" said Debbie in a graceful change of subject. "So many here are either descendants of military members or descendants of those who helped care for them and serve them as they came through. The historic significance of that is a town treasure."

Her reply flummoxed him but not for long. "Yes, yes, of course. Now about the—"

"Karl, I'm sorry, but I promised my mom we'd help get supper out, and she needs us at the moment." Janet put her hand on Debbie's arm, a gesture that made the statement inclusive. "Why don't you stop by the café one of these afternoons, and we can talk about the medals, all right? You know how it is." She smiled as she started back toward the house. "We never leave a mother in a lurch."

He moved as if about to follow them then paused. Janet caught his expression from her peripheral vision.

Their quick departure bothered him.

Why? And where did he hear about the medals?

They got inside the door and huddled in the kitchen while Tiffany helped her grandmother take burgers to the backyard grill. "Did you tell anyone about the medals?" Debbie whispered.

"Not a soul except Ian, and he wouldn't have said anything."

"Patricia?" wondered Debbie.

"She said she wouldn't tell anyone, and besides, why would she?"

No reason Janet could think of, but then she and Debbie exchanged looks. "Harry." Debbie said the old man's name softly.

"Ah. Most likely." It wasn't that Harry couldn't keep a secret. At his age it was more likely that he forgot it *was* a secret and he was excited about the medals. "We'll ask him tomorrow."

"Without making a big deal of it, of course."

Janet agreed. They hadn't even mentioned the find to Kim Smith yet. The museum curator had been swamped with preparations and promotions for the Independence Day holiday, and Janet had hoped to find out more about the medals before telling anyone about them. Karl Kurtz's claim pushed that timeline.

"And if they do belong to Karl—" She glanced toward the road then back to Debbie.

"We'll return them, no harm, no foul. But even though he might have been an honest banker in his time, there was something unconvincing about his story."

"Although the name on the tin did start with a big fancy *S*," noted Janet.

"Did Harry notice that, do you think?" Debbie drew her brows down in the way she sometimes did when solving a puzzle.

Janet shrugged. "He could have, but he didn't mention it. But for now, those burgers smell amazing. And I'm starving."

"We'll talk tomorrow," Debbie promised. "And if the medals belong to the Kurtz family, we'll hand them over."

But did they?

Janet pulled her phone out of her back pocket and tapped Kim Smith's name in her contacts. If word leaked about the medals, Janet didn't want her caught unaware. "I'm going to bring Kim up to date," she told Debbie. She glanced around to make sure no one was listening. "If Harry's spoken to Karl, he may have spoken to others. I don't want Kim to be the last to know."

"Me neither," Debbie agreed. "We're the new kids on the block when it comes to the depot. I don't want Kim or anyone else working there to think we're trying to upstage them."

"That's a big-city worry if ever I heard one," teased Janet. "I'm pretty sure small-town, homegrown Kim will be happy to share the glory of Crosby's discovery."

Debbie made a face. "I know it's different here. Everyone who works at the depot is so nice that I find myself suspecting their motives. And when I realize they don't have any ill intent, it's like the best feeling I've had in years. I love being back home."

"Not as much as I love having you here. Kim?" Janet redirected her attention when Kim picked up the call. "It's Janet. Hey, I've got you on speaker. Debbie and I have something to share with you. Can we stop over this evening?"

"Normally, I'd say yes," said Kim. "But I'm not home tonight. Mom had a spell. Nothing major, but I'm staying here at the assisted-living facility with her until morning. As long as all goes well—"

"You're being silly. I am perfectly all right. Go on home, Kimberly." Eileen Palmer's strong voice cut into the conversation from Kim's end. "I'll rest better knowing you're resting better." Clearly Kim's mother had her own opinions on the matter.

"And I won't rest at all if I'm home, so we're doing this my way tonight, Mother," Kim shot back. "I won't snore. I promise."

Hearing Eileen's voice sparked a thought for Janet. Eileen had served as the Dennison Depot stationmaster during the war years and, at a hundred years young, she knew the depot and Dennison's history better than anyone. "Hey, Kim?"

"Mm-hmm?"

"Ask your mom if Debbie and I can come by and talk to her soon. I've got some questions for her. Post-war stuff."

"You know she loves company. Mornings are generally good. She naps in the afternoon."

"I close my eyes now and again between two and four," grumped Eileen in the background. "Nothing a normal person would call a nap. Sometimes I doze off for a minute or two, but I wake right back up. I'm just resting my eyes is all."

Debbie grinned.

"Kim, tell your mom I think she's one of the coolest, smartest women around town, and I can't wait to see her. How about Sunday? Late afternoon? Pre-nap or post-nap," she teased. "I'm not afraid to wake her up if I have to."

Kim laughed. In the background, the women heard Eileen laugh too. "Sunday's good," Kim told them. "Like I said, Mom loves company. Even if it's a very stubborn daughter."

"Aw." Janet laughed softly. "You two have a beautiful relationship. It's inspirational, and I mean that sincerely. Kim, we'll see you tomorrow, and, Eileen, we'll stop by Good Shepherd on Sunday after church."

"I'll put my best pantsuit on," declared Eileen. "The light purple one with that nice, easy zipper. Fortunately for me, Kimberly is good about getting me outfits with easy zippers. Better something I can do myself than something fancier that needs assistance. I like taking care of myself, best I'm able. See you gals on Sunday!"

Janet disconnected the call and put the phone away. "Food, Debbie. And we'll talk to Kim in the morning and see what she has to say. Who knows? Maybe she'll have some insight into whose medals were buried beneath the old oak."

"And if she doesn't, her mother might. And I don't think I'll mention anything to Harry about sharing the information," Debbie continued as they moved toward the door. "I don't want him to feel as if he did something wrong."

"Agreed."

Janet's mom and Tiffany had gotten all the food outside. Burgers were ready, and they were all about to enjoy a summer evening cookout. Vintage candy tins and medals would have to wait.

CHAPTER SEVEN

Kim eyed the collection of medals with one raised eyebrow the next morning. "These were buried under the old oak tree? For real?"

Janet nodded. "A Crosby find. I helped him unearth it."

"The roots on that tree are huge," said Kim. "How did you get it out?"

"With the help of a trowel."

"Root growth may have actually pushed the box closer to the surface," said Debbie.

"Good point." Kim examined the tin, looking puzzled. "But a box of significant medals, buried like that—it makes no sense."

"Are you all right if I keep them in my safe at home?" asked Janet. "Ian knows about them, but we didn't file a police report, because there's no reason to at this point. He didn't find any old complaints of stolen medals in the records, but predigital records aren't as easy to trace. Still, nothing's come up so far."

"Fine by me." Kim opened the lid and examined the medals again. Then she said, "You know, we could be looking at something more recent than you think."

Janet raised her eyebrows.

"The military often gives out medals long after the fact, so even though these may have been earned during World War II, the soldier might not have received some of them until years afterward. That could change your timeline significantly." Kim closed the lid and handed the box to Janet. "The medals might not have been buried right after the war."

Janet hadn't considered that. "So these might not have been buried in the forties. It could have been later."

"Much later. If the growth of the tree roots nudged them up instead of down, we can't really learn anything from how deep the tin was buried."

A bell chimed behind Kim. She moved in that direction. "Keep me in the loop if you can, but it looks like you two have another mystery to solve."

"She's right," Debbie said. "I love solving puzzles. It's ingrained in me. So if these belong to Karl, case closed. But if they don't..."

"We get to delve. I'm 100 percent on board with that." Janet tucked the medals into her bag, and they walked outside. "What purpose was served by burying a tin of battlefield honors? And if Karl got them from a family member, why would someone bury them? And why here?"

Debbie double-checked the café doors to make sure they were locked. "I don't know. But it seems it's up to you and me to find out."

Janet walked backward toward her car. "We'll meet up tomorrow after church, all right? Ian's got the Sunday shift, Tiffany's going to two more parties, and I'm going to double-check everything to make sure we're ready for Monday and Tuesday."

"We've plastered the throwback doughnut celebration all over social media. Last I looked, it's been shared over eighty times. I think our early-day time frame is in our favor. We hit the ground running before most picnics take place and nowhere near fireworks time. What's the worst that can happen?" She withdrew her phone from the back pocket of her capris. "We get to eat a lot of doughnuts."

There could be worse outcomes.

Janet set her bag on the passenger seat just as Karl Kurtz pulled into the depot. The depot was still open, but the café closed at two, so why was he here?

He didn't seem to notice her or Debbie in the far parking area. He parked up the road, and Janet watched him walk back to the depot. He aimed for the museum side of the building. He marched across the bricks, a man with a mission. Looking ready for battle.

Was he approaching Kim because they'd given him the brush-off the night before?

It was understandable for him to be here if the medals were his. What they needed to figure out was how far could they go to make him prove they were his medals without risking angering him.

She and Debbie hadn't started a new enterprise to incite bad feelings. On the other hand, right was right.

She took out her phone and texted Debbie. KARL LOOKS READY TO RUMBLE. I SAY WE HAVE HIM IDENTIFY WHAT MEDALS ARE IN THE BOX. IF THEY'RE HIS, HE'LL KNOW WHAT THEY ARE, RIGHT?

She watched as Debbie heard her notification, looked at her phone, and grinned. AGREED, she responded. THAT MIGHT RUFFLE HIS FEATHERS, BUT IT'S FAIR. I DON'T WANT TO TACKLE HIM NOW THOUGH.

ME NEITHER. AND WHY ARE WE IN THE PARKING LOT TEXTING EACH OTHER? WE'RE NERDS.

Debbie sent five laughing emojis.

They were being silly, but sometimes it felt good to be silly.

Janet tossed a towel over her bag just in case she ran into someone. She didn't want anyone else getting a peek at the tin and laying a claim. Tomorrow they'd see what Eileen had to say, and then they'd go from there.

For now she had a quiet evening with Ian and Tiffany planned, and she was looking forward to that.

Dennison, Ohio
October 1948

"Hey, Buddy."

Buddy heard the familiar voice and paused. He looked up, and when he saw the nice lady in her special outfit, he smiled.

She smiled back.

She always did, like she knew something about him that made her like him real well, even though they hadn't met before he started making the walk to town. Still, she was nice to him every single day, so maybe she was the sort that just liked dogs.

She never shooed him out, and she kept a stash of old towels on hand for particular rains. Summer rains were no big deal, but the cold, driving rains had started again, and those weren't fun.

He handled snow well enough. Even deep snow, although there was a sharp pain in his left hip that made walking uncomfortable now. The snow would come before too long, but this hard, driving rain soaked his fur and sapped his soul.

Without fail he felt better once he dried off a bit. Some folks scolded him. They used the voice that no dog likes. And some said he stank—whatever that meant. Others just held their noses. But the nice lady in her special outfit would come by with a towel and dry him off. Warm him up. And when the weather got worse, she blocked off a corner by a table. Enough room for him to get by but not be right with the people. And she always laid a couple of comfortable blankets in the corner, fresh ones every now and again. He wasn't sure if she just kept blankets there or if they were meant for him.

She never seemed to mind that he'd cozy up there when the weather turned bad. He'd curl around one blanket or the other, paw it up nice and comfortable, and wait. Hopeful.

And still The Boy didn't return.

Trains came and went from both directions, but none with a sandy-haired boy.

A man now, Buddy supposed.

There was a difference between a man and a boy. Some men had a heart for dogs. Some didn't. He'd felt the front end of a boot in his time, enough so he learned to dart right and left quickly to avoid the toe's thrust.

But not with The Boy. Not with any boy, come to think of it. Boys and dogs seemed to go together, and that made things nice.

He was curled on the blanket, keeping one eye on the door—mostly, when he didn't doze off—when the lady in the special outfit came by, talking to someone. "We can't let this go on, Ray."

There was a man with her. Buddy had seen him before. He was a quiet sort. Didn't get angry.

The man glanced Buddy's way and frowned. "Seems to be doing fine from where I'm standing, Eileen."

"While he's here, yes. But what about all night?"

The lady in the special outfit sounded worried about something, and she wasn't the worrying sort. He *knew some worrying sorts. Fretters. Sometimes one of those would reach out and pet him and he'd hold still, because he knew that petting a dog made everything seem better. Calmer, even. And when they stopped petting him, they seemed happier. He didn't understand it, but he'd seen it often enough. Besides, what dog didn't like a good pat or scratch behind the ears?*

"He's got a routine of his own, I'd say." The man smiled down at Buddy, and Buddy smiled back.

"But every night, out in all kinds of weather?"

Yep. She sounded worried, all right. Something had gotten her riled up, but she'd taken care to give him a good rubdown with the towel when he'd first come in, and that meant a lot to Buddy.

"Where does he go? What does he do? He's not young anymore. And we only know his name because a ticket agent overheard the soldier saying goodbye. 'You take care, Buddy, and I'll be back quick as I can.'"

Both of Buddy's ears perked up now. He shifted slightly, listening.

"Not young but not old either," the fellow she called Ray replied. "He's a good dog and knows his way around. I say we don't try to fix what isn't broken. He likes his routine. Folks don't mind having him about, and he's happy. Sometimes a little happy is all we get, Eileen."

"Happy and safe would set my worries aside. I'm going to be moving after the wedding, or I'd take him in myself."

"And my dog doesn't take to other dogs, so I'm out for the count. I say we let it go."

She made a funny sound, like she was in pain, and Buddy paid notice because he didn't want her in pain. She was nice to him. She fed him and never talked mean. She was his friend. He didn't want her to hurt.

Humans were hard to figure sometimes. Real hard.

"It's not knowing where he holes up at night that's got me worried," she told the man. "He should be safe inside. Lying by a fire with a water dish nearby. Not curled up in some old rattrap of a building or huddled in an ice-cold dugout."

Buddy didn't know what she meant, but her concern touched him. She had a kind heart, and that was why he liked her. She cared. And he liked being cared about. That was a thing about him and most dogs, he figured.

They loved freely, and they liked being cared about.

That made things nice, all around.

They moved away, still talking.

A train rolled in, coming from the right way, so Buddy sat up, watching as people came down the metal steps and made it to the platform.

No Boy.

Maybe next time?

A brisk wind came through the door as travelers streamed into the depot. A cold wind, marking the change of seasons. Something the lady said stuck with him.

"Lying by a fire..."

He'd seen a picture of that on his walks back and forth. Down the road a bit, one of the shop windows had some pretty pictures in it. Some of water and houses and woods, but then there was one that had a big red dog in front of a fireplace. The fireplace was all lit up and glowing. The dog was curled up, sound asleep, on a round rug, the kind that goes in circle after circle and gives a body some cushion.

He liked that kind of rug, and he figured that picture was what the lady in the special outfit meant when she said "lying by a fire."

It looked nice from the sidewalk. That dog, that rug, that fire.

He thought so nearly every time he passed it, but then, that dog didn't have a Boy like he did, so he could spend his days and nights sleeping by a fire, getting fat and lazy.

Buddy's life wasn't like that.

He had a job.

An important job. A job that had merit. A job that fulfilled a promise he'd made. A promise to wait, to be there when The Boy came back.

It was a promise they made to one another, and it was a promise Buddy intended to keep.

CHAPTER EIGHT

$\mathcal{E}$ileen Palmer's face lit up when she spotted Debbie and Janet coming her way Sunday afternoon. She sat at a four-person table, one of several in the solarium of the assisted-living facility, her walker nearby. She sat up straighter and waved at the empty chairs. "You're on time. Something a train woman like myself values highly." She spoke with an excited lilt. "All those years of running this, that, and the other thing instilled punctuality in me. Running late is rude if it's avoidable."

"So true," agreed Janet. She sat on Eileen's right. Debbie took the chair on the left. "Eileen, you look positively chipper. That shade of purple looks great on you."

The compliment made her preen. "Thank you. I'm at the age where comfort ranks supreme, but it doesn't hurt a gal to look nice at the same time, does it?"

"It does not," Debbie assured her.

"Kim says the café is doing well," Eileen said. "I told her that having those two young women come on board to open a business like that is a God-thing, for certain."

The word *young* made Janet smile.

"I was a big fan of the Whipples, and you used to make me—"

"Vanilla-glazed chocolate chip scones," Janet interrupted.

"My favorite! Kim brought me a piece of that strawberry glacé pie you made during berry season. Never had better," she continued. "And the lemon poppy seed bread is delectable. The right moisture and crumb texture."

Janet smiled. "You're a baker."

"Not of your caliber," Eileen said, "but I inspired my share of smiles back in the day. I had four children, and they all had friends, so when I had time off, I baked up a storm." She leaned in slightly. "So. What's got you girls over here again? Kim mentioned old medals and a mystery."

"An accurate summation," Janet said as she lifted the tin from her bag. She set it on the table and popped the top. She'd given the edges a light coating of oil with a paper towel. That made lifting the lid easier.

"Wow." Eileen's brows shot up as she checked the medals, and she looked as mystified as Janet had felt when she first opened the tin. Eileen flipped the top down and examined it. "Schrafft's Candies," she announced.

"That's the name?" asked Debbie.

"They were big back in the day," Eileen continued. "Real big. Stores, restaurants. Oh, they were a name, let me tell you. And their metal boxes were so pretty, folks saved them all the time. Few places do metal boxes anymore, and I think the change to cardboard lessens the impact of the gift. There was something special about those old tins. In my time the gals cherished them because they were reusable. I had two for buttons, one for threads, and one for marbles. And the kids had them too. They used them for keepsake boxes, you know." She waved a hand. "A place to stash all the treasures of childhood. I must have had a dozen of them on hand to hold this, that, or the other thing over the years. I still have one in my room, an old cookie tin. It holds some of my crocheting supplies, though my right hand's been giving me trouble of late. I miss crocheting things."

"I bet you do."

"But it gives me more time to play cards. And I'm always up for a chess match with Ray." That thought deepened her smile. "We keep busy enough, and they bring in all kinds of folks and events for us, but I do miss working with my hands. But these medals." She drew her brows together. "You know, this reminds me of someone. Someone I haven't thought of in years. Donnie McGill."

Janet and Debbie exchanged looks. "He had medals?" Debbie probed.

Eileen shook her head. She lifted one of the medals and drew it closer to examine it. "No, but he loved them. He worked at the depot from the forties into the sixties. He was a wonderful help with so many things. Donnie—Donovan—was a maintenance man. He could put his hand to pretty much anything and tweak it to get through the day. He's been gone a long time. He died in the nineties, but he had a particular sadness whenever he saw medals in the lost and found. He figured if our boys had the mettle to don heavy gear and fight, they deserved those awards to be worn. But every month during the war and for a bit after, we'd add a medal or two to the lost and found box."

"No one ever called to claim them?" asked Debbie.

"Sometimes someone did," Eileen explained. "Then we were always happy to send it to them, asking them to let us know if they got it. And almost all of them either called or wrote to say they did.

But that was a fraction of the ones we found. We ended up with dozens of medals with no owners."

"And no way to track them down?"

"Not without a whole lot of effort that no one had time for," Eileen explained. "Anybody could stroll through the depot on a given day. If their service was done, they were virtually untraceable. I figured if folks wanted them, they'd come looking for them. Out of the tens of thousands of men and women who came through the station, I suppose a few dozen medals weren't really that many. These are different, of course."

Janet lifted a brow. "How so?"

"Tucked in this case with the velvet, like they're supposed to be packed nicely. Ours were in a box, a small wooden cigar box."

"So it wasn't Donovan who kept them in this tin," Debbie said, then looked surprised when Eileen shook her head.

"No, I think it could have been him. He had such respect for those achievements. Rather than let them sit in a box beneath the counter, I could see him arranging them just so, like you see them now, and giving them a proper burial. But I could be wrong about that."

"So he might have done this?" Janet posed the question quietly as three elderly women came toward them. Their walkers clunked softly on the floor.

"Maybe, but with him gone, it's hard to say. He was a few years older than me, but he never gave me a hard time about being in charge. Being stationmaster wasn't a job he wanted. He liked cleaning and fixing things, and he was good at both. And I liked running the show."

"I heard you were amazing," said Janet, and Eileen's smile brightened her eyes.

"I think I did a good job. I had a chance to touch so many lives, working at the depot. I was a youngster when I stepped up to the plate as stationmaster, but I'd been watching how Howard did the job before me. I knew I could handle it. It was a balancing act, and I was real good at walking the ridgepole, if you get my drift. When Howard left for the war, they gave me a try, and I made that station run like clockwork. I'm real proud of my time there, during the war and after."

"How smart of the railroad higher-ups to know a good thing when they saw it," said Debbie.

Eileen wrinkled her nose. "They were so busy running trains, getting this one and that one from here to there, that if they found a warm body that could actually keep things operating, they didn't interfere. They were smart enough to let me go along and do my job. Some expected it to get handed to a man when the war was over, and that happened in some stations but not here. They kept me in place, and I worked the best job ever for those years. It does me good to see Kim running the museum now. There's something about trains that feels like home to her and me. Keeping the job in the family is something to be proud of."

"It sure is. So, Eileen, does Donovan McGill have family living here still? Do you know of any?"

Eileen thought for a moment before answering. "He had two children, a son and a daughter. The daughter moved off with her husband and gave him four grandkids somewhere out west. Now and again he'd go there or they'd come here, and I remember how the oldest two just cried and cried at his funeral. His daughter cried too. We always think there's going to be more time, and when there's not, we feel it to the core, don't we?"

Debbie put one hand over Eileen's. "Yes. Yes, we do."

Eileen met Debbie's look of sympathy and laid her other hand over Debbie's. "Goodbyes are hard. And they're hard for a while. We just keep on keepin' on, as time goes by. Now there's a song for you." Eileen patted Debbie's hand and hummed a few bars of the old tune. "That song has it all. Love, sorrow, longing, joy. It's a reminder of the constants in life and that love triumphs over hatred. Kim's got several recordings of it. You know what a music buff she is."

Janet knew. Kim had a significant collection of vintage music and had distinctive playlists for the museum. "As Time Goes By" was on one of her playlists, along with dozens of other old-time favorites.

"I love the recording from *Casablanca*," she said, "but my favorite is Jimmy Durante's version, the one that came out in the sixties. Something about it calls to me."

"They used that version in one of our favorite movies," Janet said. "Debbie and I must have watched *Sleepless in Seattle* a hundred times. With no exaggeration. It's swoon-worthy, but I never thought about those song choices. Just that they were vintage."

"Jimmy put something special into his songs," said Eileen. "Unique and indefinable. He didn't try to hit the big notes like some would. But the pain he let show in the words spoke to the heart of anyone who lived through World War II and the Depression before it. He summed it all up in that song. It still brings tears to my eyes to this day."

"*Casablanca* does that to me too," Debbie said. Movies featuring star-crossed lovers made Janet's dear friend more somber, even after all this time.

"Some things surpass time. That song's one of them."

"Did Donovan's son move away too?" Janet asked.

"No." Eileen yawned, signaling that they needed to bring their visit to an end. "He stayed in town. Had two kids. Don't know if they're here or not, but with things the way they are on computers now, you can find most anything about anyone. So Kim says."

"And Kim's correct. Eileen, thank you." Janet stood and slipped her hand into her bag once more. She withdrew a tightly covered plastic container and set it down in front of Eileen. "A little remembrance for you."

"The scones!" Eileen's eyes sparkled at the sight of the plastic container filled with vanilla-glazed chocolate chip scones. "You remembered!"

"I hadn't made them since I left the Whipples' bakery. The thought of meeting with you again inspired me, Eileen. I whipped up a batch last night and glazed them this morning before church. I made enough to eat—and share."

Eileen laughed. "I'll do both. Thank you, Janet. And you too, Debbie. Oh, this visit did me good!"

"I'm glad." Debbie pressed her hand lightly against Eileen's. "Thank you for all the help."

"It wasn't much, but then, it wouldn't be after all this time."

"It was plenty," Janet assured her.

Eileen yawned again, more earnestly this time, and the ladies headed for the door. "Goodbye, Eileen," Janet said.

"See you again soon," promised Debbie. When they got outside, Janet turned her way.

"She has a way of getting to the point, doesn't she? Seeing things through a different lens."

"She's got a finger on the pulse of a time we can never get back," Debbie replied. "And I want to hear as many stories as I can while she's here."

Janet hugged Debbie once she placed the bag with the medals into the car. "Ditto. See you tomorrow, first thing, okay?"

"Yes, ma'am. And good job on those scones."

Janet smiled. "It was worth the lost hour of sleep to see her smile like that."

Debbie smiled. "Yes. Yes it was."

Black River Falls, Wisconsin
December 1950

"You've had a great year, Jerome." Allen pushed his cap back. "You aced the engineering exam to get yourself a fancy title—"

Jerome rolled his eyes. This wasn't the first time he'd been teased about pursuing coursework by correspondence, but he'd come from nothing, so he was happy to earn something no one could take away.

"Finished the Westward Link Project with three months to spare—"

"Because we brought on three more guys from the 300th." He'd lived a lifetime in the years he'd tramped through Europe with the engineering battalion. "Wisconsin gained some good blood that day, so I can't take all the credit." He grinned and clinked coffee mugs with Allen and Gordon. "Although I'll take my share."

"And a baby due any day," noted Gordon.

"What if Frances goes into labor while you're on-site?" asked Allen.

"Her dad's been instructed to come find me. So he calls her several times a day, making her wish we hadn't installed the telephone but feeling the necessity of doing it because her dad is more than a little nervous."

"You know, not all dogs take to kids." Allen had been chewing on a toothpick. He tossed it aside. "We had to find a home for one when Gordon was a baby because the dog kept growling at him. A man can't have a bad dog around his babies. A fisherman at the bay took him on, and he lived a good long time, but then the old fellow had no kids. You think Sport will do all right?"

Sport was a good mutt, one of a pair Frances had hand-fed from a pup two years before. Allen had taken the second pup because once Jane spotted it, there was little choice. Happy wife, happy life.

Jerome had discovered the sack of pups on a routine inspection. There were four of them, abandoned and alone by a construction-site pond. It was only chance that had him canvassing the catch basins that day. He'd brought them home, but even with Frances's ministrations, only two pups made it. The others were too weak. He'd buried them in the backyard.

They'd deserved more than being abandoned. Thankfully, he'd been doing a culvert check along that stretch of road after a limb-twisting thunderstorm had rained debris around town. He'd happened upon the pups before the scorching summer sun did them in. He couldn't imagine leaving creatures to die. Conscienceless choices made the hair stand up on the back of his neck. "We're hoping Sport takes to change right quick," he told the men. "We'll give it the best try we can. If it doesn't work, we'll find someone to take the baby."

It took a few seconds, but then Allen burst out laughing. Gordon too. Then Allen jutted his chin toward the stretch of new road. Not yet done but an engineering masterpiece. "I'm real glad the army had the sense to put you with the 300th," he told Jerome, "and that you sat alongside Gordon on that train. I figure things happen for a reason, and you working with the engineer corps in Europe and then taking the job Gordon offered has made a difference here. Not just to the company either."

"Sheesh, don't go getting emotional on me, boss. I might swoon." Jerome pretended to faint.

Gordon laughed.

Not Allen. "Take the compliment, Jerome. You're one of us now and not just because you married my niece. But because you understand that it takes work and a keen eye to make sure things are done right. And doing things right is always the best."

Allen's observation was on target.

Jerome fit in with the owners of Chilson Roads because they didn't let things slide. That worked for all of them.

CHAPTER NINE

The doughnut extravaganza on July third and fourth was wildly successful. Janet was glad that Monday sales were solid, because she wasn't sure how busy they would be on the actual holiday, but by cleanup time on Tuesday afternoon, they'd doubled their Monday sales, and there were only three dozen doughnuts left to distribute to family and friends.

"We broke every record we've had since we opened," Debbie said as she helped dry the mixing bowls, spatulas, and doughnut cutters they'd used. "And my dad learned how to fry doughnuts along with your dad."

"Wasn't that the cutest thing?" Janet asked. When they'd realized they were in over their heads, they'd called on their parents, and both dads had responded. One manned the fryer. The other did the sugaring or glazing while Janet prepped dough inside and Debbie waited on customers.

"I think Dad ate half a dozen," Debbie continued. "He called them breakfast, lunch, and dinner."

"I offered them real food, but they looked at me like I was a crazy person and kept eating doughnuts." Janet laughed as she turned on the big dishwasher one last time for the day. "Dad said they were the best he's ever had, and your father agreed. All credit goes to the recipe your mom found. It's amazing and simple. That's our new go-to."

"Speaking of go-to, are you going to the fireworks tonight?" asked Debbie. The combined towns of Claymont, Uhrichsville, and Dennison put on a Fourth of July fireworks show in the park near Janet's house. It wasn't a big celebration by national standards, but it was theirs, and Janet had grown up for years thinking they did it because of her birthday. She was seven years old before she realized she shared her special day with the birth of a nation. "I haven't missed fireworks on my birthday in forty-three years, so yes. Absolutely."

"Your birthday!" Debbie stopped cleaning a big bowl and whirled around. "Janet! How awful of us to not acknowledge it! You must think we're terrible friends." She looked positively distraught with the realization that Janet's birthday had passed by like any old day. "In the middle of being so busy this weekend—"

"No worries." Janet spoke firmly, even though it had seemed odd that the day had gone by with no one saying a word. But then, they had dragged family into doughnut production out of necessity, so she hadn't given anyone much of a chance. "The best gift was seeing this go well. We could even do it again sometime and make it a fund-raiser," she suggested. "It was volunteers that got all this going eighty-plus years ago. It would be a nice way to pay it back or pay it forward, wouldn't it?"

Debbie looked like a light bulb had flashed in her brain. "Friend. You have gone and done it."

Janet was pretty sure she hadn't done anything but make dough, cook, and clean all day.

"Historic fundraiser," declared Debbie. "We could get vintage dresses—"

"Instead of our very cool T-shirt attire?" Janet teased. Capris and T-shirts were her summer wardrobe in the kitchen. "Dressed up by our amazingly poofy train-themed and depot-friendly aprons."

"Yes." Debbie was on a roll. Janet could see it in her eyes. "Vintage dresses. Those cute hats or the headscarves women wore back then. Give the fundraiser a forties look to go with the music and the setting."

Suddenly Janet could see it.

The old-fashioned dresses. The style. The lipstick. "We could get a couple of banners made."

Debbie high-fived her. "Yes. That would be perfect. Banners are reusable, and we can make it a thing. Whenever a worthy cause comes up or whenever the mood strikes."

"I love that idea," said Janet firmly as the fathers came up the back walk.

Debbie's father came in first. "What a day." He grinned at them. "We're all cleaned up out there. We let the fryer cool down before we moved it to the shed. And we disconnected the propane tank."

"Perfect. Thank you both." Janet finished wiping the dough-cutting area and rinsed her cloth thoroughly before tossing it into the laundry bag. "You guys were amazing. We would never have gotten through today if you hadn't stepped in."

"I didn't know if we could keep up, but it was surprisingly easy and fun, and the people were great," said her father. "Tiffany did a great job of packaging doughnuts. We sent her home to take a shower, although I don't mind smelling like a glazed doughnut myself."

"Best perfume ever." Janet laughed up at him. He did smell like a doughnut. A spritz of vanilla with a splash of nutmeg. "We'll have to find someone to do that when she's off to school," she added. "I wonder if Greg's boys would like to help out and make a little money next time."

Debbie was putting away clean utensils, but Janet didn't miss the rise of color in her cheeks. Something that made Janet smile. "Can you check with Greg next time you see him, Debbie?" Greg Connor had lost his grandfather in World War II. He'd left from the depot when Greg's grandmother was pregnant with his father, and his grandfather never came back. The history of the Dennison depot meant a lot to the local house flipper and Chamber of Commerce president. It meant a lot to Debbie too, and Janet hadn't missed what seemed to be a spark between the two when they met last month. Greg stopped by for coffee on a regular basis now.

Maybe it was because the coffee was that good. Or maybe...

Janet smiled to herself.

Maybe it was something else.

"Happy to." Debbie didn't turn. It seemed that putting tongs, spoons, forks, and spatulas in just the right spots took concentration.

"Did you know that most people paid with their phones?" Debbie's father, Vance, asked. "That's a new one on me."

"Those apps are a time-saver," Debbie told him. "They don't charge the business to use them, and that helps the bottom line."

"Anything that does that gets my vote," said Janet's dad. "I'm heading out, unless you girls need something else done before you close up."

"No, we're good, Dad." Janet gave him a hug and a smile. "And thanks again. You guys rocked it."

"See you at the fireworks tonight."

"Yes." Janet waved. She had time to get home, shower, and make a quick supper before they'd relax into the holiday side of the day. "We good?" she asked Debbie as the dishwasher cycle completed.

"Until tomorrow." They left together. They didn't bring their cars in nice weather. There was no need.

They separated a block away from the depot. Janet went one way, and Debbie went the other, much like they'd done as kids. They'd grown up roaming these streets together. Biking, roller-skating, exploring. No one thought much of it thirty-five years ago. She'd tried to raise Tiffany the same way, but three decades made a difference. Was it because Tiffany was an only child? Or because Janet was getting older? Because Dennison was a safe town, a great community, and yet—

She glimpsed a group of teens ducking between two buildings. The cut-through was commonly used, but no one else was out on the streets at three thirty on the Fourth of July. The shops were closed. Most people were either hosting cookouts or picnics or attending one.

Curiosity took over. It wasn't that the kids were out. It was the way they'd glanced around before ducking between the storefronts and heading for the tracks.

She got to the break between the buildings and caught sight of the group as they darted left. There were more kids than she'd originally seen. She recognized one boy, Chase Monson, a kid who spent as much time out of school as in. She knew this from Ian. He wasn't a name Tiffany brought up, and Ian only knew of him from what the

Uhrichsville Police department had shared. She didn't know most of the others, but she knew two of the girls.

One was Tiffany's friend Layla. And the other was Tiffany.

Janet's heart went into overdrive, which was silly because she knew her daughter. Trusted her. Tiffany had never given them any reason to doubt her judgment when it came to her friends or her activities.

She checked her phone for a text, just in case she'd missed one. Tiffany was good about letting them know where she was and what she was doing.

Nothing.

Janet frowned, but then she came to her senses. Tiffany was a great kid. A kid who in a few weeks would be making her own choices every single day.

The group disappeared from view.

She drew a deep breath then sent a quick text. HEADING HOME. GOING TO FIREWORKS LATER, LEAVING AT EIGHT TO GRAB ICE CREAM. WHEN WILL YOU BE HOME?

Tiffany texted back quickly. SEVEN THIRTY. HANGING WITH FRIENDS. GAVE OUT SOME OF THE EXTRA DOUGHNUTS. THEY LOVED THEM.

The text didn't reflect the furtive movements of the group, but were they furtive? Or just being teens?

She turned and hurried home.

A part of her wanted to go after the kids and find out what they were doing and why they were skulking between buildings.

Her conscience scoffed and amended the word *skulking* back to *darting*. Still, why were they there? Where were they going?

She'd ask Tiffany later.

They'd always been close. She'd loved that about their relationship, and the idea of stepping back didn't just *seem* hard. It was hard.

But necessary. Ian had told her that often enough. Possibly too often.

The thought of that made her smile. Her cop-husband did like to make his points, but then, so did she. But right now she needed a long, cool shower, because the almost-ninety-degree day had left her in dire need of some freshening up. Tonight's seventy-four-degree fireworks prediction would be a welcome respite.

A quiet house greeted her.

Ian was still working, covering for an officer down with the stomach bug that was going around.

Tiffany was hanging out with her friends, and their pouting cat was nowhere to be seen, which meant she'd probably gotten out again. Despite their attempts to make Ranger a house cat, she was a born hunter. Little dissuaded the dark gray feline when she was on a mission. But Laddie woke up the moment she closed the door. He scrambled up, tail wagging, a wonderful welcoming committee of one. She gave him a good petting then let him out back to have a cruise around the yard.

No birthday cards sat waiting on the kitchen island or the table.

No cake sat in the fridge or on the counter. But who buys a baker a cake?

No one.

And that was fine, wasn't it? Birthday celebrations should end at age forty. She and Debbie had made that agreement three years before, although they always remembered each other's special day.

Until now.

She made a note on her phone's calendar to remember Debbie's birthday in October. Obviously the whirlwind of opening a new business had put them in a time crunch, and she didn't want to forget something so special.

She felt better after a long shower. And a few minutes later, as she was grabbing burgers out of the freezer to grill, her mother texted her. HAPPY BIRTHDAY TO MY FAVORITE DAUGHTER!

THANK YOU! she texted back. ARE WE MEETING BEFORE FIRE-WORKS TONIGHT OR JUST GATHERING AT THE PARK?

LET'S MEET THERE.

Janet swallowed a sigh. SOUNDS GOOD, she replied. SEE YOU THEN.

PERFECT.

She stared at her mother's perky word and frowned. Then her frown deepened at her mother's follow-up text. WAIT, CAN WE COOK AT YOUR PLACE? THEN WE CAN JUST WALK TO THE PARK.

OF COURSE.

A thumbs-up emoji followed.

She decided to use the quiet spell to check out Donovan McGill. There hadn't been a moment to think of what Eileen had shared with them on Sunday, not with the doughnut brigade at the café. Now there was. She brought Laddie back in, poured herself a cup of iced coffee, and settled in at her laptop.

Within five minutes she'd located his daughter, Alma May McGill Webster. She'd been married and was now widowed. She lived in the family home on a rural road. It was an old house. Really old. Not too far out on Route 250, but the online map gave the place an eerie feeling. Janet took one look at it and knew she would not be going alone. Or after dark.

She marked the page, sent directions to her phone, and stood as a dog started barking up the street and then another one joined in. Laddie scrambled to his feet and hurried to the front window to add his voice to the ongoing chorus.

Within seconds, two toots of an emergency siren brought her hurrying to the door.

Ian's police car headed her way, lights flashing.

Behind him, Burt Margolies drove one of the Dennison Fire Department pumpers, and on its side was a big banner that said HAPPY BIRTHDAY JANET! The banner was awash in red, white, and blue, and images of patriotic-themed balloons trimmed the edges.

And then her mother's car, decked out with real balloons. Then Debbie's car, and then her parents. Pastor Nick Winston came along behind them, and as they cruised up Welch Street, a line of neighbors joined the parade, walking alongside. And from the far side came Tiffany, Layla, and the group of kids she'd seen down by the tracks. They carried balloons, a cake box, and a small cooler.

She stepped out onto the porch, and the whole crew began calling out birthday wishes. Horns beeped, and Ian hopped out of his car in his customary quick style and grinned up at her. "Happy birthday, Janet."

"I thought you all forgot." She shook a finger at him as he jogged up the steps and grabbed her in a hug.

"Clearly not, and I'd stay here huggin' you, but I've got to get the grill going. I had to send the kids after the cake and ice cream. I got caught up on a call, and no one was answering their phones, so Tiffany and her friends went to the Whipples' daughter's place below the tracks and gathered the cake and then the ice cream. Which probably should be put in the freezer. Surprised?"

He smiled down into her eyes, and she nodded. There was a lump in her throat, not just from the surprise but from everything. Everything new. Everything changing. Good changes, yes. But good change was still change. "Extremely. I was deciding whether to be wretchedly disappointed, mildly annoyed, or ruggedly stoic."

"What was winning?"

"It was a race to the finish," she assured him with a laugh. "A mix of emotions, but this—" She reached up and kissed him. "This is amazing."

"Son, kissing isn't getting food ready, and I'm about done with doughnuts for a day or two," Janet's dad said. "So if we could get the grill fired up out back, I think there'll be time for a kiss or two later on."

Ian laughed, but he didn't let her go until he claimed one more kiss. "Happy birthday, Janet Shaw. I love you."

She sighed a happy sigh, and then she met his smile straight on. "Same here, Chief. Do we have enough food?"

"All taken care of," said her mother as the parents brought in bags and coolers. "A cookout and then fireworks. I'd say this is a perfect day." Janet couldn't disagree.

She finally had a chance to talk to privately to Debbie at the park four-and-a-half hours later. "I found Donovan McGill's daughter."

"Did you?" Debbie settled in her lawn chair. "Is she close enough that we can talk to her in person?"

"Out Route 250, in an old house that looks like it should become an exercise in firefighting for the local recruits," Janet said.

Deb whistled softly. "Oh. Well, then."

"We can head out tomorrow after we close."

"Should we call first?"

Janet nodded. "Yes. A local number was listed. Whether it works or not, we'll find out tomorrow. You in?"

"Absolutely," Debbie said.

Janet didn't mince words. She'd seen the pictures. She gave Debbie's arm a light squeeze. "Better prepare yourself. The house looks to be in rough shape."

CHAPTER TEN

*J*anet pulled up in front of the unkempt old house, but she didn't turn off the engine. She eyed the decrepit two-story structure, then exchanged looks with Debbie. "What are we thinking?" she whispered, as if the house's inhabitants could hear her. "I told you it was creepy."

"Nothing's falling down or caving in." Debbie inserted a note of cheer into her tone, but her expression said something else entirely. "Alma May Webster lives here? She's got to be almost eighty, right?"

"Eighty-two, according to the internet."

"Oh man." Debbie sighed. "The place looks like a death trap, Janet. I wonder if we could get a crew from church to help. I can't believe the people at Dennison Community know about this and haven't stepped up to help already. It's—"

"Yoo-hoo! Ladies!"

Janet and Debbie simultaneously turned to the right.

A woman waved to them from the modern ranch house across the road from the McGill place. Debbie rolled down her window. "Sorry, didn't mean to disturb you. We're heading over there to see Mrs. Webster."

"If you mean Alma May, I'm right here." The woman nearly bubbled over with enthusiasm. She laughed at their expressions then motioned to the driveway they'd just passed. "Back on up while no one's coming and pull in. I didn't realize you thought I lived in the old place—it never occurred to me to say anything." Her enthusiasm was endearing. "If you go on the internet, it gives the old McGill address, probably because it comes first on the tax records. I own both places, so I guess it makes sense." She waited until Janet pulled into the shaded stone driveway. When they exited the car, Alma May came forward. She stuck out a hand first to one and then to the other. "I get hungry for company out here," she said. She turned with the speed of a much younger woman as she led them into the pretty little ranch.

"My kids are long gone from this area. No jobs hereabouts back then, so Lynnie and Cheryl are up in Cleveland, Rob's in Southern California, and Joey has made a nice life for himself in Pennsylvania, outside Pittsburgh. He used to work for one of the automakers, but when those jobs dried up, he got into computers. I thought he was plumb crazy," she confessed as she swung the screen door open. "'No future in them,' I said, and he's having a good laugh about that now, let me tell you. Come on in. Don't mind Houdini."

A small spitfire of a dog was making a racket on an enclosed back porch.

"He thinks he needs to be the center of attention 24-7 and gets miffed if he can't be the primary meet-and-greet person, but he'll settle into his crate shortly. After a proper show of protection, of course. He earned his name long ago. That rascal is an escape artist. Now that he's got a few years under his belt it's not as bad, but keeping him alive was a job for a while. Silly dog."

The bouncy Chihuahua mix pierced them with three more barks and a dour look before he marched into a miniature crate to sulk.

"Oh, that was funny. He's a hoot," said Debbie. "I love dogs. I kept making excuses why I couldn't have one in Cleveland, but now that I'm back here, I may cave. Of course, we have Crosby at the depot, and he's like a community dog."

"Harry's boy."

"Yes." Janet nodded, glad for a quick connection. "You know Harry?"

"Oh, honey, this town is not so big that most of us oldies don't know each other. Now Harry's got ten or fifteen years on me, but he's always been such a good man. Helping this one, doing for that one. With him and Miss Eileen at the depot, they took it on themselves to look after folks. No lookin' for thanks, not a lick of it," she expounded. "Seemed like kindness and caring was born in them. People like that made this a good place to come back to as my dad got on in years. I came here in my fifties after my husband died, said goodbye to my dad, and I've been here ever since, but one thing has remained a constant in Dennison." She took a seat and indicated they should do the same. "We look out for each other, one way or the other, and if it's on the QT, even better. The Good Lord looks kindly on a joyful giver."

"I believe He does," agreed Debbie.

"We've opened a café in the depot," Janet told her. "And Harry comes by every day. His granddaughter comes by too."

"And of course, Harry brings Crosby along," Debbie added.

"Whose claim to fame seems to be digging," said Janet. "But I believe his actual claim is that he's a descendant of Bing, the World War I dog that came home a hero."

"Oh, that was a story and a half, let me tell you. There were no small number of folks claiming this dog and that to be Bing's son, daughter, granddaughter...you get the picture." Alma May looked excited to share then stopped herself. "Do you gals want coffee? Or tea? I did up a fresh pitcher, knowing you were coming along. It's sweet," she went on. "But with that no-calorie sweetener because at my age, I watch what I eat, what I weigh, and what I watch on television. It's held me in good stead so far."

"You seem wonderfully healthy, Alma May," said Janet. "And I'd love some tea. The heat wears on us, doesn't it? But better than snow in October. That's what my dad always says. Can we get it for you?"

Alma May sprang up and shook her head. "Moving keeps me moving, if you get my drift. I was in a sit-down job for years, and the effect of that was weight and exhaustion, so I decided to change jobs. I started waitressing at the diner over in Uhrichsville, not far from that bakery you helped run," she told Janet.

Janet was surprised. "Have we met before?"

"No, ma'am, but Esther Stewart used to get all the desserts from Whipples', and she'd come back talking about how that Janet Shaw was the best thing that ever happened to that bakery."

"Aw, how nice." Janet accepted the compliment with a smile. "They gave me a great opportunity."

"They're good people, the Whipples, but I think it's real nice that you gals are running your own lives and your own business at the depot now. You follow a whole line of good people watching over that train station. I'm proud that my father was part of it." She filled the glasses as she spoke and then set the stoneware pitcher back in a refrigerator so clean it made Janet want to go home and scrub hers.

"And dogs have managed to be involved with no small number of depot stories over the years," she continued as she brought three tall, icy glasses of tea back to the comfortable sitting area. She set them down then reclaimed her seat on a stout wooden chair. "I like nice furniture, but that's my one concession to getting older," she noted as she indicated their softer chairs. "A firm seat doesn't mess up aging joints the way soft ones can. Anyway, Crosby is a good boy. I've met him many times when I've gone into town, and Bing's story is well known, but I think my favorite all-time depot dog story is about Buddy."

Janet lifted an eyebrow in invitation. "Was he Harry's dog before Crosby?"

Alma May shook her head. "He was one of those who looked enough like Bing to leave little doubt about his heritage, but no one knew who he belonged to or where he came from. One of the workers—a porter, maybe, or it could have been someone who worked with my dad—overheard a young man call him Buddy as he boarded a train with hundreds of other GI Joes. And that was all they knew from that day forward. He became part of the depot from then on, showing up every day, making the trip up the road from somewhere out of town. Folks got used to him being there, like he was part of the woodwork. They'd greet him when they came in, Dad said. Some with a big smile, some with a bit more distance, but Buddy never seemed to mind. 'Hey, Buddy! Whatcha doing in the station today?' or 'There he is. Hey, Buddy! Looking good.' Daddy said that dog's one goal was to be at the station, every day, waiting on someone. Or something. Something that never happened, he said."

"The dog came to the station every day?" Debbie asked.

"According to my dad," Alma May replied. "He liked that dog. He said no other dog he knew showed up like that, day after day. Now, maybe he was just a stray, looking for a warm spot and a scrap or two, but he became the depot dog soon enough. My dad told me that as Buddy got on in years, Miss Eileen took care of him, making sure he was looked after. Making sure he had everything a good old dog needs. But you didn't come here to talk about dogs."

"Medals," said Debbie. "We found a tin box of medals, and Miss Eileen told us that your father had a particular sympathy for lost medals. That it made him feel bad that they weren't with their proper owner."

"You think my father stole those medals?" Her brows couldn't have lifted higher as her eyes widened.

"No, oh no." Janet corrected that notion quickly. "We were wondering if he may have seen fit to give them a respectable burial."

Alma May's brows drew down tight, and Janet couldn't fault her, because the idea sounded silly when said out loud.

"Like respect for the flag kind of thing," added Debbie lamely.

"Oh my goodness." Alma May fanned herself and then stood and paced the room. She looked worried. Her skin had a sprinkling of freckles and age spots, and Janet supposed she had probably been a redhead in days gone by. Alma May was silent for a long beat.

Finally she stopped, turned, and faced them. "My father did feel strongly about military medals," she told them. Her voice was firm, and her face had lost the shine of levity she'd shown them before. "He fought valiantly for this country and then worked long and hard at the depot. Seeing medals tossed into some random box hurt him to the core. A cigar box," she went on. "He said that's what they used later." She wrung her hands, still frowning. "He found that insulting. Like they were tossed into someone's junk drawer, and he couldn't bear it. He said that was his one bad memory of working the depot for so many years. And when he said it was the only bad memory he had, he meant it, because my father loved his job."

"We didn't mean to upset you, Alma May," Janet said. She could sense the change in the older woman's manor, and she didn't want to cause undue stress.

Alma May hugged herself, even though the heat of the day was peaking right then, just below the ninety-degree mark. "But you did."

Oh dear. Janet stood. So did Debbie.

"You can see yourselves out."

"Of course." Janet wanted to say more. She wanted to apologize for upsetting the kindhearted woman, but it seemed smarter to let it go. "Thank you for sharing your stories with us."

Debbie led the way out the door, and Janet followed. Alma May didn't reply to their thanks, and she didn't follow them or shut the inner door.

She stood there, rock solid, hugging herself in the living room. And she was still there, visible through the open drapes, as they backed out of the gravel drive and onto the road.

Janet sighed as she pulled away. "We hurt her."

"But how?" Debbie asked. She'd always had a more practical way of examining problems than Janet. "Because she thinks he buried the medals?"

"Or that we're accusing him of being a thief?"

"Except nothing was stolen, so…."

"Well, I suppose if you take something that doesn't belong to you and bury it, it could be considered stolen," said Janet. "Technically, because it wasn't yours to bury."

"You think that's how she sees it?" Debbie asked. "Because when she got upset, I got the distinct impression that she knew something more than what she was telling."

Janet had gotten the same feeling. "But what?"

Debbie shook her head as they drew closer to town. "I don't know, but the feeling was there. Although I didn't like upsetting such a sweet woman."

"Agreed. But I was glad we didn't have to meet with her in that old house."

"Also agreed," declared Debbie. She made a face and turned toward Janet. "It gave me the willies for sure, but then I got to thinking that maybe it could be pretty again. With some tender loving care."

"It may have potential," Janet said. "I like seeing things get fixed up instead of trashing them. But now I feel bad for worrying her. And there's Karl Kurtz coming our way, so I'm going to put my game face on and see what he has to say. Because you know what I realized?"

Debbie shook her head as Janet pulled into Debbie's driveway.

"If these are Karl's medals, Donovan McGill had nothing to do with them, because he was retired by then. And if Donovan McGill buried them, then they're not Karl's, so why is he trying to claim them? Simple math says both things can't be true."

"I hadn't looked at it that way," Debbie replied. "So"—she undid her seat belt and reached for the door handle—"let's see what our former banker has to say."

Karl came to Debbie's side of the car. "I was hoping to run into you two."

"And here we are." Debbie kept her voice light but not overtly friendly. As she exited the car, Janet didn't miss the calm note of caution her friend used.

"I went to see Kim about those medals you found."

Debbie lifted a single brow.

Janet waited, keeping her face serene.

"She said it wasn't her find and that I should refer back to you, which doesn't really make sense to me. The museum owns the depot now, so why wouldn't something found there be under her authority?"

"Finders keepers?" quipped Janet, but when his face darkened, she realized he wasn't amused.

"So then you're selling them, I assume." He narrowed his eyes. "To the highest bidder to make money for your new enterprise. That's not what I would have expected from two women whose people served this nation at one time or another."

"I don't believe we said anything about selling the medals. Did we, Deb?"

"Not a word." Debbie checked her watch. "I don't have time to chat now. I've got things I need to accomplish, but I believe we have a solution, Karl."

His frown deepened.

"Can you describe the medals in the box? What you remember of them? Or do you have a picture of them in the family? In the box or on a uniform, either way works." Debbie made the offer in a candid tone. "Or check out the national database. That could help. Naturally, we want to accurately identify the owner."

"We'd feel dreadful if we gave these medals to the wrong person and then the rightful owner showed up," added Janet.

"There are very few soldiers from World War II who are still alive," he reminded them. "And you've clearly never attempted to access the database," he added. "If a specific fact is incorrect, the results can't be viewed. And things changed quickly during the war. Rank. Awards. There's stuff that went unsung, let me tell you. And the chances of having a hundred-year-old veteran stroll into the café to gather his lost medals at this point are thin at best."

"And yet many of those war heroes have descendants who might initiate a search, and I'd hate to have to come to you and retrieve the medals. Talk about awkward, right?" Janet kept her tone friendly, but she added a note of authority underneath. "We're going to see if Jim Watson will do an article about the discovery in next week's *Gazette*."

"And we'll post the find on our social media pages," Debbie added. "In the meantime, if you could jot down what you remember about the medals, we'll compare it to the ones we found. That should give us a good idea of whether they're yours or not. Try as I might, I can't figure out a reason anyone would bury your medals though. Especially if they knew you'd lost them. That part doesn't make sense to me."

"People do weird things," he said. "And this place got a lot of traffic in its day. Who's to say that someone didn't think they were doing a soldier an act of kindness by giving his brass a proper burial?"

He was right about the traffic. Dennison had been a busy hub, but the image of some train traveler randomly finding and burying a stash of medals made no sense. Still, Debbie didn't argue, and that was good because Karl Kurtz seemed like he was spoiling for an argument. "That raises an interesting thought, but I do have to run.

Janet, thanks for the ride." Debbie started up her drive. "See you first thing."

"Bye." Janet got into the car, but when she went to back out, Karl leaned down. He tapped on the window.

She didn't want to open it.

She wanted to keep backing out, but that wouldn't be right. This wasn't some nefarious crook. Karl was a retired businessman.

Who knows a lot of things about a lot of people...

She shoved that thought aside and opened her window. "Yes?"

"You know, if I could see the medals, I'd know right off if they were mine," he told her.

"And if they're yours, you should be able to give us a description, correct?"

"It's not like they got pinned on my chest," he said, and his voice lost its friendly edge. "They were handed to me by my grandfather."

"And you've no pictures of your grandfather?"

"Of course I do. But I think he included some other medals in there too."

"You come up with a list, okay? I have to go." She rolled the window up and backed out, hoping he'd move his feet.

He did, but it wasn't any too quickly, and she felt his eyes on her as she maneuvered onto the street and headed up the road.

She knew him as a former customer at the Third Street Bakery, but she didn't know him on a personal level. She was pretty sure she didn't like him and equally sure she didn't want to get him angry, because no one starting a new business wanted to rile up the people they served. On the other hand, she wasn't about to hand over the box of medals to just anyone for any reason.

Dennison, Ohio
March 1951

Perimeter sniff: Check!

Interior sniff: Check!

And just to make sure things hadn't changed and nothing was overlooked, Buddy made his way to the train tracks and gave the platform a thorough sniffing as well.

Scent-tracking procedures were ingrained in dogs. It was an inherent trait, and even though it had been a couple of days, he was able to deep-sniff the tracks, the cleared snow paths, and the area leading away from the depot in case The Boy had returned during his capture.

The experience had taught him some valuable lessons.

Avoid cars at all costs. Not just the ones aiming your way. All dogs knew the danger in that. But now he knew that even the simple act of getting into one was a clear and present danger.

When the lady in the special suit patted her back seat to offer him a ride up the hill, he'd let her sweet talk him into accepting it.

And then they'd trapped him in the old lady's house.

He had nothing against old ladies. They were nice enough, he supposed, but most weren't overly friendly to stray dogs. This one was all right—maybe a little grumpy—but it wasn't aimed at him, so he shrugged that off.

But when morning came and she didn't open the door, he got nervous.

Real nervous.

She thought he needed to do the necessary things, and he did, but she let him out the back door, into a yard.

A fenced yard.

He barked. She let him back in. He whined. She frowned and let him out back again.

Clearly, she wasn't getting it. He barked again.

She brought him in, and he immediately trotted to the other door. The one they'd come in the night before. He stared at the door and barked three times.

"You've been out twice. You're fine, go lie down by the fire," the old lady said.

Lie down by the fire? Like a lazy old hound?

The very thought of turning his back on The Boy, of abandoning his post, made Buddy pant. He stared at the door, barked loudly, then stared at her.

She walked away.

He couldn't believe it.

Didn't she get it? He wasn't like the dog in that picture in the window. He didn't want a place by her fire. Sure, it was cozy, just like the picture seemed, but it wasn't for him. Not unless The Boy was sitting right there in a chair alongside. That would tilt his decision, but The Boy wasn't there, so he barked again.

"Hush, boy."

His name wasn't boy. Usually he was fine when folks called him that but not today. Not locked in a strange house with no way out.

He woofed louder this time. Pawed the front door. Spun around twice, pawed the door again, and then barked once more. Deep, loud barks too.

She stared at her newspaper and ignored him.

She must be hard of hearing. The Boy's grandmother had been hard of hearing when he was a pup and he'd had an accident or two—well, a few, at least— on her chipped tile floor. But he was a pup then, and pups have a lot of learning to do.

He barked louder. More times.

"Shush, boy. Shush."

So she did hear him? He trotted across the room and sat alongside her, nice and upright. Then he whined.

She frowned.

He whined again, a long, drawn-out piteous whine that made her face change. Her eyes got smaller, and the bushy brows above them drew down and in. It was an unhappy face. He took pride in never making humans have an unhappy face, but she wasn't listening to him, and so he whined again. Nice and loud.

She stared at the paper, then him, and then the paper again. Then she folded it carefully, the way old ladies do, and set it aside. She stood up. It took some doing because she had to grip hard on the arms of the chair. She made it after a time but didn't try to move until she reached for a cane.

The cane had a rounded knob on top, except it wasn't all rounded. It was like a flower carved into it, and her hand gripped the flower. Then she began to walk toward the back door and the snow-filled yard again.

Buddy made it easy for her.

He trotted right over to the other door and sat, waiting.

She looked at him, and then she came his way. "You want to go down to the station, eh?"

He pawed the floor then stood, quivering with anticipation. She knew. She understood. She—

"You know my granddaughter will have my head if I let you out."

He didn't know what that meant or who her granddaughter was, but he eyed her, then the door, and then her again. And then he patted the door with one paw. Just one. Polite-like.

"All right, Buddy, all right. I get the drift."

His heart raced.

She reached for the door. And when she swung it open, he charged out and galloped down the driveway.

Free!

Free at last!

He was ready to race down the road to the station, but he'd forgotten something. Something important.

He slid to a stop and turned.

The old lady stood framed in the door, kind of like those paintings in the shop up the road. She met his gaze and nodded.

He did the same, except he smiled at her. A really big smile too, and then he wagged his tail as hard as he could.

She'd listened to him. Understood him. And that meant so much.

He turned and ran down the road to the train depot. When he got there he left no post, corner, or tree unsniffed or unscented.

The Boy had one job.

He had another.

And they'd perform their tasks with honor until all was complete. And then they'd be together again.

CHAPTER ELEVEN

Janet had been ordering online for years, but outfitting a college dorm for her only child should be a mother-daughter bonding time. She could get the very same things with a few quick clicks, but this shopping trip was a rite of passage.

Tiffany stopped by the café on Friday morning. "Are we all set for a run to the mall tonight?"

"Debbie is closing up, and I'm out of here by two," Janet promised. "We'll head straight up to New Philly, okay? And grab supper on the way back."

"Is it all right if Layla comes along?"

Layla's family had met with hard times two years before, when her father walked out. Layla had hit a wall, but she was emerging from that difficult cycle. She'd been Tiffany's best friend for nearly ten years. Janet smiled at her daughter. "Layla's always welcome. Saves me from having to talk. When you two are together, the best thing I do is listen."

Tiffany laughed.

"Will it bother Layla that we're buying stuff for you to go to Case Western? Community college wasn't her dream."

Tiffany sighed. "Having her dad walk out rocked her, for sure. Her grades slipped. She fell off the tracks for a while."

Janet had suspected as much, but teen girls tended to talk to other teens, not their mothers, so she'd learned to listen whenever the opportunity arose.

"By the time she got her head on straight, junior year was half over. On the plus side, she's found out she likes fixing things."

"She's always had a knack for that," noted Janet as she boxed up two Boston cream pies for an order. They sold them by the slice in the café, but she'd had several bakery orders this week for whipped cream or custard-filled cakes. People loved the fresh, cold taste of refrigerated cakes in the heat.

"Belmont's got a building preservation and restoration program she's interested in," Tiffany went on. Belmont was a community college in nearby St. Clairsville. "The nice thing is that she can do some courses online if the weather gets bad and she can't commute. Going to Belmont means she can be home, help drive her brother around when her mom's working, and still get an education." Tiffany pulled her backpack over her shoulders. She was working at the local Parks & Rec summer camps for the next six weeks. It was a good experience for a girl with no siblings. "I'll see you at two, okay?" she said then paused. "Hey. Where'd you get this?" She reached around the cash register and lifted the small heart-shaped button Janet had set there and forgotten.

"Debbie found it. Around back of the vintage cars."

"That's great," Tiffany said. "I loaned Layla my shirt, and she was so upset when she lost the button. She even offered to buy me another shirt, and you know she doesn't have money for that. She'll be so happy it was found." She lifted the button to get Debbie's attention. "Thank you for finding this. I hated that she worried so much about it."

"No worries." Debbie waved it off. "You have a great day, Tiff."

"You too."

Jim Watson walked in as Tiffany went out. He held the door for her and then let it swing shut once she'd gone through. "Orientation for Parks & Rec?" he asked as he chose a seat at the counter.

Janet spotted Harry heading their way with Crosby in tow, so she poured two coffees and set them side by side in front of Jim. "Yes. How'd you know?"

"The village booked a couple of ads for the sessions in the *Gazette*. They used her picture from the swim lessons. Working with kids in the pool."

Tiffany had loved swimming ever since she'd first learned how. She was a fish in the water, like Ian. Janet was a much more cautious person when it came to the water. She preferred waving from the beach to being pounded by the waves. "She's got her lifeguard certification, so she can either lifeguard or teach lessons. She's psyched."

"And off to college soon," he added as he took his seat.

"Yes." Janet drew the word out slowly. "Elementary, my dear Watson, and since you already knew all that, what's on your mind?"

He handed her a sheet of paper. "I was hoping you'd be okay with me putting a story about the medals in next week's edition. Harry let it slip," he told her. "I figured if you haven't found the owner yet, it might be time to get the word out."

Talk about perfect timing. "We were just discussing that," Janet said. She motioned Debbie over. "I'd like to see if we can figure things out first ourselves though. We have an announcement ready for social media too, but I can't bring myself to post it, because I keep thinking we'll find something. It's only been a week." But as she said that, she realized that it *had* been a full week and they were nowhere closer to an answer than they'd been the week before. But how did one find answers to questions that might be decades old?

Kim came through for an early coffee. Patricia followed her in, and since they were both aware of the situation, Janet kept the conversation going. "Usually I'm good at puzzles," she said. "Ian has no patience for them, but I like tinkering. Figuring things out. Finding answers. And with the medals, I'm nervous that they could fall into the wrong hands. I'd feel awful if the right person came along and we had already given them to someone else."

"I heard that Karl Kurtz is fussing about those medals being his," said Patricia as Debbie made her coffee. "But before you go falling for that, you might want to have a look at the Depot Inn."

"The old place over on North Water Street?" asked Debbie.

Patricia nodded. "Karl's sister, Ellen, owns the inn. Her daughter Katie runs it with her."

"Ellen Knowles?" asked Janet. "She's hosted a few people at the inn for Pastor Winston. I didn't know she was related to Karl."

"Ellen Kurtz Knowles," Patricia said. "Her parents owned it way back. Gramps knows."

"I sure do," said Harry. "George and Edwina bought the original house a long time ago. They ran it for years while living there, and then they bought a second house across the street on North Water, kitty-corner. They moved the family into that place. Doing that gave them two more rooms for more visitors at the inn and no mess, because you know how kids are. The Depot Inn's not big, but it's charming and right here in town."

"Edwina used to collect old tins," said Patricia. "All different sorts. She displayed them on little shelves around the inn. That old building was meant for that kind of thing. She used to crochet with my mom, and she talked about those old tins like they were something special. Candy tins. Cookie tins. Crackers. A lot of stuff was sold in reusable tins back then."

"And then the place caught fire," said Harry. "They lost a wing and part of the upstairs, but they had it rebuilt just the way it had been. Edwina liked that nod toward history in a historic town. That's what she used to say. But the fire took a lot of those old tins—they were mostly displayed in the wing that burned."

"So this adds some weight to Karl's story," Debbie noted as she set Harry's eggs and toast in front of him.

Kim shook her head. "Not necessarily. Being around the tins might have just made him familiar with them. He would have been a teen when the place burned, and I'm sure his mother had a few around their house too. They were such sensible containers."

"Washable and reusable. I love tins like that," said Janet. "I think Debbie and I will pay Ellen a visit and check things out. Maybe meeting Karl's sister will give us some insight on him."

"I don't know him well," said Jim. He heaved a sigh of appreciation as he sipped his coffee. "Best coffee in town, ladies."

Janet and Debbie smiled at him.

"I do know that Karl was a fair and honest banker. I also know he likes to spend money, and unless people are exceedingly careful with finances, changing spending habits can be tough when you're on a fixed income."

"He's not working at all?" asked Janet. Most of the people who stayed local after retirement ended up with some sort of part-time or even full-time job. Sitting around doing nothing wasn't a popular pastime.

Jim shrugged. "I can't say. I'm just saying that if you don't change your spending habits, you can dig yourself into a hole pretty quick."

"There's a lot of truth in those words," Patricia declared. She raised her coffee cup. "Gotta run. Thank you for the coffee. It's delish as always!"

Janet finished icing the Boston creams. Debbie took care of the counter and the customers as the place got busier. They'd been concerned about not having enough customers the first week or two in business, but once word got out about the coffee, the bakery, and the quick short-order breakfasts and lunches, people had started calling in their orders or making them online. If business remained this active all year round, they'd make up their investments by year two, and that was a full year sooner than expected.

By the time she was back home from the shopping trip, supper with the girls, dropping Layla home, and then stowing a whole lot of bags and parcels on the living room sofa, Janet had just enough time for a quick shower and five hours of sleep before heading to the café to get the early baking prep done. Debbie was coming in at six to help, but Janet knew a four o'clock start on a busy Saturday morning made sense, and she could always sleep in on Sunday.

By the time the oven preheated, she had six seven-inch round cakes ready to be baked. Her homemade piecrusts had thawed overnight, so she got to work precooking fruit fillings on the stovetop. Precooked berry fillings didn't tend to be as runny. It was a trick Charla Whipple had taught her, and it worked. She was filling three crusts with strawberry-rhubarb filling when a sound caught her attention. An odd sound, like someone messing with the front door. Specifically, the doorknob. The kind of noise that told her someone was trying to gain entry to the café. Someone out there, in the dark, fiddling with the door. Someone she couldn't see through the curtains.

Her heart stopped.

When it dared to beat again, the instant adrenaline rush set her pulse racing.

She could see across the café but not too clearly, because the only lights on were in the kitchen area and by the back door.

She stared at the front door.

The noise came again. Not loud but not real soft either, as if the person wasn't trying to be all that quiet.

A small part of her wanted to move toward the door and confront the person.

But the larger part wisely advised her to call Ian.

CHAPTER TWELVE

Ian arrived in just a few minutes. She saw him pull up out front. The beam of his high-powered flashlight lit up wide swaths of the area. The vintage trains, the walkway, the sidewalk, the green areas. His quick diligence indicated that he took her concerns seriously. He came around to the back door a few minutes later, and she let him in.

The first thing he did was relock the door. Then he hugged her. "Hearing things, my love?"

"Real things," she assured him. "And they seem to happen mostly when I'm here alone in the mornings. Remember that thump last week that I thought might be a bird?"

"I do," Ian said. "Maybe that raccoon we found has friends around here."

He noticed her skeptical expression and filled her in while he filled his favorite mug. "Raccoons do try locks and door handles. Full-sized raccoons, that is."

"Really?" She thought for a moment then accepted the possibility. "Opposable thumbs."

"And you had the installer put one of those lever handles on the door that you just have to push down on. Much easier for a raccoon to maneuver than a round doorknob."

"Well, who would have thought?" said Janet. She set the big saucepan in the sink and checked the lattice crusts on the surfaces of the fruit mixtures. Three strawberry rhubarb, two cherry, and two bumbleberry—mixed fruit—pies would be in the oven in fifteen minutes, giving her a nice head start on the day. "We just thought it was cute and authentic looking."

"They can't get in if it's locked, and they're nocturnal, so you shouldn't have a problem during closed hours," he told her. "And they're not going to come strolling in during daylight hours. Generally," he added with a grin.

"Well, be that as it may, I'm glad to be married to the police chief and doubly glad that it's just a silly raccoon."

"I said it *could* be," he reminded her. "I didn't see or hear anything to tell me what it actually was, but having that raccoon around last week and knowing their habits, it's a possibility."

"I would prefer the word *probability*," she told him, but she decided he was most likely correct. "Although I never had this problem during the early shift at Whipples'."

"Their bakery wasn't located in the same kind of area," he reminded her. "The tracks offer a lot of natural hideouts, and you've got old industrial buildings nearby. What we'd call an eyesore could be considered a four-star hotel to our furry friends. They're great climbers. And I got the report on that one I found last week. No rabies. I don't know what was wrong with him, but it wasn't that."

"That's good to hear," she said. The timer buzzed the cakes' completion as Debbie came toward the back door lugging a reusable grocery bag. Ian opened the door for her, and she wasted no time.

"You here on official business?" she asked.

"I heard a noise and called him." Janet hated to admit her fears, but it was weird to have things trying to enter the building. Especially in the dark. But maybe not weird for nocturnal creatures that liked sugar.

"And I found nothing but a great pot of coffee and a pretty girl." Ian's smile said it was all worth missing forty minutes of sleep. "I'll head back home. Tiffany and some of her friends are spending the day at the water park near Akron. They're driving up around ten then coming home tonight. She'll walk over and get your car later this morning."

"She and Layla told me about it last night. I may have lectured them about driving carefully and being aware of their parking area and surroundings, you know. All the things mothers do."

"I'll be giving them the same advice, so they'll get it in stereo," said Ian. He gave her a quick kiss goodbye. "Nothing wrong with being aware of what's going on around you. Smart stuff, Mama Bear."

"I don't like that something is spooking you," Debbie said after the door closed behind Ian. "I'm going to come in super early with you from now on."

Janet refused that offer instantly. "You are not. That's ridiculous, and besides, there's nothing for you to do. I come early to bake, and you stay late to clean up." She slipped the cakes onto a cooling surface then adjusted the oven temperature for the pies. "I'm over-the-moon thrilled that we have so much business. Who would have thought we'd be this busy this soon?"

"Not me, but I love it," Debbie said. "I'm going to make the tuna and chicken salads for lunch. Do you need me to do anything for you right now?"

"Keep the coffee dark and the conversation light," said Janet, and that was what they did right up until it was time to stop by the Depot Inn that afternoon.

"This place is so cute," Debbie said as Janet parked the car along the curb on Ninth Street. The gracious Queen Anne oozed the charm of a small-town bed and breakfast, from the lace curtains to the edged walkway and vibrant annuals spilling from two matching hanging baskets.

They climbed the steps and knocked on the door. A young woman opened it within seconds, and the laughter of a small child came from an unseen room beyond. "I'm Katie," the woman told them as she ushered them into a lovely foyer. An impressive staircase rose on their right, and an inviting sitting room was off to the left. "Mom's just about finished upstairs," she said. "We have three guests booked for today. We like to be ready by four just in case anyone comes in early."

"Of course." Debbie extended her hand. "Debbie Albright. New co-owner of the Whistle Stop Café in the historic depot."

"And I'm Janet Shaw," Janet told her.

"From the Third Street Bakery," declared a voice from the stairs as Ellen Knowles started down. Katie's mother looked like an older version of Katie, and only slightly older, although the internet indicated twenty-five years between them. Clearly, Ellen's genetics treated aging with singular kindness. "We used to order cookies and muffins from there when I was too busy to make my own before I retired from teaching."

"I wondered why you'd stopped," Janet said as Ellen descended the final steps. "In a small town, you get to know people by their orders. Although I don't think we ever met, did we?"

"Your shift was done by the time I was able to pick things up in the afternoon," Ellen explained. She motioned to the Victorian-style living room. "Come on in here. We can talk about those old tins, a family favorite. We don't let the grandkids come and play in this room, because they're rough on furniture and people love taking pictures in here. I'm going to leave you with Katie today, though, because I have some baking to do across the street. She can fill you in on anything you need to know." She turned to Katie. "I'm taking the kids with me," she told her. "That way you can finish up here."

"Will do."

"If you ladies have any other questions, give me a call next week, all right? Weekends are busy, and I don't want to risk a bad review by being careless. Those reviews matter a lot these days."

"We found out the truth of that at the bakery," Janet said. "We'll talk next week."

Ellen nodded and hurried out the front door. Janet's seat on the sofa allowed her a view of the outside, and Ellen had just crossed the street when a car pulled up to the curb where she was standing.

Ellen paused.

She seemed to be listening to whatever the driver was saying.

Then she frowned, waved the driver off, and did a pivot that would have made an NBA player proud. She marched up the drive and into the house through the side door.

The car continued past the inn. Janet could see the driver, but she really didn't need to, because she'd seen that pricey car several times the past few weeks.

Karl Kurtz had come to see his sister. The meeting looked like it was none too friendly, and Janet wondered why. But for the moment, she turned her full attention back to Katie. She smoothed her hand over the elegant tucked-and-buttoned sofa. "Not horsehair."

Katie made a mock face of horror. "My mom showed me a horsehair sofa once, at an estate sale. It was so ridiculously uncomfortable, I just couldn't do it. We went with the same kind of style but used friendlier materials." She crossed the room and pulled two vintage tins from a shelf. "These are dust catchers now, but back in the day people used them for everything. Before plastic, this was your go-to for storing all kinds of things." She handed one to Janet and one to Debbie.

"We heard your grandmother was a collector." Debbie ran her fingers across the smooth blue finish of her tin. "We found a tin buried at the depot. It was filled with medals."

"Gran loved those tins and used them for everything," said Katie. "Years ago someone from a magazine came to write an article about her and the inn and the tins. They took a lot of pictures and gave Gran all the proofs. Those ended up being a big help when they had to come up with compensation for the fire. I brought a few to show you."

She handed some photos to Debbie and some to Janet.

"Your grandmother had a good eye," Debbie noted. "She didn't overcrowd the shelves. She placed them at their best advantage around the room."

Janet flipped through her stash quickly. Toward the back, she found what she was looking for. She held up two pictures. One with a tin like they'd found, and one from another candymaker. "I love these. The flowers. The background. They're beautiful."

"We still have the black one," said Katie. "It's in one of the upstairs rooms. But the Schrafft's tin was in the fire-damaged area. That one was burned along with about forty others."

"Did your grandmother ever replace it?" Debbie asked. If she did, Karl might have had access to the floral-embellished tin they'd recovered.

"No, they weren't easily found back then. There were no online sites like the ones that make things so easy now. If you didn't happen on something in a shop or a yard sale, it didn't exist. And Gran and Grandpa were too busy running the inn to worry about it. She gathered a few more over the years, but they were newer ones she happened to come across. Mom has replaced some." Katie pointed to the tin sitting on the end table next to Janet. "She found that one online, and the baking soda one. She loves that."

"Any baker would," Janet declared. She exchanged a look with Debbie. Should they tell Katie about Karl's claim?

Ellen's daughter was in her early thirties. Would she have been privy to something he'd done twenty years before?

Janet didn't think so. Not because it was nefarious but because she didn't think an uncle would share information about medals with a child.

"What was the tin you found like?" Katie asked.

"This." Janet held up the picture of the blue candy tin covered with flowers. "Rusted, but you could tell it was a beautiful old piece."

"That's a needlepoint tin." Katie's eyes lit up. "Those are very popular, and that one is old, for sure. You can find tins online now, and that one's always there."

"Because they were plentiful?" asked Debbie.

"Or just because they're so pretty. Gran and her parents immigrated to the US in the thirties when she was a child. She married Grandpa in the forties right after the war. That woman knew the value of a dollar. They bought this place with money Grandpa's parents left him. Both of his parents died of tuberculosis in the sanitorium up in Stark County. They didn't have much, but it didn't take much after the war. Grandma liked to tell their story."

"I'm glad you listened," said Debbie. "So often we don't take the time to hear those old stories."

"I didn't take in as much as I should have, but I know she and Grandpa worked hard to make a go of things. She had great respect for this country and for the opportunities that waited around every corner. Her saying, not mine, but I believe it."

She glanced at the clock, and Janet took the hint. She stood. "You've been a marvelous help to us."

"I don't know how." Katie smiled. "I don't know much, but I do know the tin you found isn't ours. Ours was lost, but it kept a spot in my grandma's heart throughout the years. I hope you find the owner of yours real soon."

CHAPTER THIRTEEN

*A*fter they said their goodbyes to Katie and left the inn, Debbie pulled into the Dairy Queen up the road. "Soft-serve sundae?" she asked.

"That's a definite yes," Janet said. "The heat has drained me of resistance and willpower. It also makes anything hot sound awful right now. Just a mini though. Chocolate with strawberries and bananas, please. Ian's doing hot dogs on the grill later."

"Sounds like a miniaturized banana split. The sundae. Not the meat."

Janet grinned. "Exactly."

When they had their treats, Debbie parked beneath a big old tree. "Ah. Shade."

"The comfort of trees," said Janet. "Except that it's close to ninety even in the shade, so keep the air going, okay?"

Debbie laughed. "We're such wimps. Okay, let's talk about what Katie said while it's fresh on our minds."

"First, let me tell you what I saw out their window." She explained Karl's encounter with his sister, and Debbie frowned.

"He couldn't have known we were coming, could he?"

"Should we check for tracking devices?" asked Janet.

Debbie rolled her eyes, obviously skeptical. "Like those things they put on cars in the movies?"

"Oh, honey." Janet laughed. "That's so 2010. No, the tiny discs someone can slip into your purse or under a seat. Anywhere they're not likely to be found. Luckily, some smartphones can tell you when one's been placed near you."

Debbie stared at her. "You've been watching too many cop shows."

"I'm married to a cop show," Janet said. "I hear all the fun and updated ways people can get into trouble and cause trouble for others. You can buy a four-pack of those things for a hundred bucks on Amazon. Two clicks, and bingo!" She snapped her fingers. "They arrive the next day."

Debbie's expression displayed her outrage. "How can this be a thing?" she demanded. Clearly, she'd had no experience with this tracking technology. "How can that be legal?"

"Because it's marketed as a great little device to find lost items," Janet explained. "Bookbags. Keys. Remotes. Use one of those, and you can pinpoint it with your iPhone."

"Well, a four-year-old Android isn't going to work then, so I'll pass. Do you really think he's tracking us?"

Janet shook her head. "I think he's wanting to find out what he needs to do to make us think those medals are his. But why?"

Debbie rolled her eyes. "Money, of course. Isn't that always the bottom line?"

"Are they worth anything, though? I mean to someone else? Is there a resale market for medals?"

Debbie did a quick search on her phone. "There is a market for them. A bigger one if you can identify the recipient. The ones we found are in great condition. And if they were given to someone in Karl's family, he's got a personal association with them. So we're looking at several thousand dollars' worth of medals."

Jim Watson's words came back to Janet. "Remember what Jim said about changing spending habits when you retire? Maybe Karl's underwater right now."

"But to sell family military medals?" Debbie frowned. Then she ignored her ice cream and scrolled on her phone. After a few minutes she whistled softly. "Holy moly, I think we've got a clue." She held up the phone with the logo of a popular resale site. "Say hello to Banker 1041."

Janet frowned.

"Base: Eastern Ohio. History: Financial services. Served: US Army, four years, honorable discharge." Debbie stopped reading and met Janet's gaze. "And guess who lives at 1041 Alameda Street in Uhrichsville?"

"Karl?"

Debbie nodded. "The very same. So our retired banker *does* have a side job. Online sales of vintage items, specializing in military and Americana."

"So he's just after the medals to sell them." Janet took a deep breath. "He's lying to us."

"And if he is, then we're done with him," Debbie said. "I'm not a fan of anyone misrepresenting our military or our nation. So that's that."

"We need to ask him again to describe the medals. He can't possibly know what's in the box if they're not his, right?"

"Right. When should we see him?"

"I'll set it up and let you know."

"Sounds good," said Debbie. Her phone buzzed a text. She glanced down, sent off a quick reply, and went back to her ice cream. "Mom needs help moving furniture. I'm going to head over there after I drop you off."

Debbie tossed her empty cup into the small garbage bag she kept up front. "I say we visit Eileen again. See what she has to say."

"I'll make a treat for her to share with her friends. Can we go tomorrow afternoon? I've got a two-hour window between church and helping Ian move a shed. He's got it in his head that it's way too close to the house. And Jim wants to meet with us about the medals," she added. "I'd rather let him run with the story first then post to social media after. He's such a good guy. I think he'd get a kick out of having an exclusive."

Debbie's quick smile showed that she agreed. "Perfect." She put the car in gear. "I'll set up tomorrow with Eileen and text you if it works out."

"And I'll see if Jim can come by after closing on Monday. That will give us quiet time to talk and show him the medals. He wants pictures," she added.

Debbie nodded as she backed out of the parking spot. "Understandable. It's time to get the word out, see if anyone knows anything. Now that we've pretty much kicked Karl's claim to the curb."

"Which brings up another question," said Janet. "How will he react when he realizes we're not buying his story?"

Debbie shrugged. "I have no idea." She pulled onto the road. "I don't like making enemies. There's a part of me that likes to avoid

controversy at all costs. After all, new businesses have enough chal-
lenges without making people angry. And yet there's another part of
me that wants to stand my ground." She shrugged as she turned east
on North Water Street. "In the end, doing the right thing outranks
all the rest."

She was right.

Janet knew the risks. Being married to the chief of police had
schooled her in a lot of things, but she agreed that doing the right
thing was the only way to go. They'd just have to mend what they
could when they were done.

Black River Falls
May 1952

*Sport peered out the window of the pickup as Jerome
pulled into a parking space at the little market.*

*Grown now, the pup had taken on a spaniel appear-
ance, like one of those Brittany dogs—red-and-white
splotched, good for hunting birds. Neighbors had kept
a pair of them when Jerome was young. They had been
up-the-road neighbors, closer to town, where places
were generally better kept, although no one had much
back then. He'd been blessed to hire on with Ed Zink's
gravel-laying service in the late thirties. The old*

fellow needed the strength of a muscled youth, and Jerome fit the bill. He'd learned a lot from old Ed, but his trek to work meant he had to pass his neighbor's house with those dogs every single day. They bellowed as he approached, barking and lunging, pulling at their ropes. The rope on the bigger dog broke one day. The liver-and-white dog came after him like a fireman on his way to a working blaze, and Jerome knew better than to try and outrun him.

He'd stopped and turned, not knowing what to expect, but when he instinctively put his hand out, the dog slid to a stop. Then he sat, quiet-like.

The owner charged out of the house about then, calling the dog's name. When the dog turned to him, the man brought his open right hand diagonally to his left shoulder, and the dog trotted peacefully to him.

Jerome faced the man. The guy was big. Not heavy—no one got to be heavy in those days—but big, nonetheless, and Jerome thrust his chin toward the dog. "How'd you teach him to sit and come like that?"

The man rocked back on his heels. "Trained him. Read it in a magazine for hunters. It's quiet. Using hand signals doesn't rile the game."

Of course. Jerome nodded. "Makes sense. Surprised me, is all. They're pretty dogs too."

"Looks are all right, but a dog that behaves is the best," the man replied. "Dogs need to be trustworthy. I know they bark at you when you go by. I appreciate you not egging them on."

Jerome didn't try to hide his surprise. "Who would do that?"

The man drew his brows down tight. "Mostly kids. But the dogs need to be tied up in front right now. Fencing comes dear, and they can't be out back diggin' up the garden or we'd go hungry come winter. So they're out front with the tree for shade. You have a good day, now."

Jerome had pondered the man's words, his sensibility. He started teaching hand signals to Buddy the next night, and his friend knew a few before a month was up. The only thing that dog had ever wanted was to make Jerome happy, and he did, right up until the day Jerome stepped onto that train full of new recruits.

He sighed.

Sport seemed to sense the change of mood. He brought his silky head around and nudged Jerome lightly, as if comforting him. The dog's trust and affection felt good.

He'd only owned two dogs in his life. His mom let him keep Buddy because the dog seemed to exist on *little food, which made him affordable. Although he wasn't sure if he kept Buddy, or Buddy kept him. It worked, either way.*

And Sport was an all-around good dog too. He was calm in the house and got his exercise running around their place in town.

"I'll be right back, Sport." He hopped out of the cab and walked into the small grocery store. They were low on milk and laundry soap, and a toddler and a newborn sure did create a lot of laundry.

Two sons. Beautiful boys. And Frances already letting him know she intended to have a daughter at some point.

Thoughts of a daughter made him think of his sisters.

Funny how moving on and doing all right made one think of when things weren't all right, but Dale was doing well. She was the oldest and living in California now. His mom and Patience were in Florida, and Cara had married a Texas soldier and moved outside of Houston.

Fourteen years had brought a lot of good and a lot of change for all of them. Buddy moving on with old Henry Burton, who'd said he'd care for him, the older girls moving on from their wartime work in Cincinnati, and Patience still living near or with their mother. His mother's letters made that sound like a back-and-forth thing, but she said nothing more, and he didn't pry.

None of them were going without anymore. No one was hurting for food or clothing. And everyone had a sound roof over their heads. A man couldn't ask for more than that.

He took care of his errands then climbed back into the cab.

Sport looked happy to see him. He nudged his head toward Jerome again, and Jerome obliged him with a good scratch behind the ears.

He still smelled of wet fur, but he was mostly dry now. Dogs got fleas in the summer—big ones up here—but if he gave Sport a good long swim two days a week, there were no fleas. He didn't know if they drowned or jumped off, and he didn't much care. He only knew that Frances had learned that trick from her mother. And it worked, which was good, because no one with two little kids needed fleas.

They headed for home just as the bars came down on the rail crossing. The train rumbled by, a passenger one this time, and for a moment he was transported back to that confluence of tracks and the old depot, crowded with soldiers and sailors, Salvation Army workers, and the scent of fried doughnuts filling the air with hints of cinnamon and nutmeg.

He'd left on one of those days.

Left and never looked back, but he'd never forgotten the scent of that oil, frying puffed-up yeasty cakes, the sort that melt in your mouth when you bite them.

Nobody made doughnuts like that up here. There were good ones here and there but nothing like those mouthwatering ones the volunteers served up all day, every day, to the thousands of troops passing through. Some boys were there for only fifteen minutes or so, barely enough time to use the facilities, but the volunteers spread out, carrying trays of warm doughnuts and fresh, hot coffee.

The caboose trundled through the intersection, and the gates rose. He went on, heading for home, with the thought of that last day stuck in his mind.

Final goodbyes.

One last walk with his trusty four-legged friend before entrusting him to Henry.

And a handful of doughnuts that became food for a day.

Nostalgia hit him. Not hard. But it was there, nonetheless, and when he pulled into the driveway of their big old place, he sat in the cab a minute. Then he left the past where it belonged and climbed out of the truck. Sport jumped down, tail wagging, still too fragrant to be inside. He let the dog out back and headed for the side door.

Frances liked old houses. She liked the imagination she could put into them. He'd thought one of those new ranch-style places would be easy upkeep, but he'd learned a solid lesson from working with Allen. Happy wife, happy life.

And when her face lit up as he strolled through the door carrying a jug of milk, a box of detergent, and half a dozen of Ernestine Worth's doughnuts, he knew he'd chosen well.

CHAPTER FOURTEEN

lashing lights greeted Janet when she drove into the Good Shepherd Retirement Center parking lot on Sunday afternoon. Two fire engines took up the No Parking/Safety Zone area. Twin ambulances and a police car stood nearby, and the home's residents were walking or sitting on various parts of the lawn. The heat-stressed grassy area linked the assisted-living center to the parking lot just off the road. She pulled off to the side and hopped out of the car, worried.

Debbie called out to her from the small grove of spruce trees nearby.

Janet went her way. "What's happening?"

"A report of a suspicious smell. The fire department is here to check it out. No one's hurt, but everyone had to come outside until we get an all clear."

That was a relief. "Good."

Debbie motioned to her left.

A group of senior women sat fanning themselves at the far end of the building. Some of the home's residents would be fine outside, but the heat index in July was no laughing matter, especially for people who weren't acclimated to the higher temperatures. The thin shade from meager ash trees wasn't enough to make the women comfortable.

Eileen spotted Janet and Debbie and waved them over. Janet wasn't sure if there were rules about visitors during emergency services, but Eileen seemed unbothered. As they approached the outdoor table, she clapped her hands in glee. "There hasn't been this much excitement here since I moved in. It does an old body good to have a little dustup now and again!"

Debbie laughed, but Janet noticed that the other two women didn't look comfortable. "Can we move you all into the shade?" she asked.

The woman nearest her sniffed. "You'd think a place like this would have more trees, wouldn't you? And these ash trees are barely leafing."

The other woman replied in a scolding voice, "Blame the bug, Lucille, not the place. That ash borer thing rolled through this part of Ohio a few years back and killed a bunch of the trees. What a mess that was." Her dour voice had taken on an instructional tone, but then she turned and sniped at Lucille. "You're not in memory care yet!" she declared. The unfriendliness of her voice surprised Janet.

Lucille kept fanning herself with a newspaper. "I remember well enough, but I haven't seen a body out here planting new trees, have I?" She stood and gripped the table momentarily to get her balance then grabbed her walker and moved off. The other woman got up and did the same, leaving Eileen alone with Janet and Debbie.

"Did we scare them off?" Janet asked.

Eileen followed the two elderly women with her eyes. "Lucille has been sad for a long time," she said. "She's got no one left who comes to see her or sends her notes. She's alone in this world except for us here, and that's not the same, is it? Not the same as family that checks in on you. And Joyce, she was an administrator over at Nordstrom Manor, but they didn't want her to come there as a resident when she lost her mobility. The Nordstrom folks figured she'd be second-guessing everything the staff did. This isn't where she wants to be, so she takes that out on others from time to time. Now"—she turned her attention back to them—"to what do I owe another delightful visit from Dennison's newest entrepreneurs?"

Debbie took a seat and began. "Donovan McGill's daughter mentioned something about a dog."

Eileen's brows drew down in confusion. "Any particular dog? I've loved a lot of pups in my time. One of the gifts and sorrows of a long life," she added, but it wasn't a lament. More like quiet acceptance.

"Alma May remembered her dad telling a story about a dog that came to the depot every day," added Janet.

Eileen's expression changed. A mix of joy and sorrow darkened the circles beneath her eyes, and her hand shook as she reached for a cup of water just out of reach.

Debbie slid the cup closer.

Eileen grasped it with two hands, and Janet had to fight the urge to help as Eileen drew the shaking cup to her mouth.

But Eileen managed. She took a long drink from the protruding straw and set the cup back down. "Buddy."

Debbie leaned in and nodded. "That's what she called him."

Eileen clasped her hands and leaned forward. "I loved that dog." She said the words softly, glancing at Debbie and then Janet. "He was a good old boy. So good. He came to visit the depot every day without fail. He'd come early in the day in the spring and summer and a little later in the day in fall and winter. You know how bad our winters get."

"We get some rugged storms, for sure."

"And still he came. Every day."

"Whose dog was he?" asked Janet. She'd taken out a small pad and pencil and was scribbling notes as they went.

"No one knew. He was just a good old boy looking for his soldier. Waiting, like so many of us did back then. Waiting for our boys to come home or missing them because they never did." A tear snaked its way down her face. She reached up and wiped it away. "I lost a brother and a father in the war. And the town lost its share, Uhrichsville and Claymont too. Every town in the nation paid its dues to defend freedom's call, and that dog waited with the rest of us."

"Loyal," said Debbie.

"To a fault," Eileen said. "I arranged for him to have a warm home with my grandmother toward the end of his years. He'd been staying in an old farmstead that had long since fallen apart out on Route 250. Harry followed him one day and saw him duck beneath an old barn. He'd hollowed out a cozy den in there. When he got on in years, Grandma took him in. I helped," she continued. "I figured he'd be warm and fed, cared for. Kind of like what we've got here, you know? It was my assisted-living plan for Buddy."

Debbie and Janet both nodded.

"Well, he lasted one night there before he made his escape and came straight back to the depot. Grandma said he was desperate to leave and she couldn't keep him locked in when he so clearly wanted or needed to be at the train station. She told me the longing in his eyes wasn't something a good person could ignore."

"He had a mission," said Janet.

"He did," Eileen said. "He made that trek as long as he could, and when it got too hard for him, I made a nest in a corner of the depot with a couple old blankets. He lived over a year with just going in and out as he chose. Oh, he was a good old boy." She paused, sighing. "Stocky when he was young. Not so much as he got older. Cream-colored with a couple of spots of brown. It was a more chocolate brown, good and dark. Not that lighter tone you see on some. He kind of reminded me of Crosby. Not so much how he looked, but there was a devotion in his eye that grabbed hold of your heart. He had strength and valor. And he smiled."

Debbie frowned. "He what?"

"He smiled," Eileen repeated. "The funniest thing with some dogs, how they mimic what we do when we smile. All those sharp teeth can make it a little odd, but he smiled at people. From the time he first started coming around. I was still somewhat new at my post then, with so many soldiers and marines and sailors going through. It was…" She paused again and swallowed hard. "Humbling," she said finally. "Who knew when or if they were coming back? And there was Buddy, hanging out at the station, waiting. He started to look lean after a while, so we made sure to have treats on hand. When neighbors around the depot heard about him, they'd bring food by. Within a couple of months he looked healthy again. And that's how it stayed for years," she said. Her expression drooped slightly. "I hated to say goodbye," she said. "He and I stepped into the depot about the same time. Watching him fade away just broke my heart. I may have given him a place to rest. We may have provided food. But Buddy didn't come to the station day after day to see me. In the end, we knew he'd had a good life, such as it was. A life of faithfulness is nothing to shake a stick at, is it?"

"No." Janet kept her voice soft, and she put her hand over Eileen's. "It's a pretty amazing thing, all in all."

"It still makes me cry." Eileen had a box of tissues in the pocket of her walker pouch. She pulled a couple out and dried her tears. "Saying goodbye to him was hard. So hard. I didn't have much in the way of money at the time, but the local merchants took up a small collection."

"To bury him?" asked Debbie.

Eileen shook her head. "No. Raymond Zink's family had some farmland south of here, and we buried Buddy there. The merchants used their funds to buy a bench. They set it under the oak tree there at the depot. The tree wasn't so big then, and it made a nice sight for folks to sit and watch the trains. A place to sit in the shade as the tree grew. Oaks don't grow fast, but they give proper shade once they do."

"The bench Winifred Gayle used to sit on," said Janet.

"Winnie." Eileen's eyes widened slightly. "Yes. That bench was like a second home to her for a while, and no one knew why. Winnie Gayle was like one of those figures out of an old story. Strong but frail. Mindful with a splash of mindlessness. Some called her touched in the head, but I think Winnie just lived on a different plane than the rest of us. She wrote stories, you know."

Janet nodded. "She mentioned that she used to like to write."

"Not under her name," Eileen explained. "She used what she called a nom de plume."

"A pen name," said Debbie.

"Yes, it was very common back then. Actors, actresses, authors, singers. They made them take different names, you know, so they had more appeal. Kim said they don't do that anymore, and that's a good thing, I say. A melting-pot nation should sound like a melting-pot nation. Anyway, that bench got weather-worn over time, and by then the depot was different. Trains were different. Transportation was different. Folks jumped into their cars and headed here, there, and the other place on the interstates, so rail travel diminished. There was a memorial plaque too."

A plaque? Janet kept making notes as she posed a question. "For?"

"Buddy." Eileen wiped her eyes again. "It was done on metal, like one of those historical markers you see. A friend of Harry's did it at no cost. He even etched an outline of a dog. It read 'Ever Faithful, Ever Trusting, Ever Loyal, I Wait. Buddy 1953.' We placed it right next to the bench. It was a story all its own," she said. "Life went on. I'd gotten married. Then I had a family. The bench eventually weakened. The tree grew, and the flowers we planted in Buddy's memory couldn't live in the shade. The roots got big and strong. Time changed everything, but it never changed that dog's love and devotion, and that's a lesson I keep with me every day of my life."

She stared off, remembering, and Janet was pretty sure she wasn't seeing the patches of sparse grass, always more apparent in the heat of summer, or the trees, some healthy, some struggling. She thought the former stationmaster was seeing a faithful cream-colored dog, loping into town, taking his spot at the station.

Eileen took a deep breath. Then she sat back. "I haven't traveled down that particular section of memory lane in a while," she said. "I think about it often enough. That's one thing. Telling the story out loud?" She raised her thin eyebrows. "That's quite another. But it was a good story then and a good one now about man's best friend. And that's something to smile about."

"Where's the plaque?" asked Debbie.

Eileen shrugged. "It disappeared years ago. Before the bench got old and the legs grew weak. We figured someone took it. Maybe someone that meant something to the old boy. Or just a common thief. I always felt bad about that," she confessed. "One day I came to work, and the plaque was gone. Just gone." She shook her head. "Harry's friend made me another. I kept that one in my office before I retired, and now it's here, in my room. On the wall. But we never did find the original."

A nursing assistant came by and announced that they were clear to go back inside. Janet and Debbie walked Eileen in, and when she yawned, the friends took the hint. "We'll let you rest in the coolness of the AC," Debbie told her. She gave the elderly woman a hug. "Thank you, Eileen. Thank you so much."

"For telling you the story?"

Debbie shook her head. "For loving Buddy the way you did. He was blessed to have you."

"Not nearly as blessed as I was to have him," she replied. Her voice had regained its strength. "We stood by one another during a tough time, and I'd do it all again if need be."

After they left the building, Debbie paused. "Two things. First, I'm really starting to think I need a dog."

Janet laughed. She'd seen that coming.

"Second, do you think the person who took the plaque was the person who buried the medals?"

"I thought about that," said Janet. "If they could be connected. Although when you're talking decades, I suppose that's a long shot, isn't it?"

Janet wondered the same thing. "Let's get Jim on this tomorrow. Spread the word. Maybe getting the medals in the news and on social media will stir something up. Someone, somewhere, must know something about them. But who that is and where they are is a mystery. Maybe with the help of newsprint and technology we can narrow things down. See you in the morning."

"You need help moving that shed?" Debbie asked.

Janet smiled. "I'm pretty sure my dad and yours conspired to tag-team the effort while I was gone so I wouldn't have to. I overheard my father say something about surprising me, and not having to move a twelve-by-twelve shed would be a wonderful Sunday afternoon surprise."

Sure enough, the shed was moved when she got home. The men had enlisted the help of Greg and his boys, and the six of them had used long wooden poles to roll the shed into place. She marveled at that while Ian grilled pork chops over a wood fire in the fire pit once the men had gone home. "I wouldn't have thought of that," she told him when she brought a dish of barbecue sauce to the backyard. "I'd have had everyone hoisting the ends of extra-long four-by-fours and carrying the silly thing. Clearly, I wouldn't have been the person inventing the wheel," she added ruefully.

"That's where it all began," he said as he accepted the dish. "Wheels, axles, and levers. And now—" He tapped the ever-present cell phone in his pocket.

"Modern conveniences galore, and we still like cooking over a wood fire best," she said.

"As long as I have a wood fire and a smoker, I'm a happy man," said Ian, but then he paused quickly. "And the best wife, of course."

She laughed. "Well, there's that."

"Except I mean it, love." He grinned at her through the puffs of smoke. "Absolutely. Completely. Every day."

She rounded the grill to nab a kiss. "I love that you're a romantic. It makes me happy."

"I do what I can." He smiled as one of Tiffany's friends pulled into the driveway and Tiffany got out of the car. She came through the front door and raced upstairs as Janet entered the kitchen from the back.

Janet smiled and handed Tiffany a container of cookies when she buzzed through the kitchen five minutes later to say goodbye. "Mom, you baked? When it's this hot?" Tiffany gave her a hug. "You're the best."

"Straight from the freezer a few hours ago. Whose pool tonight?"

"Alicia Jones. There are twelve of us heading over. She lives by the football field."

Janet didn't know Alicia.

She'd never met her. For seventeen years she'd made sure she knew everything she could about anyone Tiffany hung out with, but with college just weeks away, she had to let go. She knew it.

She hated it, mostly. But she knew it. "Have fun, and if anyone is drinking or—"

"Alicia's mom would kill us, but I hear you, Mom. These kids aren't like the ones that got into trouble last week." Tiffany saw Janet's surprised reaction and made a face. "Dad didn't tell you."

"Dad didn't tell her what?" asked Ian as he came into the kitchen with a plate of roasted meat.

"About Charlie's party last week?"

"Stupid kid stuff. Just glad you and your friends weren't there." He paused. "Well, most of your friends weren't there."

"Who was there and what happened?" asked Janet.

"One of the guys brought a bottle of vodka, and half the kids got wasted. Knowingly," Ian added. "He didn't trick them, but he used a fake ID to get the liquor."

"Your friends were there?" Just asking the question made the hairs on Janet's neck stand up. "Which ones? And were they drinking?"

"Chase and Alan were there, and neither one drank."

"They also didn't leave," noted Ian. "Or call it in."

"Dad, snitching out your friends at a pool party?" Tiffany's phone buzzed. Probably her friends, wondering where she was. "You know I don't drink, and I know better than to ride with someone who has. I'd never feel funny about calling you or Mom to come get me, but I don't think I could report my friends for drinking at a party. I'd feel like a rat."

"Two of those kids were driving," Ian reminded her. "They might have given their keys to someone to drive them home. But they might not have. Chase said he'd promised to be a designated driver."

"These are eighteen-year-olds we're talking about," said Janet. "They're underage and drinking."

"Except my friends weren't," Tiffany reminded her. "I think it says a lot about a person if they're around temptation and resist it. You and Dad taught me that. And not to sound like a total geek, but the idea of drinking doesn't appeal to me. So you're pretty safe. Promise." She tucked the cookies under her arm, kissed her dad's cheek then Janet's, and headed out. "If I need a ride, I'll call, okay?"

"And I'll answer," Ian called back. He set the meat platter on the counter next to the salad, and then he faced Janet. She folded her arms. Then she unfolded them.

Ian made his living by keeping peace and order in their town. He made assessments and judgment calls. And he was quick to remind her and others not to borrow trouble.

He was right.

Tiff wasn't at the drinking party, so there was no real reason for Janet to know what happened there. She crossed to the microwave, withdrew the bowl of fresh German potato salad, and set it on the counter. She smiled at him. "Let's eat."

Dennison, Ohio
May 1953

"Hey, old fellow." The lady with the special outfit squatted down next to Buddy's little area inside the depot. She'd put a cushion in there a while ago. Two winters back?

He wasn't sure, really. He couldn't see all that well anymore, so he could only tell what season it was by the blasts of hot or cold air as travelers came through the door and by the angle of light through the windows that looked toward the rising sun. She'd made his corner so he could see those windows without having to get up. That was so nice of her.

His feet used to be a part of his weather guide, but he didn't feel much on the soles of his pads anymore. His nose, yes. Not his feet. They weren't exactly numb, but they weren't to be trusted either.

He could always tell the lady in the special outfit was close because she smelled like a spring day. Clean and fresh, sunny and bright. She reached out a hand to pet him. "How're we doing today?"

He thumped his tail twice.

The second time was hard.

It didn't used to be hard. Leaping up, jumping to his feet, and hurrying toward the tracks used to be something he did without thinking. Natural as breathing. Just as easy too.

But getting up was hard now. Even sleeping was hard sometimes, because he had aches in places he didn't know could ache. They'd crept up on him, surprising him. Once he got up, he could stay up for a bit, but he didn't dash for the tracks anymore.

He'd pick his way tentatively to the window and sit, gazing out. He'd keep his eyes trained down the track, toward the rising sun, and when folks came strolling in, he'd try to smile at them, but even that tested his mettle.

His chest felt heavy inside, as if carrying a burden, but there was no burden. It just felt bad, is all, and so he stayed inside the station, watching the tracks between naps and making necessary trips out back once or twice a day.

"You don't have to get up, boy. It's all right. I just thought you might like a little company." The lady in the special outfit whispered the words as she stroked his head. She did that a lot now. She'd taken him up the road to see someone. A man, older like him, and the fellow had stroked his head just like she was doing

now. Then he'd shaken his head, sad-like, and the lady in the special outfit had brought him back to the depot.

She didn't say too much. She was busy running things—working and telling folks what to do. She was good at that. When she looked at him, she would smile, but it wasn't her normal smile. Even through his fading vision, he knew that because he understood what smiles meant. From the time he was a pup he understood the value of a smile, even if a dog's smile looked a little different. He'd seen his smile reflected in shop windows from time to time. It was kind of toothy, and almost looked "growly," but no one seemed to mind, because he never growled. It wasn't in him to growl.

He couldn't smile like he used to though.

Couldn't walk like he used to either. Couldn't even eat like he used to, because nothing tasted good and it hurt to chew and to swallow.

But her touch meant something. Something good and nice and kind, so he leaned into it, like he'd done with The Boy on those long, cold nights. They'd stayed warm together, best they could, and even if The Boy didn't make it back—

Even if The Boy couldn't make it back was a better way of looking at it. If he could have come back, he would have. Buddy knew enough about folks to know that. The Boy loved him in a way no one else had, and *he wouldn't have forgotten his old friend. It wasn't in him to forget like that.*

"You're such a good old boy," crooned the lady in the special outfit. "So good. I'm glad to have known you. Mighty glad."

He peered up at her.

She looked different. Sad.

Like really sad, the way some folks looked when they came to the station as if their very hearts were breaking. That was how she looked now. Only it was just him and her.

"I love you, boy."

She kept petting him, so gentle. So nice. A smooth touch, like the touch of a mother dog.

She leaned in and down, whispering now. "I'm sorry your friend never came back, boy. So sorry. But I hope you know that we loved you just as much. That we all hoped and prayed he'd come walking through that door, like something out of a storybook or one of those feel-good movies." Something warm and wet touched his cheek when she put her head to his. "You taught us a lot, my friend. About faith and devotion and keeping promises and sacrificial love. I'll never forget it, boy. Never. I love you."

Fainter.

The touch of her hand was such a comfort, but as his eyes drifted shut, he couldn't feel the touch anymore. He sensed it. Sensed her. But he couldn't feel it.

She made a sound then. A crying sound, like when The Boy would huddle against him at night after he gave his bread to his sister. He said he'd eaten in town, but the dog was witness to the empty gurgling of The Boy's belly, and he knew the truth. That made him snuggle closer to him. He couldn't give him food, but he could provide warmth, and so he did, but he never forgot that sound. So like the sound he heard now, although it was fading. Growing softer. Much softer, with every breath he drew.

And then there was no sound.

There was—

He moved his head onto her lap.

Tears fell onto his face, but that was all right. It would always be all right.

He couldn't open his eyes, but he didn't have to. She knew. He knew. It was time.

He let out one long, soft breath right there in the train station, like he'd done so often before.

Then he fell asleep one last time.

CHAPTER FIFTEEN

*J*anet pulled into the depot parking area early Monday morning. She wanted a head start on the day. Once fresh breads were in the oven, she'd pull anything from the case that should be donated. Ian would run them to the food pantry, and she'd refill the bakery shelves with fresh offerings. Then they had an early meeting with Jim Watson to discuss his article and a late-day meeting with Karl to let him know they knew the medals weren't his.

She grabbed a small sack of supplies that had been delivered to their house and headed for the back door.

Something shifted in the deep shadows. Something light-toned and not small. Definitely not small.

Her pulse ramped up.

Was it a person, crouched low?

Her heart hit overdrive. Her breath caught low in her throat, choking her. She'd lived in Dennison all her life and had worked predawn hours for years, and she'd never been afraid to challenge the early darkness. Until now.

She withdrew her phone. With a one-finger swipe, she switched the flashlight on then trained it in the area of the old oak tree.

A dog slipped through the beam. A good-sized dog. It darted between the tree and the fence then moved to the vintage rail cars.

"Hey, boy."

The dog paused and looked back. Even in the shadows cast by the lights, his lean physique cried hunger, and when she turned toward the door, she saw a dusty pawprint, clearly distinguishable next to the doorknob. The doorknob was coated with a similar dry dust, not uncommon in the drought days of July.

The dog was hungry, looking for food.

She unlocked the door quickly and set her bag down. In less than five minutes, she had a scrambled egg and a slice of toast sitting on the counter. She let it cool while she blended lemon pound cake batter in a mixing bowl. By the time the loaf pans were in the oven, the egg and toast were cool enough to set outside.

She didn't put it right next to the door. The dog might not approach with her inside. She placed it a little farther out, closer to the wrought iron fencing. A bowl of water would probably help him too. She set one nearby.

Would he smell breakfast?

As she mixed cookie dough in the commercial mixer, she kept one eye on the window.

Shortly after six a silvery shadow slipped across the brick walkway. The oblique lights cast a grayish tinge to the dog's coat, like moonlight on fog. The dog drew up short, and Janet thought it looked like he inhaled the food. Then he turned and gave the door a look of expectation, but Janet resisted the urge to put out more food. If he was really starving, small meals were the best beginning.

Debbie's car pulled into the lot.

The dog stiffened. He sniffed the air, spotted the car lights, and loped west. She didn't know where he was going or where he'd been, but for the moment he wasn't weak with hunger, and that meant the world to Janet.

Debbie came through the back door. "Was that a dog I just saw?"

"It was. It appears this depot attracts its share of canines."

"Dad saw a crew of coyotes walking the tracks the other night, just before dark," Debbie said as she grabbed an apron. "We didn't have coyotes here when you and I were little. Now they're commonplace. Was the dog a stray?"

Janet shrugged. "It seems so. He was hungry and not afraid to beg. There were pawprints on the door from the dust."

"For real?" Deb reopened the door and whistled softly. "Sure enough. Well, I'm glad you gave him a bite. Do you think it could have been him messing with the door last week?"

Janet slipped the pound cakes onto cooling racks and set the oven mitts down before answering the question. "It's possible. That late June rain kept things under control. It wasn't so dry and dusty then. There was no mistaking his intent this morning. He was on a mission for food. And he had no collar that I saw."

"I'll send a question to the lost-and-found group later this morning," Debbie said. "Just in case anyone is looking for him."

"Do you think that stray is what's got Crosby sniffing here, there, and everywhere?"

Debbie nodded. "Maybe. So we should thank the stray for the medal quest?"

Janet laughed. "Possibly."

A little after six thirty, Jim Watson came through the back door. "You remembered." Janet pointed to the coffeepot, and he nodded briskly.

She set the timer for the cinnamon coffee cakes and then poured Jim's coffee. Then she took the box of medals from her bag and brought it to the table. "Thanks for doing this early. I didn't want to make plans out in the open."

"Glad to do it." Jim opened the box and gave the medals a look of frank appreciation. "That's a collection and a half." He lifted a medal and pointed to the ribbon above it. "See this oak leaf cluster?"

Debbie brought her coffee over as Jim noted the pin that was attached to the ribbon. "Yes."

"That means he was a double bronze star awardee. Everyone that served got a bronze star. But if someone earned a second award for bravery or facing danger at great personal cost, it was usually displayed like this, attaching the leaf cluster to the original ribbon." He ran his finger along the metallic pin and then pointed to the opposite side of the ribbon. "The *V* indicates that this star isn't standard military issue to all who served. It's issued for valor. So this person served with courage and honor."

"Are you a World War II history buff?" asked Debbie.

"No." He grinned and sipped his coffee. "I did an internet search. It's amazing how much you can find by punching in a few keywords."

"Harry recognized several of these, but he was in the dark about others." Janet pointed out four nested medals.

"Those two are Polish awards," Jim told them. He scrolled down on his smartphone. "And that one..." He lifted another award. "British. In fact, these two are British, so if this is one person's collection, it means they were internationally awarded for their war efforts."

"Wow." Janet was surprised and impressed.

"The thing is," Jim continued, "most United Kingdom awards were given to people who served in the UK, and Polish awards were given to people who helped liberate Poland. Did this person serve in both areas? That might be a way to trace these. I don't think there were too many outfits that worked in both England and Poland. It could narrow our search even more. If these all belonged to one person, that is."

The back door swung open, and Bernice Byrne came through. Bernice was well known around town. She was a cat lover who had earned the title of Dennison's cat lady, but Bernice was atypical. She didn't keep a houseful of cats. She hunted high and low for new owners. Bernice liked to say she could read a good person like most people read the *Gazette*, and the thing was, she was right. None of her placements went bad, and when someone passed away or had to leave their home, they called on Bernice to reshelter their cats.

Not dogs. Bernice was not a dog person.

But when it came to cats, Bernice knew her stuff. On the other hand, she was constantly forgetting this, that, or the other thing. It wasn't Alzheimer's. She'd had that ruled out a few years before. And it wasn't dementia. It was simple "dis-remembering" as she called it, and many a Byrne belonging had disappeared over the last five or six years. Some missing items were eventually found, while others stayed hidden. But, memory issues aside, Bernice Byrne had a heart of gold and the sweetest nature known to man.

The middle-aged woman glanced left and right, and then she frowned. "Are you open?"

"In thirty minutes." Debbie stood and met her as Bernice came their way.

"I saw the lights and thought I'd pop in for a quick coffee," she said. "Then I realized it was probably too early when I saw you all sitting around." She peered at the table. "Well, that's a box of something, isn't it? Those are some great medals. I never served," she said, as if she needed to explain. "But my father served in Vietnam, and he had a cluster or two of his own. Harley wanted to bury those medals with Dad, but I put my foot down and said absolutely not." She went on as Debbie poured coffee in a to-go cup for her. "'Those awards aren't going to be buried anywhere,' I told him. 'We're going to show them off and be proud of Jasper Matthew Byrne.' Of course, Harley wasn't proud of anything, so that didn't go over too well, but I put those medals aside a few years ago. I haven't seen them since." She accepted the coffee with a quick smile. "I thought Harley might've snuck 'em into Dad's coffin—he's sneaky like that, you know—but he says he did no such thing and that I probably forgot where I put them, which is something I do from time to time."

Janet held back a laugh. She didn't dare make eye contact with Jim or Debbie. She gave Bernice's free hand a sympathetic squeeze. "We all forget sometimes. It happens."

"More for me than most, but I don't sit and fret over that or anything else. Life's too short." Bernice raised her cup. "This is good coffee," she said, smiling at Debbie. "You know just how I like it. Not too much sugar but a generous dash of cream. How much do I owe you?" she asked.

"Not a penny," Debbie said. "You're a member of our Bottomless Cup Club, remember?"

"I do now," said Bernice. She grinned and hurried toward the door. "I'll get on so you all can get on. Thank you!" She left, and Debbie turned back to Janet and Jim.

"You know she'd likely be homeless in Cleveland."

Jim grimaced. "You think?"

"People look out for her here," said Janet. "She's got such a good heart. Ian takes day-old bread and cakes to her now and again. And he's not the only one."

"Towns like ours have a way of looking after their own," said Jim.

"The pastor calls it 'holding Sunday church on Monday,'" said Janet.

"'Making every field a mission field,'" added Debbie. She exchanged a smile with Janet then filled Jim in. "Those were some of our mottoes from church camp in our teens. Old lessons I've never forgotten. Being home brings that all back to mind."

"So you're okay if I run with a story about these?"

"We are," Janet replied. "But if we show a picture of the medals, how do we ask someone to describe them? They'll have seen them."

"I'll just show the box and the Purple Heart." Jim had returned the medals to their velvet nest. He closed the lid snugly and stood. Then he took a couple of shots of the box. "That's enough to tweak a memory but keep the contents unknown."

"Thank you, Jim." Janet stood and crossed to the coffeepot. "Refill for the road?"

"Yes, ma'am, and do you two want right of approval before publication?"

Debbie grinned. "That sounds very New York, but no. You write the story, and I'm sure you'll do it justice. People around here love your writing. Mom even had a subscription to the paper sent to me in Cleveland."

Jim grinned. "I'm aware."

"I loved seeing your take on stories," Debbie said. "It gave me a taste of home. The article will be in Thursday's edition?"

"Yes." Jim accepted the refilled coffee cup from Janet and headed for the door. "Thanks for bringing me on board, ladies. See you later. I'm going to stop by when the old boys are jawing about heat and humidity."

"See you then."

Debbie checked her phone once Jim left. "I sent my text to the lost-and-found group when Jim came in. Nothing about the dog. No replies other than sympathy for his plight."

"His plight improved this morning," said Janet as Harry strolled their way. Crosby dashed ahead, sniffing every area the stray dog had walked. The door, the handle, the oak, the fencing. When he found the empty plate of food, he turned, looking indignant.

Debbie laughed. "Yours is coming, my friend. Promise."

Janet filled a mug for Harry. He liked more sugar and less cream than Bernice. He pointed to the metal box when he came inside and settled into a chair. "Any luck finding the owner?"

"Not yet," Janet said as Debbie started eggs and toast for him and Crosby. "Jim's writing an article for the *Gazette*. If it's someone local, they'll most likely see it."

"If they're still breathin', that is."

Harry grinned when Janet rolled her eyes, but she couldn't dispute his logic. "World War II was a long time ago."

"And our numbers are decreasing yearly," Harry said frankly. "But if that soldier or marine is gone home to God, someone in his or her family would recognize the box or the medals, most likely. Although a lot of men I knew put them out of sight and out of mind after VE Day and VJ Day. They'd seen enough, and we were all ready to get back to work. Back to life. Back home."

"Put the war behind you," said Janet.

"It was easy to do in some ways, because the whole world was on fire for change and looking forward," Harry said as Debbie brought the plates their way. "Everything building and growing. I'm not saying it didn't wear on some more than others," he explained. "Many of my buddies ended up struggling with PTSD and other ailments that were hard to shake. But we came back feeling like winners, and that thrust things forward."

Debbie set his plate down in front of him and Crosby's on the floor. "The thrill of victory made a difference, for sure."

"Always does," Harry said. He glanced upward. "Lord, I thank You for this food and these good friends who came to the depot to start something new. Bless them today and every day. Amen." He picked up his knife and fork, same as he did every morning since just before they had opened.

They'd just gotten through a fairly steady coffee-and-breakfast wave when Karl Kurtz came through the front door.

Janet met him before he reached the counter. "We were going to meet right after closing today."

"I was over this way. Hoped it wouldn't be busy. I can see it isn't."

His assessment stung a little, and Janet had to fight the urge to assure him that they'd been busy up until fifteen minutes before. She took a breath and sent him to a table near the window looking out over the nearby tracks.

Debbie had just finished wiping the grill. She washed her hands and moved their way, and she didn't try to hide her frown. "Karl, this is work time for us."

"I know." He looked down. "Janet said you wanted me to describe the medals. At least some of them," he continued. "And I can't." He admitted that with a sheepish expression. "I can't, because they're not mine. I never lost any medals, and I was clutching at straws because I needed money and this seemed easy. I thought I might as well sell them because whoever put them in the ground obviously didn't care about them."

"We don't know that," Janet said. "The owner would care about them more than someone who's out to make a buck."

"I disagree. Most collectors I know respect the history of what went on back then," Karl said. "They're not in it for the money but to preserve a spot of history. That's what the museum does here, right?"

"For public viewing," Debbie reminded him.

He nodded. "I'm not saying what I did was right. It wasn't. I came by early to apologize, because I shouldn't have lied. It was stupid, and I knew it the minute I spoke to my sister. She's always had my number," he added as he stood. "But she's loved me in spite of it. Good luck with your mission, ladies." He slid his chair back into place. "I'm getting a part-time job to bring in some needed cash for the next year or two. I thought retiring was the thing to do, but it's left me with too much time on my hands. And it's never good to have too much time on your hands. And if you don't mind, Mrs. Shaw—"

"Janet," she assured him.

"I'll be ordering a cake from you come April."

It couldn't have been easy for the banker to come clean, but he'd done it. Janet smiled at him. "I look forward to it."

He left, and Debbie met Janet's gaze. "Wow."

"Yes. That took guts," agreed Janet as she moved toward the coffeepot to offer refills to the two remaining tables. "And him mentioning the cake reminds me that I promised Tiffany I'd make a lemon version of it. I'm going to get that into the oven before we get busy for lunch."

The week sped by.

Janet put out an egg and toast each morning. She added kibble to the mix but only spotted the dog once. He was good at slipping in below the radar while she was busy at the baking counter. When Debbie arrived between five thirty and six each morning, the food dish wasn't just empty. It was licked clean.

On Thursday afternoon Ian came by and installed cameras on both the front and the back doors. "It's like a doorbell cam," he explained once the tiny units were in place. "Your phone will let you know when someone enters the frame, and it will video the encounter."

"Amazing technology," said Janet. "But what about our customers? They're not going to want to be on video, are they?"

"Everyone has cameras," he reminded her. "Even the depot."

"Although Kim said the system hasn't been working right," Janet told him.

"This device will help you identify the dog," he explained. "See his habits. We might be able to get a leash on him. Get him a place to stay."

"I did get a couple of comments from people who are down the tracks a ways," Debbie said. "Someone saw him heading up the creek, someone else saw him along the edges of McCluskey Park, and someone spotted a dog that looks like him under the Center Street bridge."

"Cool and shady gets my vote," said Janet.

"It gets all our votes this time of year," said Ian. He indicated the front door with a jut of his chin. "That's one pretty dog right there." Greg Connor had just parked his work truck in the shade, and he reached up and opened the side door.

Hammer jumped out. Greg scratched the border collie's ears, and the dog's black-and-white tail wagged in quick appreciation. Greg never brought Hammer to the front door, nor did he leave him in the cab of his work truck. He and Hammer came around back.

Janet was the one closest to the door. She could have taken Greg's to-go mug and filled it for him, but she didn't. Debbie angled a look her way, crossed to the door, and swung it open. Seeing her friend's smile cemented Janet's decision. "Hey, Greg. A quick cup before we close up?"

"And a dozen chocolate chip cookies. The boys are helping groom the baseball fields for the weekend tournament, and they're going to be hot and hungry when I pick them up."

Greg was a single dad with two athletic sons, Jaxon and Julian. "I'll bag them for you," said Janet.

Debbie filled Greg's coffee.

"No sugar, just cream," Janet reminded her as if Debbie wouldn't remember Greg's order.

"Got it, thanks." Debbie kept her tone light, but she poked Janet in the back as she went by. Not hard but enough to say she knew all her friend's tricks.

"Hey, ask Greg about the old McGill place on Route 250," Janet called over her shoulder as she counted out the cookies. Ian turned the lock on the front door and flipped the corded sign to CLOSED.

"What's going on with the old McGill place?" Ian asked as he came across the room.

"It needs help," Janet said. "I hadn't been out that way in a long while. I didn't realize how run-down it's gotten."

Greg smiled his thanks to Debbie and raised the to-go cup in salute. "Best coffee around. I'm glad you all are here." Janet noticed that he held Debbie's gaze a moment longer than necessary before shifting it back to her. "The church was going to do some work on the McGill place three years ago, but Alma May declined the help. I'm not sure if she was afraid we'd find something, wreck something, or nose around in something that wasn't our business, but she made it clear we should stop asking. We're still willing, but she got real nervous when she realized we'd be taking out a few walls and shoring up others. All necessary to the longevity of the house."

"Raising the question, what is she hiding?" asked Ian, and the way he said it sent shivers up Janet's spine.

"She's a sweet old thing," she protested.

Ian and Greg exchanged grins. "Doesn't mean she doesn't have a secret or two hiding in a closet, Janet," said Greg.

Debbie groaned as she bent to feed Hammer a treat. Greg's grin widened when she straightened up and sent him a doubtful look. "I do tend to find secret things in old places," he insisted. "Flipping houses comes with treasure-hunting possibilities. One of the perks."

"It also comes with crime solving," said Ian. "Remember the pile of bank statements you found in that old pawn shop?"

"Old Mr. Ritler was sitting on a gold mine," said Janet.

"And Greg was the one who discovered the dump site for that transmission place south of Uhrichsville," Ian added.

"That one got the government involved," Greg said. "The mechanic had long since died, but he managed to pollute a lot of ground. Not everything I find is valuable. But sometimes it is. And sometimes it's touching, like a bundle of old love letters. And sometimes it's criminal."

"So no one ever goes into the old McGill house?" asked Debbie. "That only makes it more intriguing."

"She's very particular about that." Greg frowned. "A nice enough woman, but she's protective of that place, and no one knows why."

"I'm going to say it's preservation of old memories," Janet announced.

Ian smirked and patted her shoulder. "You go right ahead and think that, darlin'. I'm heading back to work. What should we have for supper tonight?"

Janet's phone rang.

So did Debbie's, followed by a notification. Then another. And another.

Janet's notifications sounded too, and when she scanned the texts, she waved the phone for Ian to see. "This week's edition of the *Gazette* is out, and all these people are asking about the medals, so—"

"Grilled cheese sounds good to me." Ian gave her a quick kiss. "I'll make yours on rye with Swiss, okay? But I'll wait until you're on your way home. Let me know when you get done tracking things down."

Ian left but not before taking time to give Hammer a thorough scratch around the ears. Hammer, a real people-lover, thumped his tail on the wooden floor.

Greg lifted a brow as he accepted the sack of cookies. "You two are tracking something down? Dare I ask what?"

"We found some medals two weeks ago," explained Debbie.

"World War II medals," added Janet. "Buried out back, under the old oak tree."

"Who would bury medals?" Greg asked. Then he paused as he seemed to make the connection. "Ah. Alma May's father worked here for a long time."

"Yes, he did," said Janet, nodding.

"And he used to talk about searching for people to match up with lost medals. He'd come to the ballfield years ago—before I was married. I umpired there for extra money when my contracting business was new. Donovan loved sports. He'd walk to the fields and watch teams play. He liked to talk."

"How could he track down soldiers back then?" asked Debbie. "So many of those men were just passing through. That doesn't make sense."

Greg shook his head. "I don't know. He talked about it pretty much every time I saw him. He served in Korea and had a lot of respect for the military. And for doing the right thing. Finding the owners meant a great deal to him."

"That's exactly what Eileen said." Janet finished wiping down the counters as they got ready to leave. She motioned to a table and posed a question to Debbie. "Do you want to contact people from here? Or should we try to see them in person?"

"In person." Debbie crossed the room and did one last sweep to make sure everything was turned off. "That way we can see them face-to-face."

Janet locked the door as Greg and Hammer headed for his red pickup.

She motioned to his departing truck once she got into the car. "He's such a great guy."

Debbie sent her a look. "He is. And he did a great job on my renovation. But I'm not here looking for romance, despite my mother's broad hints about Dennison being the perfect place for people to settle down."

"There's more than one way of settling down," Janet replied. "You had the gumption to make a big leap, Debbie. A leap I love," she said with a smile. "Plenty of time for other things to happen. If they're meant to be."

Debbie had her fingers poised over her phone.

She paused. "How do we know when something's meant to be versus when it simply happens?"

Janet grimaced. "That's a big question."

"We pray, of course," said Debbie, answering herself. "But how do we discern the rightness of something?"

"I try to determine if it's a life-and-death matter," Janet replied. Debbie frowned.

"You know me. I used to be even more of a worrier than I am now."

Debbie acknowledged that with a nod. "I've noticed that you're not as anxious as you used to be over every little thing."

"I'm not. Part of that, I think, was having one child and knowing she was my only try at doing it right. And having Ian in law enforcement. Eventually I realized I was borrowing trouble where none existed. I started reading the Bible more, and I found a couple of great, uplifting podcasts. And Christmas music," she added. When Debbie looked confused, Janet went on. "I stream Christmas hymns year-round. And some favorite worship tunes. They soothe me and remind me of God's real purpose. And my own."

"I love the idea of Christmas music all year round," said Debbie. She watched as Greg backed his truck out of his spot. He had to come their way to make the turn onto the street, and when he did, he waved. Hammer wagged his tail and pushed his snout out the window to say goodbye, and he woofed twice.

Debbie smiled and waved back.

"You know one of the nice things about having you here, Debbie? In Dennison and running your own business?"

Debbie raised a brow.

"You have all the time in the world. So does he. Or whoever. There's no rush, there's no stopwatch ticking minutes, days, or months away. He's busy. You're busy. I figure what's meant to be will be."

"That's twenty-some years of marriage talking."

"And you're bringing that same twenty-plus years of experience to the café table, to life, to whatever happens. It doesn't matter that it's a different experience." Janet held up her phone. "Ellen Knowles from the Depot Inn texted me. She said she's got some information she'd like to share if we have a few minutes."

Debbie buckled her seat belt. "I've just been reminded that time is not an issue. Let's roll."

Janet started the car. She put it in gear and started backing up when her rear sensor sounded an alarm.

The cream-colored dog sat near the car, watching them. When she applied the brakes, he glanced toward the café and then the car, as if in question. "He wants food."

"I'll text Ellen that we'll be there in ten minutes or so, and you can feed Isaac."

"Isaac?" Janet pondered the name for a moment. "It fits. I like it."

"Me too. Although I'm not keeping him," Debbie announced as Janet hurried toward the door.

The dog didn't run, but he didn't sidle closer either. He seemed content to let Janet do all the running, and when she set out a bowl of kibble with a bit of cheese, he stood and faced her, tail wagging. Then he walked sedately to the food.

The museum had been busy earlier. It was quiet now. No one was around to spook the dog, so Janet took a few pictures of him with her phone.

Should she approach him and try to pet him?

Although tempted, she decided not to. Not because he was a stray. She'd never entertained a fear of animals, and the dog seemed skittish but not dangerous. She held back because she wanted him to be comfortable with people who frequented the café, on his terms. That might take a while, but like she'd just said to her best friend...

They had plenty of time.

Black River Falls
July 1959

"We did it." Allen clapped one hand on Gordon's shoulder and the other one on Jerome's as the local press snapped a few pictures of the three men, Jane, Frances, and Allen's brother, Lyle, with a generous section of I-94 rising in the background. "Chilson Roads will always be part of the American Interstate System. My grandpa wouldn't have imagined this," Allen whispered as a photographer rearranged them to get the taller of them in the back. He'd even brought along a small ladder so he could position himself to get the shot he wanted to commemorate this moment. "He had two mules, a horse, and a cart. Who would have thought that would come to this?"

"He had vision," said Jane. "He saw what would be happening and knew he wouldn't be around to see it, but that didn't stop him from jumping in with both feet. Just like your daddy did, Allen, and like you've done. And now this younger generation."

Jerome had just secured contracts for two more major sections of the growing I-90 and I-94 system in their section of the country, and they'd also won a bid on structuring an entire neighborhood set outside the city.

Jerome had flown to the East Coast to study neighborhoods that had aged successfully and avoided major issues of bad drainage or erosion with their roads.

And now he was back, having his picture taken and living a life he would never have imagined fourteen years ago. An amazing family. A wife, three kids, and another on the way. A cozy home, warm in the winter and muggy in the summer, but when one lived this far north, one took that warmth and basked in it.

He had investments.

That in itself was amazing. Jerome Peter Flaherty had money in the bank and money in stocks.

And the faith that had gotten him through long, cold nights and scant food days back in Ohio was still his.

He'd clung to what he believed, and he had made a difference in the world. The major four-lane divided highway behind him bore testimony to that, and there was more to come. Much more.

Thirty-seven years old and on top of the world.

He'd done what he needed to do every step of the way, and he'd arrived.

Thank You, sweet Lord above!

CHAPTER SIXTEEN

*E*llen had asked them to come to her personal residence across from the quaint Depot Inn. There were two cars in the driveway, so Janet parked on the street. They walked up the sidewalk, and Debbie rang the doorbell.

A dog barked.

Funny how Janet hadn't realized how many dogs there were in Dennison until lately. Something about having a café in the center of the village seemed to bring dogs into closer inspection. And she couldn't get the lonely, hungry stray off her mind.

Ellen opened the door and ushered them into a modern but retro-style kitchen. "I'm so glad you came right over," she told them. She pointed out the room's theme with a smile. "The kitchen decor was my mom's idea. They owned this house for years, and she loved the fifties-into-sixties look. It's not my style, but when I've had the money to renovate, there's been no time, and when I have the time, something else always needs fixing. That's how it goes in an old house. And the thought of having my kitchen down is scary. I do a lot of my inn work in this kitchen. Although Greg Connor did tell me he could do it step-by-step when I'm ready. He's a great guy."

Janet almost laughed.

She didn't, because her best friend sent her a scolding look, but she thoroughly appreciated Ellen's assessment of Greg. She perched on a cute breakfast bar stool. "You said the picture in the *Gazette* reminded you of something."

"It sure did," said Ellen. "I started helping Mom and Dad at the inn when I was about eight or nine, and the minute I saw that picture, I remembered seeing a box just like that on the dresser in a guest's room. A Schrafft's candy box, with needlework flowers on it. I remember it distinctly, because we had two of those in Grandma's collection. They were burned in the fire just a few years before. They were pretty tins, in pristine shape. The one in the guest's room was a little rusty. I remember when I straightened up his room, the box was sitting there, plain as could be."

"Did you open it?" asked Debbie.

Ellen shook her head. "I wouldn't have opened anything that belonged to a guest. I moved it to dust the dresser, and I could tell it was empty."

"Do you remember anything about the person who was in that room?" asked Debbie.

Ellen nodded. "There was a uniform hanging in the closet. Nothing else, just one of those clear plastic bags with some sort of uniform inside. But here's another reason I wanted you to come over. There were so many medals on the uniform! I remember lifting the plastic bag so I could touch them. The ribbons were so colorful and the medals so shiny, I was mesmerized."

"Do you remember what day of the week it was?" asked Janet.

"Mama wouldn't let us neglect our homework during the week to work in the inn, so it had to be a weekend. Like I said, I wasn't real old. Old enough to be helpful but not old enough to really pay attention to guests. Except when that rock star came a few years later." She chuckled. "We all noticed that. But then my mother made me stay over here because 'you never know about rock stars.'" She added that last in a scolding kind of voice but grinned as she repeated the words.

"A point that could be made about most anyone," noted Janet.

Ellen didn't disagree. "Anyway, that guest—it was a man—had that exact box here then. Maybe not the same box, but it was a Schrafft's candy box. I know because Mama asked him if he'd sell it to her to replace one that was lost, even though it had a spot of rust over a couple of letters. He didn't want to sell it, he said, because his wife had fixed it up for him. Whatever that means."

"Do your guest records go back that far?" asked Debbie.

Ellen shook her head. "No. We've done a ten-year-limit for a while now, although with digital files, we could easily keep older records. But nothing from back then. It had to be 1976 or 1977 when I saw the tin, because that's when I cleaned guests' rooms." She smiled. "All of us kids couldn't wait to help at the inn. Mama started us out with dusting the rooms and changing sheets, but once we turned ten we could help out in the kitchen. Getting old enough to work in the kitchen was a huge deal at our house."

"Thank you, Ellen." Debbie stood. So did Janet. "That gives us something to think about. If the medals belonged to someone from out of town, I wonder why he would bring them with him to Dennison?"

"And wear them?" Janet wondered out loud. Then she addressed the elephant in the room. "Ellen, we appreciate you talking to Karl and getting him to drop his claim that the medals were his."

Ellen sighed. "Karl's not a bad guy, but he's gotten in over his head a time or two with his finances. I think he's scrambling now. I don't have any recollection of anyone in the family having a bunch of medals. One or two here or there, but my parents and grandparents were immigrants. Neither one had siblings who came over until later in the fifties, so they wouldn't have had American medals, right? My dad just missed serving. I think my brother is trying to find a way to get his finances back in order. I know that last stock market dip hit his retirement fund hard. He's got reason to be concerned, but that doesn't excuse trying to get those medals and sell them on his military memorabilia page."

Which was exactly what Karl had told them. Janet extended her hand to Ellen. "You've been a huge help. Thank you, Ellen."

"Not as much as I'd like, but I was happy to do it," she assured them. Her phone rang just then, so Debbie and Janet let themselves out.

"A guest with a Schrafft's candy box and lots of medals," Janet mused as they settled into the car. "Donovan would have been alive then. And working at the depot. Do you suppose the guest lost the box and Donovan found it and couldn't locate the owner?"

Debbie lifted one shoulder. "It's possible. The time frames match. But then we come back to the question of the hour. Why would Donovan bury them?"

"Why would anyone bury them?" asked Janet, but then she paused as awareness washed over her. She touched Debbie's arm. "Because they were painful reminders."

Debbie's eyes widened. "Of course. The likelihood of someone burying stolen items in a public place like that is slim, but with all the sadness and losses of war, some hurting soul just wanted to put them someplace they'd never have to look at them again."

"There's really no other reason that makes sense," Janet agreed. "Which means Donovan is unlikely to be our man. But who do we know who had a personal connection to that tree? The bench?"

"Miss Winnie."

Debbie was right. Janet nodded. "Should we ask Marcy if we can see her soon?"

"Yes. But we still have a number of people reaching out to us," noted Debbie as her phone chimed with another notification.

"And here's someone sending me pictures of Isaac going down the road toward McCluskey Park again." Janet raised her phone to show Debbie the new picture.

"That's another mystery to solve," said Debbie. "No one has stepped up to claim this guy yet. Just these random sightings."

"If he got dumped off, no one will be claiming him," Janet said. "He's another stray, depending on the kindness of strangers."

"You know what I've discovered?" Debbie posed the question as Janet made a turn. "Being kind to him and Harry and Crosby is a pretty solid way to start our days." Compassion shone through Debbie's smile. "Knowing we're bringing sunshine into lives makes getting out of bed an absolute delight. And I can honestly say I didn't always feel that way in the city."

"Hometown therapy," declared Janet. "It's the little things, like a grilled cheese sandwich with my name on it back home. Want me to have Ian double the order?" she asked as she headed south.

Debbie thought a moment and then nodded. "I sure do. Then we can see if Marcy is open to another visit. And what about Ray?"

she asked. Raymond Zink was a longtime Dennison resident and one of the last survivors in town to have served in World War II. He'd moved into Good Shepherd months before, and Debbie had bought his classic craftsman-style house. "Ray Zink is a treasure trove of trivia when he gets going. Being a military man, he might be able to think of why someone would have been here in the seventies wearing military medals."

"Maybe they came for a funeral," Janet suggested as she made the turn toward Dennison. "Between World War II veterans, Korea, and then Vietnam, I'm sure there were lots of military funeral services going on."

Debbie made a face. "I never thought of that. I pictured some big ceremony—"

"Not too many of those around here," Janet said. "Although they used to have parades. Fairly regularly, I think. I remember Grandma Slater talking about that."

"I miss parades."

Come to think of it, so did Janet. "Me too. So maybe someone was in town for a parade? Or funeral? Or military ceremony?"

"We can google that on my laptop tomorrow," said Debbie. "How many events could there have been in the two-year span based on Ellen's memory of seeing that candy box?"

"Hey." Janet parked the car in the driveway and reached for the handle. "If we've gone from eighty years to two years, I'm thrilled. If the tin Ellen saw is the one we found, we just made major progress. And"—she yawned and stretched as she climbed out of the car— "I'm chalking that up as a win."

CHAPTER SEVENTEEN

Raymond Zink met the friends in the solarium the next evening. The elderly gentleman looked chipper as they approached him. He'd drawn his wheelchair to a grouping of chairs, and his first words made both women smile. "It does this old heart good to know my house is in such capable hands now, Debbie Albright. How's everything going? No big issues? You know I'd feel bad if there were, and I'd hire someone to fix 'em straight away."

"It's all good," she assured him, laughing. "I've fallen in love with that old house. After decades of renting, I'm enjoying having a place of my own, Ray. I'm sorry you needed to move, but I'm grateful that this fell into place when it did. I love it. That house is the perfect mix of quaint and classic."

Her reply made his eyes twinkle, and he brightened even more when Eileen joined them a few moments later. "Prettiest lady in the place," he announced as she came their way.

Janet thought Eileen blushed, but as the former stationmaster drew closer, she realized that Eileen had put on a bit of makeup to add color. She stood and drew out a chair for the elderly woman at the small table. "Is this good?" she asked, and Eileen rewarded her with a quick smile.

"Perfect," she declared. "Kim called me earlier to tell me you might have found out more about those medals."

Janet withdrew the candy tin from her bag, set it on her lap, and then popped the top open.

Ray nodded appreciation. "I'd whistle, but my whistler's been broke for a while," he said. "But if ever a group of medals deserved a whistle, it's this one. You don't often see this many commendations over the span of a few years. That makes me think this person's a lifer, that he or she made the military their choice. Of course, in times of war, more medals are given out," he added. "Or maybe this person served in a lot of different ways."

"Many folks waited an inordinate amount of time to be recognized for their valor," Eileen cut in. "Including Raymond. So some of these may have been given out long after they were earned."

"Ray." Janet turned, surprised. "I didn't know you were awarded medals after the war."

"I didn't fight for medals," he said. "I fought because there wasn't much in the way of choice. You can't sit back and let bullies have their way. Otherwise, you end up with nothing but bullies."

"He was wounded in Europe," Eileen explained.

"Not much more than a nick here or there," he argued, but he seemed pleased that she told the story.

"They found two pieces of shrapnel in his left leg when he went in for a knee replacement about twenty years ago. So he was hit and kept on."

"Which brings us right back to lack of choice," Ray said. "We kept on for those who couldn't."

"Our state senator heard about it—"

"Can't imagine how." Ray winked at Eileen. "No one's come right out and owned that piece of information."

She kept her gaze trained on Janet and Debbie, but her natural color rose beneath the peach-toned blush she'd applied. "And the senator instigated a push to get Ray recognized."

"Winning the war was recognition enough," he reminded her, but it was plain that Eileen's admiration pleased him.

"It was and is, but it's good for our local youths to see what men and women of courage can do," Eileen said as one of the nursing assistants brought a rolling cart of water and juices over to them.

"So did they do a big ceremony for it?" Debbie asked, and there was no denying the heightened look of interest on her face.

Janet caught her drift. "And did lots of military people come?"

Ray tapped the can of medals on his lap. "You're wondering if this box has anything to do with that ceremony, but tell me something first, because I know a good share about trees and growing. I did landscape work for the county in some of our nicest parks. How deep was this buried?"

"About so deep." Janet indicated the depth with her hands. "Ten inches down. More or less."

"Tree growth is pretty consistent," Ray told them. "Root growth for a protected tree not growing in a forest wouldn't have allowed anyone to dig ten inches deep twenty years ago. A tree in the forest has a fight on its hands," he explained. "It's vying for sunlight, for water, for room to spread out both in the earth and toward the sky. But a tree planted as part of a landscape can really show its stuff. All the power goes to tree formation. The energy goes to growth, not fighting stress, so to find the box buried ten inches down means that it wasn't put there twenty years ago. The roots were too established. Twice that, maybe, but doubtful. Fifty or sixty years ago, give or take?" He nodded and tapped the can with one finger. "That's the most likely. That tree was young then, about ten years in the ground at that point, because it was planted back in the early fifties. But I'm pretty sure this box wasn't put there twenty years ago. Sorry to disappoint."

"You didn't," replied Debbie. "Your expertise might have just helped us pinpoint the timing better. Ellen Knowles remembers seeing a box like this in a guest's room about fifty years ago."

Ray's eyes widened. "You don't say. She was a mite then, wasn't she?"

"About eight or nine years old."

"And always a helper," added Eileen.

Janet nodded. "But we weren't born sixty years ago…"

"So…" Debbie added the open-ended word with a raised brow.

"Were there military parades or anything then?" asked Janet. "Or maybe a funeral and someone wore his or her dress uniform? Ellen said there was a uniform in the guest's room with a lot of medals on it."

"It could have been a number of things," Ray said. "A funeral's most likely. Folks were big about giving a proper send-off, and not everyone who served wanted to be buried in the national cemeteries. And that newer one up north wasn't open yet, so if it was a funeral, it would have been local."

Another good tidbit of information. Janet scribbled it down. "We can check the records."

"Jim Watson has access to announcements from old issues of the *Gazette*," Eileen said. "His mother, Tansy, converted the microfiche records to digital a couple of years ago. She worked at the paper for decades, so when the change to put everything on floppy things or those little sticks began, she took a course over at the high school and figured it out. The Watsons have worked at the newspaper as far back as anyone can remember. If it came to writing or telling a good tale in Tuscarawas County, there was probably a Watson behind it."

"That'll make our search a lot easier," said Debbie. "Jim published the story for us, and we got lots of tips but no real solid ones except for Ellen's. But if we've managed to narrow the timeline down to a couple of years, that's huge. Eileen, do you still think that Donovan would have done something like this? Found the box, maybe, and buried it?"

Eileen exchanged a glance with Ray. "Not anymore. Ray and I discussed it, and he convinced me that Donovan would never have given up like that. He would have kept looking for the owners."

"But how did he locate people back then?" Janet asked. "No internet, no social media, and no central location. It's not like you could just put a notice in the *Gazette,* because not every soldier was from here. They were passing through the depot."

Eileen and Ray both shook their heads. "I don't know how he did it," Eileen said. "I do know he was seldom successful. But he sure was happy when he could package a medal up and send it to the rightful owner. That put a smile on his face, every time."

"Well, if he could do it without all the resources we have, we're determined to do it now." Debbie stood. "We've got to get on, but thank you both for taking the time to talk to us. What a wonderful help you've been."

"We brought a little treat to go with your dinner or the evening card games." Janet slipped a container of brownies onto the table. "Enough to share. And I'm happy to send more when this gets low. I know it's one of Eileen's favorites."

Eileen beamed appreciation. "Thank you! And the card players thank you too." Her smile brightened the cloudy afternoon. "I don't envy you baking this time of year. I was never a friend of heat and humidity. I can add layers to be comfy all winter, but there's something oppressive about ninety degrees of temperature and seventy percent humidity on top of it."

"Exactly why I start my day when I do," Janet said. "I can turn the oven off by nine in the morning and let the AC take over. If the baking's done, the frosting can begin."

"Words of wisdom."

When they got back to Debbie's car, she turned it on quickly to let the air conditioning soak through. The thick cloud cover didn't just darken the day. It sealed the heat and humidity in like a smothering blanket.

"My hair blows up in this weather." Debbie leaned back against the seat. "Thick hair is a blessing and a curse."

"Mom would *tsk-tsk* you for that remark." Janet slipped her notepad into her bag. "She talks about how my grandma's hair started thin and ended thinner, so whenever I gripe about my hair, she reminds me that starting thick is pure bonus."

Debbie laughed. "She's right, as always. So, fifty years ago, hmm? Do you think that's a solid time frame for the burial we might be looking for?"

"We have a witness sighting an identical tin and an estimate from a man who is self-proclaimed to know trees. Did you know that Ray worked in landscaping?"

Debbie shook her head as she put the car in gear. "I knew he worked for the county. My dad said something about that, but goodness, Ray was in his midfifties when we were born, so the oldest memory I have of him is him pitching horseshoes at McCluskey Park or seeing him sitting at church on Sunday mornings. Oh, and of course the awesome wooden things he made in his garage. He had that garage turned into a small factory to produce all those wooden ornaments."

"Mom has six of them," Janet replied. "She puts them away every winter to prolong their life. That man kept busy until he couldn't. Dad is quick to mention what a fine example he is."

"Are you ready to see Miss Winnie?" Debbie asked as she turned onto the highway.

"Marcy says it's been a good day so far, so yes. I have butterscotch cookies."

"Who doesn't love those?"

"Right? Marcy said it's a Miss Winnie favorite, so I whipped up a small batch. Let's go for it."

"All right."

They pulled up to the barn twenty minutes later. Several cars were parked along the landscape timbers that separated the parking area from the walking area. Big fans had been placed at several points inside the sprawling building. It was still hot, but the fans broke the oppressiveness. Marcy spotted Janet and Debbie right off and came their way. "You made it."

"Yes." Janet handed her the plastic container of cookies. "Family favorites."

"We'll love them," Marcy declared. "Let me walk you up to the house. Aunt Winnie has air in the apartment. She doesn't venture out much when it's this hot and humid. But it's not slowing down business, so that's a plus."

"Don't you have to be at the barn?" asked Janet.

Marcy shook her head as they approached the old farmhouse. "That's the beauty of a cooperative. There are several vendors taking care of things back there. And you never know how Aunt Winnie will react to things."

"Then thank you for being a buffer," said Debbie. When they got to the apartment, Winnie wasn't inside. She was sitting on the shaded side porch of the farmhouse. Twin ceiling fans churned above her. The old porch, her faded look, and the dress that walked right out of an old Sears & Roebuck catalog completed the picture.

"That's a painting if ever I saw one," whispered Debbie.

The pale green dress, almost sheer, had tiny pink and ivory rosebuds on the collar. The wide collar was open to a *V*, and the bodice was shirred and tucked.

She watched them approach and lifted one arched brow as they drew near. "Your mothers lacked the wisdom to instruct you on proper dress, I presume?"

"I believe our invitation to tea got lost in the post," Janet said, "so this is quite unexpected. We have no wish to intrude," she added.

Winnie huffed. "And yet, you have."

"We did bring cookies. Oatmeal butterscotch. A favorite, I believe. May I sit?" asked Janet as Marcy peeled off the top of the container.

"Etiquette requires one to be cordial to drop-ins at the very least. Even when annoyed."

"I invited Debbie and Janet to come over, Auntie." They all took a seat, and Marcy held out the small tub. Winnie didn't take just one cookie. She grabbed two in a less-than-ladylike move. "They were wondering about the bench at the depot. Where you used to sit. They found medals there, remember?"

Winnie stared at Marcy as if she were speaking another language, and then she blinked.

It was another light bulb moment, like they'd seen at the depot.

She tipped her head graciously, the cookies temporarily forgotten. "I hate war."

CHAPTER EIGHTEEN

*J*anet said nothing. Neither did Debbie. Interrupting the elderly woman might halt the flow of memory.

"So much taken. Gone forever. Our men. My man."

Marcy's mouth dropped open, but she didn't interrupt.

"Vietnam," Winnie said. "Killed within two weeks of getting there. So young. Both of us. He'd have turned seventy-one next month. Gone the last year of the war. He never even knew about the baby."

Janet tightened her grip on the arms of the chair she was sitting in.

"I wasn't myself, you know. After." She gazed off into the distance. "No one paid much attention to Richard's death. He wasn't from one of the more acceptable families. He was an up-creek kid who didn't have much of a future handed to him, but he liked to say he didn't need handouts. He'd do fine on his own. We married quietly, down at the courthouse, so everything would be legal if anything happened to him. Of course it did, and then I found out about the baby."

"I didn't know what to do," she said softly. "I knew I was in the wrong place. I knew I didn't belong here. I knew I was married even though they couldn't find the registration. They said I couldn't get survivor benefits, because I wasn't his wife, and then I lost the baby, and it was as if the whole universe was yawning open before me with nothing going right, no one really caring, and me in the wrong place, still."

She reached for a glass of tea, but her fingers shook too much to grasp it. She stared down at the tea and sighed. "So I waited. I don't know for what," she whispered, giving them a glimpse of how sorrow could hollow out the light in someone. "For my real family to find me? For Richard to come home? For it all to be a big mistake? Or maybe that the baby I lost would reappear, that I could at least be a mother, but that was denied too. And I kept waiting. Watching. Wondering. There was little else to do, you see."

Janet saw, all right. Winnie's fragile brain couldn't accept her losses, and so she sat vigil at the station, waiting for time and fate to play their hand.

"That tree was small when I started sitting there. Richard and I sat on the bench for a few minutes before he boarded the train. Not too long but long enough to know the risks and pray for rewards. He wasn't much on dogs, but he sat on that bench and said 'a good dog like that is something, ain't it?'" A winsome smile touched her face, her lips. "I didn't correct his English," she explained in a more normal tone. "It didn't seem right in light of his mission. I've spent time regretting that, believe me, because good speech is often overlooked these days, and we're the worse for it. Don't you agree?"

"I appreciate well-spoken people," said Janet.

Debbie and Marcy both nodded agreement.

Janet slipped the candy box out of her bag and set it on her lap. "We found this under the tree, Miss Winnie."

Winnie glanced her way and sniffed.

But then she turned a more studied gaze to the metal can. "Tears over that one, let me tell you."

Janet scarcely breathed.

"I saw him put it in the ground, you know." Winnie's eyes moistened. "So sad. So much heartache. So much sorrow. It dripped right out of him, and him without a hanky of any kind. He used his sleeve until I came forward and handed him my handkerchief. The box was on the bench, and the man was off to one side, the side closest to the tracks. He'd dug a good-sized hole, and then he took that box and set it down deep. So deep. Tears flowing, flowing hard, almost sobbing as he put all that dirt back on top.

"Miss Eileen had mulched the ground real nice." Her forehead creased as she continued. "She liked a good mulch to keep weeds away, and she'd put all these pine shavings on top of the soil. When this man was done, you'd never even know he'd been there. He covered it up that well. Finally, he straightened up and stood there, all hollow-eyed, as if he'd put heart and soul into the ground. And then he left. Just walked off, head down, his hands in his pockets. He was coughing some. I remember that, and I remember wondering if it was the crying that made him cough. But then I got sick a few days later, so maybe he had something."

"He buried the box."

Winnie stared at Janet and nodded. "And part of his soul with it, I believe. I looked into that man's face, and it was like seeing the sadness in my own every time I saw a mirror. I stayed away from mirrors for that very reason. No one wants to see that."

She'd seen the man who buried the box.

Janet's brain went on high alert, but she kept her voice easy. "Was it someone from town, Miss Winnie?"

Winnie frowned.

"The man who buried the box," Janet continued. "Was he from around here?"

Winnie drew her brows tighter and then shook her head. "I stayed a good while back then. On another bench, I mean. He got on a train a bit later. Not one of the big ones. A local one. And after he left, I noticed the sign was gone."

"The sign?"

"The one about the dog being ever faithful. The one near the bench. I thought maybe the crying man took it."

"I'm sorry for your losses, Miss Winnie," Debbie said softly.

"Yes. Well." Winnie's expression relaxed. "Most days it's so long ago. Others it feels like yesterday. I've never known quite how to fix that."

She looked tired and worn.

Janet stood. "May I hug you?"

Miss Winnie seemed shocked then managed to surprise her by standing and reaching out for the hug. "I miss hugs," she whispered as Janet embraced her.

"Then we'll share more of them," promised Marcy.

Winnie had brought a sheer shawl out with her. She shivered, despite the oppressive heat, and drew the shawl over her shoulders. "I'd like that. Although a rest now would be nice." She moved off to her apartment in the old carriage house.

The three younger women exchanged looks. "She actually saw the man bury the box." Marcy's eyes were wide. "What are the odds of that?"

"Pretty good if she was there as often as Harry suggested. When did her husband die?" Janet asked.

"She said he was killed during the last year of the Vietnam war," Marcy said, "so that would have been in 1975. Although this is the very first time I've ever heard she was married. And how dare they deny her benefits? I'll have Bob look into that right away. A lost document shouldn't mean loss of income or insurance. But if she saw a man bury the box—"

"Sobbing," added Debbie.

"Then he buried the box sometime after 1975," Janet said. "Which matches what Ellen said about seeing the tin and uniform in a guest's room in '76 or '77. Do you think he took the sign?"

"Anyone could have taken the sign," Debbie replied. "So maybe or maybe not, but it looks like we've got our time frame narrowed down. And we know it was a man who buried the medals."

"And that Auntie gave him her handkerchief," Marcy added.

Janet reached out and gave her a quick hug. "You've been a huge help. Thank you for letting us talk to her. I hope it doesn't do any harm."

"I think bringing things out might actually do some good," said Marcy. "It's not good to hold everything in. Sometimes we need to expose everything and clear the air."

Janet took a moment to breathe when they got back to the car. Not so much as a respite from the heat as the AC bathed the car with cool air, but to envision a younger Winnie at a much younger tree and the scene she'd described. "We were right about the emotional part."

"I'll say." Debbie tapped the steering wheel lightly. "Can you call Jim and ask about seeing those old funeral records? See who might have had a military funeral back then?"

"Sure." Janet placed the call. When Jim answered, she explained their mission. "Can we access the files and see if anyone looks likely to have had a decorated soldier at their funeral? And is there a way of tracing someone who might have had military honors coming to a wedding or some other function? Someone who would need to wear their dress uniform?"

"I'll do you one better," he said. "I'll do a scan with keywords and see what comes up. My mother had a good hand at digital filing, and there's been a lot of times when I've thanked the Good Lord for that. I'll come by tomorrow with my laptop, all right?"

"That would be awesome." She hung up and turned toward Debbie. "I get chills, thinking we're this close."

"I do too, but mine is more of a reality check."

"A reality check?"

"Yes. I think of all that's gone on at the depot before us. The history, the people, the stories, the lives." Awareness shadowed Debbie's expression. "It's not that I don't know about the history, but I'm wondering about what kind of effect something that happened so far in the past will have on the present. When we find this guy, will his family be happy to get the medals? Or sad? Was his life filled with anger and remorse, or joy?"

"There's no way for us to know," Janet conceded. "We can't predict the outcome, but I've always thought that if I do the right thing, the best I can, good will eventually come from it. And who knows?" She lifted her shoulders in a shrug. "We might be bringing needed closure to someone." She held up the bag that held the candy tin. "Maybe finding the medals is part of God's timing. At the very least, it's taught us a few things."

"I can't deny that." Debbie slowed down as she neared the turn onto Janet's street. "I was worried that moving back home would end up with every day being predictable. My life in Cleveland wasn't predictable. It was busy and chaotic, and people sometimes did their jobs and sometimes didn't. It seemed like everything was in a frenzy all the time. I wanted to leave the frenzy behind, but I didn't want to be bored. I was worried that might be the case by coming here. Coming home. Janet, let me just say this right now." She pulled into Janet's driveway and blew out a breath of air. "I am not bored, and life in Dennison is not nearly as predictable as I feared. That's not only a relief, it's a reason to jump out of bed every morning to see what the new day brings. See you tomorrow."

"I'll be there. Sugar-topped blueberry muffins are first on my morning priority list."

Debbie smiled as Janet climbed out of the car. "One of my favorites."

Blueberry muffins had been a favorite of Debbie's ever since they were little kids. Seeing the smile on her friend's face was reason enough to do the muffins first thing. "I know. We aim to please at the Whistle Stop Café."

Debbie laughed as she backed out of the driveway.

Coming here had been a big change for her. Huge. She'd been upbeat about the whole idea, but Janet recognized the worry she tried to hide. Change was often good but not always easy. Debbie was doing all right. No, she was doing better than all right.

Janet was pretty sure her best friend was truly glad to be home, and Janet was just as happy to have her here.

Black River Falls
June 1976

"Dad!"

Jerome turned. His son—their oldest—waved to him across the Green Bay terminal then came his way.

"How'd it go? How was Dennison? I'm sorry I missed it," Michael said as he reached for Jerome's bag. "We'll add this latest award to your collection," he continued. "Mom's having guests over for supper to celebrate another medallion in your trophy case, and Cassie is feeling better."

Their youngest had gotten sick the day they were scheduled to fly out to the service in his hometown. That meant Frances stayed home with Cassie and he made the trip on his own.

Michael kept talking as they made their way to the car. "I'm glad school's over and I can stay with you for a couple of weeks."

Michael had just finished nailing down his degree in journalism. Peter, Jerome's second son, had gotten the itch to build things. He was slightly younger than

Michael, and from the beginning had a discerning eye when it came to puzzles and building.

Michael was the perceptive one. He sensed things. About life, about people. He pushed his way through the exit door then paused, the door half-open. His expression changed. "You all right, Dad? Did you catch Cassie's bug?"

Jerome shook his head. "Tired, is all. It's been a long three days."

Michael frowned but took him at his word. "Do you want me to find a pay phone and have Mom cancel supper plans?"

Hurt Frances's feelings, or bury himself in the what-ifs confronting him now?

There's no changing things. No going back. No do-overs.

"I'll be okay."

"You sure?" Michael was looking at him closely. Time to put on a more normal expression.

"I'm sure. Just tired, most likely. I'll close my eyes and rest on the ride home. Everything good here?"

"Better than good. Gordon's developing a plan to extend north of Eau Claire."

Another road. Another destination. Another goal to keep people safe and ease the sudden curves of life.

"The governor's on board, and Pete's over the moon. He's a chip off the old block." Michael put Jerome's bag in the back of the eight-passenger station wagon and closed the door snugly.

"It's okay that you're not, Mike."

Michael had rounded the wagon. He paused. "Not what?"

"A road builder." Jerome met his son's gaze and held it. "It's okay that you're exactly who you are. You don't have to be like me. Not now. Not ever."

Michael moved toward him.

He seemed concerned. Worried, even. He drew close and felt Jerome's head. "You've got a fever, Dad."

He might. He felt hot and cold and angry inside. Angry and disappointed.

He shivered.

"Hop in." Michael opened the door of the second seat. "I'm going to go call Mom. You hang out here, and I'll get you home, okay?"

Jerome half-crawled into the back seat.

He never heard Michael return to the car, and when he woke up, he was in a bed at Sacred Heart Hospital in Eau Claire.

Frances was curled up in a chair nearby. She looked tired and uncomfortable, but the moment he moved she jumped up and came his way. "Hey. You woke up."

He blinked. *"So it would seem. What happened?"*

"A virus. Flu, they think, but it dropped you like a brick. You've been out for three days. I've never been so worried." She pressed her forehead to his. "You were so sick, Jerome. It scared me, darling. Don't do that again. Okay?"

His head hurt. His chest hurt too. And his arms felt like jelly, but he was able to loop one up, around her. "Give me a day. It's all good."

She laughed softly, and the sound meant something dear, something wonderful.

Cling to that.

The advice seemed to come from someone or something far away.

Cling to what you've got, for you are truly blessed.

He was. He knew that. He understood the gratitude of a life well-lived, the amazing accomplishments he'd achieved with Chilson Roads, the blessings of his family, his faith, his country, his church.

But there was a lead ball of regret lodged beneath his heart, and he wasn't sure how a heart could keep beating around such a weight.

Frances's gentle embrace meant so much. She loved him. He loved her. He loved his life.

But if he had it to do over again...

Exhaustion blanketed him. He felt warm and cold and fairly awful and wasn't sure he had enough breath to handle today, much less fix things from so long ago.

His heart tightened, his brain fogged, and he slept.

CHAPTER NINETEEN

Isaac licked his bowl clean the next morning, and when Janet saw that through the window, she took a chance.

She opened the back door slowly. The dog cocked an ear but didn't run. Then she took a seat on the nearby bench and offered him a piece of bacon. No smart creature could or should resist bacon, and Isaac was no exception.

He moved her way cautiously. He eyed her.

She returned the favor. He didn't grab the bacon and run. He sat, politely waiting for her to give him permission.

What a good dog!

"Here you go, Isaac." She waved the bacon and moved her hand closer. "All yours."

He took it gently. Another indication that he may have been someone's pet at one time. He didn't look old, but he wasn't a pup either.

Would he let her pet him?

She reached out and touched his head lightly, and Isaac leaned in as if grateful. "Oh, you sweetheart," she breathed. "You do like people, don't you? You've just had to be shy to get by. Have you lost a little trust along the way?"

Isaac accepted a scratch behind the ears before he backed away. He started to dash off, but he only got about ten feet before he paused and sent her a doggy smile over his shoulder.

Then, tail wagging, he headed west like he usually did.

She washed up before she returned to work, and by the time Debbie arrived, the blueberry muffins were cool, banana muffins had joined them on the counter, and bran muffins were in the oven.

"This place smells so good." Debbie breathed deep as she came through the back door. "I almost hate to start the bacon because it will cover up the baking smells."

"Customers love both, so we're good." Janet set a timer on the primary oven. "It's going to be a beautiful day. Not as hot as yesterday, and Isaac let me pet him this morning."

"No. Really?" Debbie settled her purse at the far end of the counter and grinned as she grabbed an apron. "That's such good news. He was friendly?"

"Very. He smiled at me when he walked away."

"I've never quite known how to take a smiling dog," Debbie said. "Something about those sharp teeth—"

"It was a cute smile," insisted Janet. "But yes, it was toothy. I can't disagree."

Harry and Crosby came across the brick-lined walkway just then. By half past seven a crew of old-timers chatted about this and that as they sipped their coffee. Two women stopped in for a pair of lattes with whipped cream, and Patricia dropped by earlier than usual for her peppermint mocha. "I have a lot on my plate today," she explained as Debbie built her drink at the coffee station. "Not the least of which is helping an elderly woman over on Route 250 fight the demolition of her family home even though the place will most likely fall down before too long. Which is why the county is looking to condemn it, but the sadness in her face is heartbreaking."

"Route 250," Janet repeated. "Would that be Alma May McGill?"

Patricia frowned. "I can't tell you that, but the county's petition is public record. They're citing that the old place isn't just an eyesore but a hazard and that it needs to be removed."

"Did this just happen?" asked Debbie.

"Two days ago," Patricia said. "The owner came to see me immediately. We've requested a continuance with an additional request for more information and a hearing, but the old dear is rattled."

"Patricia, did you know that Greg's church offered to come in and stabilize that house a few years ago?" Janet asked. "They were doing it as an act of service at no cost to Alma May, but she refused. I don't know why."

"I'll call Greg and check it out," Patricia said as Debbie handed over sweet-smelling coffee. "Can you ladies package me up one of those blueberry muffins and a bran one too? My assistant loves your bran muffins, Janet. They're one of her all-time favorites. She used go to the Third Street Bakery to get them when you were there. And can I order a dozen mixed muffins for this weekend? I'm hosting a gathering on Sunday, and the muffins will be a perfect addition to my spread. I'll pick them up midday on Saturday if that's all right?"

Janet jotted the order down on a pad, pulled the page off, and stuck it to her order board. "Consider it done."

"Perfect. Have a good day now, you hear?"

"We will," Debbie promised. "You too."

It was busy all day long, and not just with museum visitors. Locals stopped by to grab a quick lunch and called in to-go orders. At one point, the coffee line wrapped around the room and almost out the front door. By the time they got to the afternoon, they'd done a booming business, the bakery case had been hit hard, the pie case was down to just a few pies, and Debbie had flipped burgers, dropped fries, and filled sandwiches for over two hours straight without a break.

By one thirty the friends were fairly wiped out.

The tables were mostly empty, and there was only one person left at the counter. Jim was due in with his laptop. No cleaning or restocking had been done, and Janet hadn't even thought of prep for tomorrow's baking.

She met Debbie's gaze from across the room as the last counter customer walked out. "What just happened?"

Debbie laughed, delighted. "We got mobbed!"

"We sure did, and you know what that means don't you?"

"More money in the account?"

Janet laughed. "More help. We need to have someone here from nine until one at least. A solid four- or five-hour shift."

"A server."

"Yes. And the sooner the better," she added as Greg Connor came through from the museum side. Hammer wasn't with him, but he took one look at the café and whistled lightly. "Whoa."

"Yeah. Great for business. Not so much for cleanup. Do you want a cup of coffee, Greg?" asked Janet.

He nodded. "I do, yes. I wanted to make it over here before you closed up so I could thank you for giving Patricia Franklin a heads-up on the old McGill property. I just stopped by to see her, and we might be able to work something out that will put the county's mind at ease and save some of Alma May's history. It seems her reticence goes back to her father's concern about medals."

"Military medals?" asked Janet. "The ones he found at the depot over the years?"

Greg nodded. "He bit off more than he could chew, she said. He tried to find owners through available means and ended up with a bunch of medals that weren't his. He was embarrassed to give them back to the depot, and she was afraid of consequences. She has a fairly high guilt meter."

"That's why she didn't want people roaming through the old house," Janet said.

"Yes." He included both women in his relieved expression. "Now she understands that the medals aren't an issue. I've returned them to Kim, and the church is planning to begin work on the old place in late September."

Debbie moved forward, smiling. "Greg, that's amazing. How wonderful."

He smiled back at her and, for a moment, Janet was sure they'd forgotten all about her. Then she saw Jim Watson heading their way. She rounded the corner of the bakery display case to retrieve the Schrafft's candy box. Cleanup could wait.

She bent low to retrieve the medals and stopped short.

They weren't there.

The candy box filled with buried valor was gone.

She'd put them on the lower shelf, knowing they might need to compare the real medals to any pictures Jim may have found, but the spot was empty. Absolutely, indisputably empty.

Her heart fell. Had she forgotten them? Left them in the car? At the house?

She spun around just as Jim came through one door and Greg headed toward the other. "The medals." She almost choked on the words. "They're gone."

"They're what?" Debbie, Greg, and Jim moved her way. Debbie stared at the blank lower shelf and swallowed hard. "They were there before the rush, Janet."

"You're sure? I was thinking maybe I'd forgotten to bring them this morning. Or left them in the car."

"No, they were right there two hours ago," Debbie said firmly. "Then the masses descended, and I never noticed them being here or not, but I can guarantee you they were here before we got slammed for lunch."

"But they're not here now." Janet's heart sank, and a chill ran up her spine. Not because the medals were all that valuable, but because she'd been tasked with taking care of them and she'd failed.

Her eyes filled.

Debbie slung an arm around her shoulders. "Don't blame yourself. We were both here. Who would have thought anyone would even notice them there?"

"We had Jim write an article about them, and I posted information on social media," said Janet. She wiped her tears, mad at herself for not hiding the medals better. "Then I left them under the counter nearest the back door. That puts it on me."

"It doesn't, because I saw them there and I didn't move them," Debbie insisted. "And who would think anyone here would steal military medals?" she continued. "Dennison isn't that kind of town."

"It made for easy picking while we were slammed," said Janet. She slumped into a chair, mad at herself. "I'll call Ian and file a report. And Jim, here you were, ready to help us again."

"Ready to help still," he said firmly. "Regardless of where the medals are right now, we need to figure out their rightful place. That way, when Ian finds them, we can put them back in the owner's hands."

Janet blotted her eyes with a napkin. He was right.

"Can I help?" asked Greg.

"Pray," said Janet, and her voice broke a little when she said it. "Pray that we find them and the owner. I know it doesn't seem like a big thing—" she added, but Greg interrupted her.

"God doesn't just care about the big things in life. He hears every prayer and concern. Like those sparrows we talk about. I'll pray." He sent her a comforting smile before he left through the back door.

Jim shifted the conversation as he opened his laptop. "I did a search, like I said," he said as the computer powered up.

Janet hauled in a breath, rolled her shoulders, and listened.

"I came up with a lot of funerals and a few military-type events. There weren't so many of those, although we did have Memorial Day parades back then, so there's one of those for each year. I made two copies of each list so you can both look through them. I thought if you wanted to look now, while I'm here, you could flag a date and I could look it up for you in the archives. See if there are any articles or pictures that would help."

"I won't say no to that," Debbie replied. "Cleanup isn't going anywhere, and I've got the rest of the day."

They started down the list, and when they pinpointed an event Jim searched the town and newspaper records, looking for identifying characteristics. They were halfway through the list when the back door opened and Becca Albright came in, followed by Ian.

Debbie stood, surprised. "Mom?"

"I heard you could use a little help on cleanup, so I came right over," Becca announced.

"How did you know that?" asked Debbie.

"Greg called to see if your father could help him put together a layered molding for an old house on Fourth Street and mentioned something about lunch. You girls go ahead with your meeting there. I'll tidy up."

"And I'll get a cup coffee and start the police report," added Ian. "The medals are missing?" Janet appreciated that he kept his tone gentle and didn't tease her. "Where were they?"

"In a fairly obvious place," she told him. She pointed to the open lower shelf along the back counter. "To the left of the luncheon plates. That empty spot, just perfect for a small metal box."

Ian winced. "Sorry, honey. That's a tough spot, for two reasons. The proximity to people walking by, and the back door is right there."

Remorse hit Janet again. "I know. It was dumb."

"Oh, it was not," scolded Becca from the dishwashing area. "Who would have thought anyone here would steal anything?

Nothing dumb about it. It was tucked away, out of sight. Someone had to be deliberately looking for it to even notice a spot like that. Was anyone here today who'd expressed interest in the medals?"

Debbie and Janet exchanged looks. "No," said Janet. "Not that I noticed. It was busy, and there were moments we were both out here on the floor, delivering orders," she explained. "Debbie was doing double duty on food and the occasional table. But it's not a big area, so it was very bold for someone to waltz in here while we were busy and steal the tin."

"The guy who ordered the burger with extra onions and mush-rooms was the closest to it when it first got busy," Debbie said, "but he didn't look like a thief. Did he?"

Janet frowned. "I'm pretty sure you can't tell a thief just by look-ing at someone."

"The woman with the roasted chicken and strawberry salad sat there next," Debbie continued. "She doesn't seem likely either. Of course, anyone could have made a grab as they went out the back door."

Ian didn't say anything, but Janet read the confirmation in his expression.

Jim returned the discussion to the lists. "Why don't we do this later? I know you all are—"

"Well, what have we here?" Becca had been bent low in the cooking area. She straightened and held up a surprising find. "Is this what we're looking for?"

"The medals!" Janet stood, excited.

So did Debbie. "Mom, where did you find them?"

"Right behind the bread rolls. You need more sesame seed rolls, by the way," she added, as if sesame seed rolls were as important as military medals. She came forward with the tin, and Debbie met her halfway. Then she turned back to Janet. "How did they get there?"

Janet glanced from face to face. "Not me. I put them right on that lower shelf. Debbie is my witness. She saw them there."

"I did, but they didn't walk to the other storage area," Debbie looked at Janet. "You sure you didn't second-guess yourself and figure out of sight—"

"Out of mind," quipped Ian.

She frowned at him. "I am not out of mind, thank you very much, and I know exactly where I put them. Which turned out to be a terrible place, but I'm so glad you found them, Becca! You saved the day! But how—"

"I've learned never to question Providence," Ian told her. "Pop it open, make sure they're all there, and be happy they were found. No matter how they got behind the sesame seed buns. That reminds me of food, though, and I'd love roast beef sandwiches on sesame seed buns sometime soon."

"We'll do that this week," Janet promised. "And thank you for coming over."

"I was on a call not far from here. Came over as soon as I was done." He swept a quick kiss to her forehead. "I'm out. See you tonight."

Janet carried the tin to the table. They'd drawn two tables together to have sufficient room for the lists, the laptop, and now the medals. As they returned to the lists, Becca's happy hum provided calming background noise.

They were on the fourth Memorial Day parade when Jim snapped his fingers. "Ladies, I might have something here."

He shifted the laptop toward them.

There, riding on a patriotic float behind a John Deere tractor, was a man wearing a chest full of medals. As Jim zoomed in, it was clear that this man sported every one of the medals now held in the candy tin.

"It's him," Janet whispered.

"Sure seems to be," added Debbie. "What year, Jim?"

"Nineteen seventy-six," he said. "Thirty-one years after the war ended. The sign on the side of the float says he's Jerome Flaherty."

"'Renowned former citizen of Dennison comes from Wisconsin to be honored at this year's Memorial Day parade and ceremonies,'" Janet read from the inserted article. "So he used to live here."

"And maybe came back for the celebration?" Debbie tapped his name into her phone then whistled softly. "Oh, wow. Look at this. What this guy's done. Did," she corrected herself. "He was a war hero who came home and helped initiate and build the northern extensions of the Interstate Highway system. And received presidential commendations for his contributions to the safety of all Americans."

"I can't even imagine how one goes about designing a massive interstate system," Jim said. "But here's the question."

Debbie beat him to it. "Why is he riding on this float, looking happy, then crying while burying those very same medals?"

That was the more important mystery. Janet sat back and faced Debbie and Jim. "I have no idea, but at least we can contact his family and let them know we have the medals. Then the rest is up to them."

Debbie sighed. She glanced around as if dissatisfied before meeting Janet's gaze. "I'm a little lost," she explained. "I just now realized it. It's not enough knowing where the medals should go. I want to know why he buried them in the first place."

"Me too." Janet trailed a finger over the tin. "But even if we never find that out, even if we never learn the reason why they were buried, we know where they most likely belong. Should I contact the family?"

Jim pulled up several listings of Jerome Flaherty in Wisconsin and then slid the laptop her way. "You figure out which number to call or address to use. I'm glad we found him. And I'm okay with you being the one to reach out."

Janet chose a number listed to a relative of Jerome Flaherty of Black River Falls, Wisconsin. She tapped out the number on her phone, and when a voice said hello, she jumped right in. "Hi, my name is Janet Shaw. I'm in Dennison, Ohio, and we've stumbled on a box of military medals that I think might have belonged to a man named Jerome Flaherty. Do you—"

"Jerome's my grandfather. Was my grandfather," the man corrected himself. "I'm Mike Flaherty Jr., his oldest grandson. You found his medals? For real?"

Janet put the phone on speaker. "We believe so. The medals match a date when he was here for—"

"A military parade," the man cut in. Excitement laced his voice. "Gramps was being honored for his courage and commitment and his skill at understanding the ins and outs of roadbuilding. I'm sorry, I'm prattling a little. We thought we would never see those medals again. According to family legend, they were lost decades ago—"

Janet didn't interrupt him to explain that they hadn't been lost. They'd been deliberately placed. She would send him a copy of the article and write a personal note. He'd learn the medals' fate soon enough.

"The family had lost hope," he continued. "Despite our best efforts, we could never find them. I can't tell you what this phone call means to me. To us," he added.

"If you give me an address, we'll send them right out," Janet told him, but Mike squashed that idea instantly.

"No, we'll come get them. The family's been itching to get out of town. The mosquitoes are eating us alive, and several of us have this week off. Dennison is only a day's ride, and I'd like to see the place where the family began. My grandfather was one of those bootstrap people. He came from nothing and ended up being a classic American success story. He set the bar high for all of us. We'll head down on Thursday and come see you on Friday. If that's all right?"

"It's fine," she assured him. "I'll text you a couple of places to stay. We've got the typical hotels nearby, but we've also got a nice bed and breakfast right here in Dennison. In fact, one of the inn owners gave us a clue that led us to you. To Jerome's identity."

"Then I'll book rooms there if they're available. The best way to return a favor to a small business is to use their business," he added. That was an adage the people in Dennison would appreciate. "Wow." His breathing was shaky, as if he was choking on emotion. "This is great. Really great. My grandpa didn't have a lot of joy in his youth, and it was like a light went dim in his later years, but he was an incredible man. We'll see you Friday. And thank you! Thank you so much!"

He hung up.

Janet set the phone down, and then she faced Debbie and Jim. "They're coming here."

"Isn't that amazing?" Debbie reached out and gripped Janet's hands. "He sounded so happy."

"He sure did." Jim sounded happy too. "Well done, ladies. And thanks for letting me jump in on this. It was like old-time fun, when papers did this kind of thing all the time."

"You were wonderful, Jim." Debbie grinned at him. "I'm going to let Katie and Ellen know he might be calling. Then we can finish up here."

"Almost done." Becca sang out the words, and she was right. While they'd been scouring the papers and the internet, she'd loaded the dishwasher and gotten it running, plated and wrapped pies, and polished counters and tables. Other than giving the floor its daily mopping, they were ready to lock the door.

"You call the inn," said Janet. "Your mom and I can finish this."

"I'll move chairs," Jim offered. He upended the chairs onto the tables and shifted a few things as Becca wheeled the big yellow mop bucket around the corner of the display case. In ten minutes the floor was washed, the dirty water discarded, and the bleached mop head was left to dry.

They were getting ready to leave when a quick rap turned their attention to the front door. Bernice stood there, looking expectant.

Janet moved toward her and unlocked the door. "Bernice, I'm sorry. We're closed. Everything's put away."

"You found it!" Bernice pointed to the tin on the table and gave Janet a delighted hug. "Oh, I'm so glad! I didn't have your number, and I was just five minutes away, but I realized I never told you that I moved that precious box of medals out of sight. I spotted it there, right on the shelf." There was no denying the excitement in the quirky woman's voice. "And you were all so busy, like I haven't seen in a long time, and I realized straight off how someone could just waltz by and slip that box off the shelf and hightail it out the back door, and no one would be the wiser."

She finally paused for breath.

When she did, Janet hugged her. "You did good," she told her in a kind voice. She didn't berate her for moving it without saying anything, because the picture Bernice painted was accurate. They were too busy to notice, and her actions proved that. "You saved the day."

Bernice blushed with joy and pride, and Janet couldn't remember ever seeing her this happy. "Really?"

"Yes, really, because you were right. The box was in plain sight. That was silly on my part."

"All's well that ends well," Bernice said, and the satisfaction in her tone was Janet's reward.

"How about I wrap you up a piece of pie to go, Bernice? We've got chocolate cream, lemon, and bumbleberry."

Bernice's face lit up. "I wouldn't say no to bumbleberry. It's my favorite."

After Janet boxed up the pie, they all trooped out together.

Jim headed toward the newspaper offices that sat just down the block from the police department and town hall, Bernice went west, and as Janet, Becca, and Debbie began moving to their cars, something caught Janet's eye. Isaac, hiding in the shadows of one of the rail cars, watching them go.

She paused. "You guys go on." She handed the box of medals to Debbie. "I'm going to put out a little food for our friend. I don't want him to wait until morning."

"I can stay," Debbie offered, but Janet shook her head.

"No, go ahead. Ian isn't home for a couple of hours, and Tiffany's at another party. This one's over in Claymont, so I've got time. I'll see you tomorrow. Great job today," she added. "Both of you." She gave Becca a hug.

"We might want to put a sign in the front window about needing help," Debbie reminded her. "I'll print one up tonight."

"Sounds good." Janet hurried back to the café. She fixed Isaac's bowl, took it outside, and settled it beneath the old oak tree.

The dog eyed the food and licked his chops.

But he waited in the shadows until she retreated to one of the benches.

When she took a seat, he moved forward. He seemed at home beneath the shady tree. He glanced around now and again as he ate, keeping an eye on his surroundings. "I suppose that's a good habit to have," she told him as he ate the kibble mixed with a dollop of leftover soup. It was beef with barley, and the dog seemed pleased with it. "Being on your own and all."

Isaac finished the bowl, licked it clean, and then sat. He met her gaze.

She met his. And when she tapped her lap in invitation, he came her way. This time when she reached out to pet him, the dog smiled. When she paused her hand, he nuzzled into it as if asking for more.

Janet thought about what she knew, trying to piece it together.

A soldier goes to war. He serves his country with courage and valor.

His loyal companion waits for him. Faithfully. Day after day, month after month, year after year.

And then one day the soldier returns, to be honored for his service. And he discovers, too late, the steadfastness and devotion of the dog he left behind.

Isaac gazed up at her.

His eyes met hers. And in that moment she realized why Jerome Flaherty buried his medals.

Her heart swelled to match the lump in her throat. Tears ran down her cheeks as she gave Isaac a good petting. A petting he so clearly deserved.

She wasn't sure how long she sat there, bonding with the big cream-colored dog.

She wanted to take him home. But she wasn't sure their diva Yorkie would accept a rival for their attention.

Isaac made the decision for her.

He backed away a few minutes later as if sensing capture. He didn't back away in a normal dog-step though. It was more of a prance. Almost a dance. Then he wagged his tail, turned and headed west, like always.

He seemed content.

Not as lost.

That was good, and if he made a daily trek around the depot for food, that wasn't a bad thing. They'd found the owner of the medals. The dog seemed satisfied. And the café was busy beyond their expectations.

But as she locked up the back door, all she could think of was Miss Winnie's story of the heartbroken man burying his cache of military honors next to a memorial honoring a faithful friend.

Washington, DC
May 2013

"Gramps, are you all set? Anything you need before we head to the bus? The weather looks wonderful today." Cory motioned toward the window overlooking the skyline of the nation's capital. He tapped his watch. "Gotta head out."

Jerome couldn't do it.

As nice as this all was, there was no way he could do the Honor Flight monument tour.

He didn't deserve it. Any of it. The clapping, the cheers, the special attention. None of it.

Stall him.

Pretend to be sick.

Pretend to have gut issues. Frequent bathroom calls get old folks out of a lot of things. You could—

Cory bent low.

Jerome was in a wheelchair, not because he couldn't walk, but because the amount of walking in Washington, DC sunlight made the chair a smart alternative for Honor Flight veterans. His grandson met his gaze. "We don't have to do this, Gramps. I can send your regrets."

Regrets.

His heart ached.

For one short moment he imagined what life might have been like if he'd made a different decision all those years ago. One short detour before he set off on a life and career that helped change the face of the national map, adding fifty years of interstate highways and neighborhood roads. A job that began with delivering gravel for an old man and ended with more money than any one man could use.

Success had been his goal after living through the Depression with his mother and three siblings.

He'd achieved the goal, but he couldn't look back without guilt, regret, and sorrow.

He'd made a promise all those years ago. A promise to a friend. A promise he hadn't kept.

The war had come with its darkness, and in that darkness his talents had shone bright to his commanders, earning him a spot in the 300th and learning how to engineer ground access on multiple levels.

He didn't want to rain on Cory's parade. Cory and his sweet wife had submitted his name for the trip as a grand surprise. He would spend the day being applauded, appreciated, and accompanied from monument to monument, a celebration of courage and valor shown.

He'd messed up. Nothing he could fix now. Frances said the Lord had long since forgiven him. She'd said that right up until her final breaths. She worried about him. Him and the kids. Always.

Problem was, he couldn't forgive himself.

"Gramps?"

He took a breath. A deep one. Then he met Cory's gaze straight on. "Can you send my regrets, Cory? Please." Cory had gone the distance for him, and he didn't want this wonderful young man disappointed. "I want to tell you a story."

"Of course. Anything for you."

Cory made the call from the adjacent room. Then he came back into the sitting room of the hotel suite and poured two cups of coffee. He fixed them the same way, a fun connection between old and new. Then he brought the coffee to the chair nearest Jerome.

"Here you go." He handed one mug over and kept the other for himself. He sat and gazed Jerome's way, expectant.

Jerome couldn't fix old wrongs. He knew that. But he couldn't go on pretending to be something he wasn't.

A hero.

God and timing had given him a long life and a chance to come clean, and he did what any good soldier would do.

He seized the day.

CHAPTER TWENTY

he HELP WANTED sign lasted about an hour before Greg's mother popped in Tuesday morning. She was medium height, on the stocky side, with a smile that lit a room. Her short and trim hairstyle was never mussed, and her outgoing nature kept her in good standing with almost everyone in town. "I heard you might be looking for someone to jump on board." She pointed to the sign that Janet had put in the window. "I thought I'd come right over."

"We do need help, Paulette." Janet didn't hesitate. The midday rush the day before had taught both her and Debbie a lesson.

"You're Greg's mom." Debbie came forward with a smile. "He texted you were coming by. He mentioned that you'd been a server before."

"I loved my job," Paulette said. "I'm retired and bored, so if I worked here for four or five hours a day, that would be marvelous. I ran shift at the Red Rail Diner over in Uhrichsville for ten years and waited tables at the steak house before that, but the coziness of cafés and diners appeals to me. They're more personal. Of course, in a small town like ours, everything is personal."

"That's the truth," Janet agreed.

"We're informal here," explained Debbie. "T-shirts and jeans or capris, and cute aprons."

Paulette indicated the T-shirt and jeans she'd chosen for today. "Greg said as much. And he said it's the kind of atmosphere I'd love." She pointed to the daily chalkboard. Janet had changed the saying that morning to *This is the day the Lord has made.* A smile brightened Paulette's face. "'We will rejoice and be glad in it,'" she said. "That's my prayer every morning."

Janet exchanged a look with Debbie. "What do you think?"

Debbie grinned. "I think she's heaven-sent."

"By my wonderful son!" Paulette added with mother-pride.

"He is amazing," agreed Janet. "Right, Debbie?"

Janet didn't miss the color in Debbie's cheeks "He did a great job on the renovation at my house," Debbie said. "And he's been wonderful to my father."

"Well then," Paulette said. "When shall I start?"

"Now," Debbie replied. She hooked a thumb toward the aprons behind the counter. "Take your pick."

Janet burst out laughing, and Paulette's smile widened.

"I don't prefer waiting tables," Debbie said. "I like flipping burgers. I like slapping sandwiches together. That's like food therapy after being in an office for twenty years. But when twenty-plus people are calling your name, the burgers are burning, the circuit breaker goes off and shuts down the fryer and you don't notice it because you're trying to not be rude to a sweet elderly man who can't quite figure out how he wants his eggs... I was this close to losing it yesterday." She pinched two fingers together. "And I would be happy to never feel that way again."

"Well, you will feel that way again, from time to time," Paulette assured her as she moved toward the aprons. "That's the restaurant business. But when there's enough help and everyone knows their job and their place, things generally go smooth. Smoother," she corrected herself with a laugh. "Nine to one, unless we're really busy?"

"Yes," Janet and Debbie said at the same time.

"Good." Paulette lifted a dark blue apron covered with old-fashioned train engines and cabooses and settled it over her head. "Let's get to work."

By Friday morning it was like Paulette had been with them forever. She was smart, amiable, and quick, and people loved her. On top of that, she wasn't above slipping Crosby and Isaac a treat, so the dogs were on board too.

Mike Flaherty had called. He and the family were visiting some of the local places his grandfather had mentioned over the years, and then they were coming to the Depot Museum. They would finish their tour and Mike would let Janet know when they were on their way into the café.

She received his text at twenty minutes past one.

Janet hurried to meet the group as they came through from the museum side of the depot. A middle-aged man hurried forward and held out his hand. "You must be Janet. I'm Mike Flaherty."

"My goodness," Janet said. "You told me you were bringing a crew, and you did!"

Mike laughed. "We've been meaning to do this for years. Your phone call inspired us to just get in the cars and drive. Janet, this is my wife, Beth, and my daughter, Izzie. And my son, Cory, and daughter-in-law, Lisa." He gestured toward an older couple. "And this is my aunt Cassie and uncle Frank and their grandkids, Rachel, Brian, and Jerome."

"I've put tables together," Janet told them as she led them across the room. "Hungry?"

Jerome didn't hold back. "I'd go straight to starving."

Janet laughed. "Then food first?" she asked with her eyebrows raised. They nodded agreement.

"Ellen and Katie made a great breakfast this morning, but that was nearly five hours ago," Mike said. "So despite my impatience, food first would be great. And lots of coffee too."

"I'll fill waters," said Paulette.

"And I'll do coffee." Janet retrieved five mugs and a fresh pot of their house blend and then crossed to their table once they'd settled into seats. "Here we go. What do you think of the inn?"

"We love it," said Izzie. "Ellen and Katie are amazing, and their attention to detail is inspiring. Not just with the inn, but the food, the presentation, the whole setup."

"Izzie's an event planner, so she notices everything," Cory explained. He grinned. "It's kind of a pain in the neck, but we put up with it because no one throws a party like my big sister."

They continued to tease each other and laugh together during their meal. As much as Janet enjoyed their banter, she wanted to urge them to chew faster.

But she didn't. She did, however, sweep empty plates off the table at lightning speed. By the time the Flaherty family had finished, most of the daily cleanup was complete. Paulette had discreetly flipped the sign on the door and was setting out baking supplies for the morning.

The table had been cleared of everything but coffee mugs when Janet and Debbie approached with the candy tin.

Mike swallowed hard when Janet set the tin down. His wife squeezed his hand then let go.

When he lifted the lid, awe filled his gaze and his eyes filled with tears. He gripped the raised lid with both hands and stared at the medals.

He turned the box so everyone could see the contents. "These were my grandpa's medals," he explained. "From World War II. This is how brave he was while building roads and keeping troops safe by giving them getaways and bridges and ways to escape."

"He built roads in the war?" asked Rachel. "Real ones? Like he did here?"

"He did. Your great-grandpa helped soldiers and marines get to safety. Lots of times."

The older boy—Brian—touched one of the medals. "Can I see them?" he asked, and Mike handed the box over.

His eyes widened, and as Brian lifted the awards to get a closer look, Mike turned to Janet and Debbie. "But where were they all these years? Why didn't they turn up before now?"

"A dog," Janet replied. "In fact, in the end, this story is all about a dog."

Cory shifted his gaze to Janet as Kim came through the door. She'd brought Eileen at Janet's request, and the quiet thump of Eileen's walker marked the seconds as she moved their way.

"I asked Eileen to come because I think she can shed light on the mystery," Janet explained. "She was the stationmaster here for a long time."

Cory stood and moved toward Eileen, and as she approached the table, he drew out a chair for her. He helped adjust the chair once she'd sat down, and then he squatted next to her to minimize the height difference. "You're the one who took care of him, aren't you?"

Surprise lifted Eileen's brows and brightened her eyes.

Mike frowned. "Took care of Gramps?"

Cory shook his head. "Buddy."

Mike and Beth exchanged looks, but Eileen reached out and grasped Cory's hand. "You know."

"I know part," he said softly as his eyes moistened. "I know that my grandpa never got over being disappointed in himself for not coming back. Not checking in. Not making sure Buddy was all right."

"And yet he was," Eileen told him in a firm voice as she gripped the young man's hands. "He was loved and cherished, and faithful to the end."

"The dog's faithfulness is what broke Gramps's heart. Gramps wasn't faithful, and he couldn't forgive himself for that."

"You mean Jerome was the soldier who said goodbye to Buddy at the train station?" Paulette asked, looking just as surprised as Eileen.

Cory nodded. "Gramps told me the story when we took that Honor Flight before he died, but he made me promise to keep his secret, at least until he was gone. We were supposed to go down to the lobby and meet everyone to visit the monuments, but he couldn't go. Wouldn't go. Said he didn't deserve to be honored when he broke the most important rule of all. To make sure those he loved were all right.

"His family was poor," Cory went on. "Depression poor, and maybe just starting to get on their feet when the Japanese attacked Pearl Harbor. Grandpa was working for a man who helped scrape driveways and roads and build culverts for ditches. He joined up after the attack. They sent him to an engineering division because of his experience. While he helped build the Alaskan Highway, his mother and sisters left the area. They couldn't afford to keep Buddy with Gramps gone, so they gave Buddy to a family. That family also left the area."

"There was a lot of movement at that time," noted Debbie. "As awful as the war was, it offered new opportunities for a lot of people. The war effort created jobs, and people went after those jobs."

Cory met her gaze across the table. "Yes. Gramps always figured Buddy was with that family. That he was okay."

"But who was Buddy?" Mike asked.

Cory's expression wavered with emotion. "He was the dog that kept Gramps warm at night. The house had one heater, and Gramps insisted that his mother and sisters use it. He'd huddle with Buddy under an old blanket, and that's how they got through the winters. Buddy's the dog that shared his meals. The dog that waited for him every day when he walked all the way home from the road job he had. The dog that watched out for rats and mice and owls or raccoons and didn't let anything invade their rundown old home. Buddy was Gramps's best friend. He was his protector when a teenage boy needed protecting."

"And he was the dog that came to the station with Jerome the day he left for basic. And every day after," Eileen whispered. Her eyes were wet. Kim reached for her mother's hand and clung tight. "He must have been left by those other people. Or just plain wouldn't go with them. He had a mind of his own," she explained. "He made the trek into town every morning. He smiled at people, that kind of funny doggy smile. He'd sit there, every day, gazing out the east-facing windows if he was inside or watching from under the over-hang if he was outside. We loved him. Folks would pet him and say 'Hey, Buddy, where do you belong?' and he'd wag his tail and stay right there. But he'd stand and watch like a soldier at attention every time a train rolled in from the east until age got the better of him. He never paid one lick of attention to the trains coming through on the western tracks."

"Gramps headed east for basic, but when they learned he had roadbuilding skills, they sent him west," said Cory. "Not something a dog would know."

"It was as if Buddy knew his boy went that way and had to come back that way," Janet said. "He was an amazing animal."

"He must have been." Mike's expression reflected wonder at this revelation. "Grandpa served with great honor and courage," he said. "Then he came home to build a great career, mostly by chance."

"I'd say divine guidance," his wife corrected him. "He took a seat on the train alongside a road builder's son, and the rest is history. A history they built together throughout the upper Midwest."

"So the dog lived with you?" Mike asked Eileen.

She shook her head. "He lived on his own for years. When he got old I tried to get him to stay with my grandmother, a widowed woman who needed something to care about, but Buddy would have none of it. He broke loose as quick as he could and hightailed it back to the depot. We made him a corner all his own. And when he got too old to make the trek in and out of town, he stayed right here. He was my friend. That good dog's loyalty stirred many a heart. Hurting hearts. Happy ones too. He never gave up. He passed away in 1953, and it about broke my heart to say goodbye." Her voice softened, and then she sighed. "We set up a memorial out there for him. A bench, right beneath that oak tree—it wasn't much more than a sapling then—and a plaque that honored a dog's devotion. Janet told me about the man who wept as he buried the medals," she went on. "And now we know why."

Cory filled in the next part, and he didn't hide the sorrow in his voice. "It broke his heart to hear of Buddy's devotion. He felt like he'd abandoned the one creature that cared more about him than anyone else ever had. Until he married Gee Gee, that is."

"That must be why he never got another dog after Brandy died," Mike said. He looked at Janet and Debbie. "Brandy died soon after Dad came back from Dennison. I'd just graduated from college."

Cory nodded. "He said he didn't deserve a dog's love. By the time we were done talking, I think he felt better. He seemed to, anyway. I think admitting it made it seem less awful. Knowing that Buddy was loved by the town and cared for by the stationmaster eased his mind. Not his guilt." Cory sighed softly. "But his mind."

A noise pulled their attention toward the back door.

Isaac sat there, chin up, looking in the window that overlooked the railyard.

Eileen gripped the table hard. So hard that the knuckles on her aged hands strained white. When she spoke, it was as if the very word choked her. "Buddy."

"What?" asked Kim, looking from the dog to her mother.

"The dog there." Eileen whispered the words. "He's the spitting image of Buddy."

"No." Janet frowned.

Eileen nodded. "A dead ringer, Janet. And look. He smiles."

Sure enough, Isaac's mouth was open in a doggy smile.

Debbie moved to the door and swung it wide.

Isaac didn't shy away.

He walked through the door as if he'd done it a hundred times before. Then he sat, watching them all, patiently waiting.

"Whose dog is he?" asked Eileen.

"A stray we've been feeding," Janet said. She sent a somewhat guilty look Kim's way. "We're not trying to attract strays, Kim. He was hungry."

"And alone," Eileen whispered.

That summed it up perfectly. "Yes," said Janet.

Cory stood up. He crossed the floor slowly and stooped down by the dog's side. "Hey, fella. How you doin'?"

The dog looked right at him, and then he nudged Cory's hand, asking for a petting. Cory obliged, and the dog smiled.

So did Cory. And while he petted the young dog, he shifted his attention to his wife. "Lisa, do you—"

Her eyes glistened as she met her husband's gaze. "No need to ask, darling. The answer is yes."

He turned back toward Debbie and Janet. "Can we take him home with us? Would that be all right?"

Debbie looked at Janet, and Janet cleared her throat. It took her a moment, but then she nodded, speaking for both of them. "It wouldn't just be all right, Cory. It would be absolutely perfect."

The three kids gathered around Mike and the dog.

Janet worried that Isaac might shy away, but he didn't. He sat there, smiling a toothy grin, as people showered their love on him.

The medals had found their home with Jerome's family.

So had the dog.

Was it chance that Isaac resembled Buddy and that Buddy might have been related to Bing and Crosby?

Maybe.

And maybe it was God's plan, mending the old while blessing the new.

Janet's eyes filled. Someone thrust a napkin into her hands, and she looked up.

Debbie met her gaze, and her eyes were just as moist, but then she smiled.

She stepped back and put her arm around Janet's shoulders. "We did it," she whispered, and there was no denying the joy and pride in her best friend's voice.

Janet exchanged a happy grin with her and nodded. "We sure did."

Dear Readers,

I love dogs.

After reading this story, you know the truth in this!

The loyalty of a good dog is so precious and fun and sometimes messy and sad and goofy and…everything. Just everything.

When Guideposts offered me the chance to work on this series, I jumped in, because coupling dogs, history, valor, the Greatest Generation, a great café (I waitressed in a diner for eleven years, so I'm right at home in Whistle Stop!), the Salvation Army support of military…. Well, this touched all of my buttons as an all-American girl. And I was a professional baker for years, so Janet's role is not only fun, it's natural!

But I loved Jerome's story too. A guy from the "sticks," a guy who sacrificed as a child, then as a soldier, then as a construction worker. Jerome sets the bar high for getting things done. He's a man of faith who believes in doing right. When he discovers a major misstep, it hits him hard because he truly is a man of valor.

I hope you loved this story. I hope you're cheering for Janet and Debbie's success at the depot as they launch this new endeavor—a business that touches hearts and souls and makes folks smile with great food and the best little bakery around!

This coffee drinker from Western New York raises a mug o' joe in your honor. Thank you so much for reading *As Time Goes By*!

Ruthy

ABOUT the AUTHOR

Bestselling, inspirational author Ruth Logan Herne has published over seventy novels and novellas. She is living her dream of being an author, and in her spare time she is co-owner of a rapidly growing pumpkin farm in Hilton, New York. She is the baker-in-residence, the official grower-of-the-mums, and a true people person, so filling her yard with hundreds of people every day throughout fall is just plain fun!

She loves God, her family, her country, dogs, coffee, and chocolate. The proud mother of six with a seventh daughter of her heart and fourteen grandkids, Ruthy lives in an atmosphere where all are welcome, no mess is too big it can't be cleaned up, and food is shared.

ON the HOMEFRONT

I have long been a big fan of William Booth and the Salvation Army. William Booth started a mission to bring the Gospel to the poor, the broken, the lost, and the shunned. He brought the Bible to the teeming streets of London in 1865 in a way so different from traditional means that his "army" of helpers grew into an international organization that has since helped millions of people.

In World War I, Salvation Army workers visited the trenches in Europe, offering clean clothes and frying doughnuts in soldiers' helmets—seven doughnuts at a time! Who would have thought such a thing possible?

By World War II the support of the Salvation Army was embedded into American culture and "Doughnut Lassies" took their comfort skills to wherever military gathered, including places like our beloved Dennison Railroad Depot. The women fried doughnuts, poured coffee, and gave the servicemen (and servicewomen!) a taste of home as they shipped out.

The kindness of these volunteers, those doughnuts, and smiles and good wishes were sometimes the last thing a soldier saw before shipping off to an assignment that didn't include doughnuts. That valiant military rose up to do what had to be done at monumental sacrifice, earning the name "The Greatest

Generation." They not only survived the Great Depression, they shined in the foxholes, trenches, tanks, ships, and planes of a world war. It is a pleasure to honor them and their valor in this wonderful series!

FROM the HOME-FRONT KITCHEN

The Salvation Army Doughnut Lassie Recipe

Thank you to the Salvation Army for providing this original recipe for their doughnuts. And yes, Ruthy and Janet have both made them, and they're marvelous! Janet doesn't use lard. She uses canola oil or vegetable oil, and she offers several varieties: cinnamon sugar (1 part cinnamon to 6 parts sugar), glazed (simple recipe below), and powdered sugar, often called "confectioner's sugar" until the turn of the century—a quaint and accurate name!

Janet also sets the doughnuts on paper towels to drain the oil before finishing them with glaze or sugar.

Yield: 4 dozen doughnuts

Ingredients for doughnuts:

5 cups flour

2 cups sugar

2 large eggs

1¾ cup milk

5 teaspoons baking powder

¼ tablespoon salt

1 tub lard (Janet uses vegetable oil and a fryer, but you can use a kettle with 2–3 inches of oil and do this on the stovetop or over a campfire.)

For the glaze:
Whisk together 2 cups powdered sugar, ¼ cup milk, and 1 teaspoon vanilla until smooth.

Directions:
1. Combine all ingredients (except lard or oil) to make dough.
2. Thoroughly knead dough, roll smooth, and cut into rings less than ¼ inch thick. (When finding items to cut out doughnut circles, be creative! Salvation Army doughnut girls used whatever they could find, from baking powder cans to coffee percolator tubes.)
3. Heat oil or lard to 365 degrees. When frying doughnuts, maintain temperature between 350 and 365 degrees.
4. Drop the rings into the lard or oil. Turn doughnuts several times.
5. When browned, remove doughnuts and allow excess fat to drip off.
6. Dust with powdered sugar or dip in glaze. Let cool and enjoy.

Read on for a sneak peek of another exciting book in the Whistle Stop Café Mysteries series!

WE'LL MEET AGAIN

BY JENELLE HOVDE

Dennison, Ohio
April 1943

Oh, please, please let him like my gift.

Ignoring the nervous flutter in her chest, Eileen Turner handed a wrapped package to the man who had stolen her heart. He loosened the string and peeled back the paper with a small cry.

"You bought me a book?" Samuel Lapp turned the blue volume over in his calloused hands. Gold lettering glinted in the sun as he examined the spine with an expression of something akin to awe. The Odyssey by Homer. His smile, however, beamed far brighter than

the elegant gilding. How tiny her gift looked, cradled within those long fingers.

She sucked in a quick breath, dazzled by that dimpled smile. Feigning nonchalance, she raised a shoulder. "I know you wanted a copy, and I ordered it for you over a month ago."

A delighted laugh broke free from him as he carefully opened the cover, the faint sound of crisp papers clinging to each other finally separating and breaking free. Gingerly, he used his index finger to flip the fragile pages edged with gold. She took advantage of the moment to observe him. Already, he was lost to her, his eyes rapidly skimming the words, his mind drinking them in like a man in desperate need of a soda pop on a sultry day.

And who would have thought Samuel Lapp, furniture maker extraordinaire and heir to Lapp Lumber, with his tanned arms beneath his rolled sleeves and his suspenders looped over his broad shoulders, would have such a keen desire for the written word? With the summer sun beating down, he pushed his straw hat up from his forehead, and his longish blond hair curled damp about his ears and neck from a morning of hard work. His mouth formed silent words as he continued to study Homer's writing.

She certainly didn't have the same insatiable desire to read. She had barely mustered a solid B in

Mr. Hanson's English class, forcing herself to endure Shakespeare's Hamlet. To be or not to be, that is the question. *Well, if Mr. Hanson had asked her—and he hadn't—*Hamlet *proved pure agony, truth be told.*

But making Samuel smile? It was worth the cost of the book plus the ninety-three-cent shipping and handling charges, all the way from Baker's Books in Columbus, Ohio.

She reached into her worn leather handbag and pulled out the second volume, feeling like she was about to dole out sarsaparilla sticks to the neighborhood kids. This book, The Rights of Man *by Thomas Paine, had been hesitantly recommended by her papa.*

When she slipped the books into her purse this morning, Papa had turned white around the gills. "Samuel isn't like us, sweetheart. I know you met him during his rumspringa, *and he's been a special friend these past few years. But he's got a world he can't leave. Are you willing to abandon your way of life for him? Don't you give that boy false notions, you hear?"*

"Eileen!" Samuel's cry broke through her thoughts, including Papa's chiding voice. "What have you done?"

She handed the book to him, her gloved fingers brushing his. A thrill rippled up her arm, aiming straight for her chest. And judging from the way his blue eyes startled, Samuel had felt the same electric spark.

"Eileen," he said again, this time with a hint of warning in that mellow baritone, "you should not have spent so much money on me."

"I know you can't get to the library easily, especially when barn-raising season comes," she said as her cheeks flamed. "Besides, it's important to have your own copy to read over and over again. You can make notes in the margins and memorize the parts you like best."

And think of me. *Of course, she would not admit that thought out loud.*

He transferred both books to one arm and reached for her hand, his thumb brushing across her knuckles. Despite the fabric barrier, it felt as though she wasn't wearing gloves at all. "You are so gut to me. I cannot imagine my life before I met you, and to think it has been three years. The best years I can recall in a long time."

He raised her captured hand to his mouth, and...

Was he going to kiss her? Goodness, she just might melt right into the lawn in Dennison's McCluskey Park for all to see. Sure enough, he brushed his soft lips against the back of her hand. Mercy.

"Samuel Lapp!" *A strident voice shattered the tender moment.*

Eileen gulped as Samuel tore his gaze from hers to look over her shoulder. His eyebrows dipped downward in alarm, and he dropped her hand. She pivoted on her sensible heels, only to witness a young man yank on the reins, forcing his black buggy to a jerky halt on the road running parallel to the park.

"Oh no, it is Jacob," Samuel breathed. He edged past Eileen, the books pinned firmly beneath his arm. "It appears our date will be cut short."

The youth glared, squinting at Eileen as if she were a loathsome sight. Thinner, and with a ruddier complexion, Jacob offered a younger, far more irritable version of Samuel. "Daed needs you back at the lumberyard. Why didn't you tell him you had plans to whittle away the afternoon?"

The look Samuel shot her was part regret, part resignation. A sigh escaped him. These stolen moments together seemed all too few these past months.

"It's okay. If you have to go, I understand. I've got another shift at the train station. Margot needs help with the sandwiches for the soldiers," she said. Although that wasn't entirely true. Margot had plenty of female volunteers ready to bat their eyelashes at the departing men who shipped out from the Dennison train station.

Besides, a more troubling thought took hold. Why hadn't Samuel told his family he was meeting her for lunch at the café? He had found a ride with his cousin, planning to deliver a hand-carved bench to Mrs. Healy, the first-grade teacher, and then meet for lunch with Eileen. Was he ashamed to be caught with an Englischer?

Samuel glanced over his shoulder as he headed toward the buggy. "You know how my daed can get in a snit when I am not at the workshop. Hopefully, I will see you later. In two weeks at our special spot, ja?"

She nodded, her throat tightening at Samuel's sudden reserve. Though her handbag felt infinitely lighter, her heart sank. He climbed into the buggy, his jaw clenched, as Jacob's loud chiding rose in pitch. Then Jacob clucked his tongue while slapping the reins against the horses, and Samuel's solemn gaze sought hers.

Her afternoon ruined and her dignity in tatters, she readjusted her white gloves with the seed pearl buttons and headed toward the train station. Samuel's gentle touch lingered on her hands.

Perhaps Papa was right. Perhaps this connection with Samuel Lapp, one of the best furniture makers in all of Ohio's Amish country, might prove too risky in the end. Yet she felt drawn to his quiet strength, to his mysterious demeanor, and to the charming way he asked for her advice on Englischer ways. Didn't he seek her out when he came into town, never pressuring her for more than the pleasure of her company over a cup of coffee? Those visits had blossomed into something sweet and heady.

No, Samuel wasn't ashamed of her. Every time he found her in the train station she felt he cared deeply, flashing that winsome smile, his eyes alight when he saw her. His family? Well, that was another matter entirely.

Two weeks later, Eileen waited in McCluskey Park, shading her eyes as she searched the road for the familiar sight of a black buggy and chestnut workhorse. The sky overhead arched bright blue, and a young mother pushed a gray pram down the winding path, pausing every so often to coo to the baby nestled inside.

A tiny cry brought a pang to Eileen's chest as she furtively watched the woman reach into the pram and snuggle a small bundle of white. So many mothers and new brides faced long months of loneliness and uncertainty as their husbands left Dennison. Thousands of soldiers slipped through the train station, their hands outstretched for the canteen sandwich bags and doughnuts, now a famous treat served by the Salvation Army. Within less than a year, the train station had garnered nationwide attention. Beaming girls offered delicious food and one last glimpse of home as the men headed off to war. The GI's called Dennison

Dreamsville, USA, *in homage to Glenn Miller's song with the same name.*

Since receiving a coveted promotion after the previous stationmaster enlisted, Eileen loved the work—found purpose in it—but she also felt more tired than she could remember. The lunch dates with Samuel remained one bright spot in her days; a chance to escape, even if for a moment. She shifted on the bench, glancing at the silver watch pinned to her dress. Twelve forty-five. No Samuel.

Her afternoon shift started in fifteen minutes. She had no choice but to return to the train station a few blocks away from the park. Disappointment sliced through her as she left. Had an accident occurred at the Lapp lumbermill? Or had Samuel's father finally put an end to their friendship? Samuel was nineteen, only a year younger than she was. A man, by all accounts. Surely his father wouldn't continue to interfere?

With increasingly heavy steps, she hurried back to her post and the shifting train schedules and never-ending maintenance issues that demanded her attention. But neither her duties nor the low rumble of the engines and the steady stream of travelers could distract her, and after her shift ended, she continued to mull over what had happened to Samuel. He rarely canceled.

That evening, when she entered the house, a pile of letters lay scattered across the kitchen table. Bless Papa, he tried so hard to help her. Some days he retrieved the mail from the post office, but other days he forgot.

"Is that you, Eileen?" her father called from the living room.

"Yes, Papa. It's me," she answered as she hung her hat on the coatrack in the hallway and tugged her gloves free. She cast them onto the console pressed against the wall.

She peeked around the corner. He sat in an over-stuffed club chair, unfolding a newspaper with a rattle. With his left leg propped up by a tufted footstool, he appeared the picture of comfort. But she knew that leg ached something fierce from an old war wound, courtesy of the First World War. A breeze ruffled the living room curtains, a few of the windows open despite the afternoon heat. Already her dress clung to her skin, thanks to the humidity within the stifling room. Perhaps he hurt too much to get up and close the windows.

"There's a letter for you in the kitchen. Samuel Lapp, I believe," he said.

Her pulse skittered as she recognized the bold scrawl. After tearing open the envelope, she pulled out a sheet of blue-lined paper, the kind a child would use during his grammar lessons.

Eileen,

I read the books you gave me. Read them twice, in fact. I have never received a gift that so spoke to my soul. I cannot help but think that *Gott* placed you in my life for a reason. Every night, I sleep with the books on my nightstand, and I dream of you.

Daed wanted to burn the books, but I would not let him. I fear the neighbors heard our horrible fight. I cringe, thinking of it. I said hard things to him, things a good *sohn* should never say. He is a decent man and deserves far better than rebellion, but he does not understand my need to read and see more of the world. You do, however. And with you, I feel more alive than I have ever felt.

I have been thinking about many things since our last meeting. This dreadful business with Germany and the brave men who ship overseas to protect their hurting brothers and fight for the freedom to think and worship as one pleases, to exist fully as our Creator intended. *The Rights of Man* challenged me to my very core. Long ago, my people fled persecution, hoping to find religious freedom.

Why should I not fight for those I love? Why should I not fight for you and everyone else in Dennison? There. I said it. I wanted to say it to you before Jacob rudely interrupted us. But I love you,

Eileen. I will always love you, my *liebling*. From the moment I bumped into you at my rumspringa, knocking the ice cream cone right out of your hand, I was smitten. There you stood at the soda counter, wearing that pink dress. And clumsy oaf that I was, I nearly trampled your shoes. But you merely laughed when you saw the ice cream staining your outfit. Not at me—just the situation. I thought you had the prettiest laugh, like little bells tinkling in a row. And you even let me replace your double vanilla scoop, suggesting I try the chocolate sprinkles on top.

Was that our first date? Listening to the Mills Brothers sing from the radio while eating ice cream from the Revco Drugstore? If so, I felt like I had tasted heaven. How I looked forward to being with you, snatching moments dancing to Sinatra, with my arms wrapped around you as you pressed your cheek against mine. These things I had remained blissfully unaware of until I met you. You changed me, Eileen. And now, like Odysseus of *The Odyssey*, I find I am embarking upon a journey of doing what is right and noble. How it fires my imagination!

She lowered the paper, tears blurring the rest of the black letters, slanted and bold, telling her of his plans. Why had she ever thought to offer him those books, of all choices? Never in her wildest imagining would she have pictured him, a conscientious objector, leaving his family and business behind to fight overseas in France, or wherever the Good Lord would send him.

How could she possibly say goodbye to the man who had meant everything to her? Yet... Papa had fretted Samuel would reject her for the plain life. She had wrestled with whether she would fit in with the Amish community, abandoning her favorite music and all she held dear. Because of her, Samuel had held off baptism, signaling his hesitance to embrace his Amish heritage.

Was this God's plan? To change him and, somehow, bring them closer in the end?

If so, why this path, Lord?

She sensed no discernible answer to that prayer other than the cooing of a mourning dove settled in the nearby oak tree just outside the kitchen window. As she headed toward the living room, two thoughts battled, each one fighting for dominance as she clutched the precious letter to her chest.

He loved her! And he was leaving.

A NOTE FROM the EDITORS

We hope you enjoyed *Whistle Stop Café Mysteries series*, published by Guideposts. For over 75 years, Guideposts, a nonprofit organization, has been driven by a vision of a world filled with hope. We aspire to be the voice of a trusted friend, a friend who makes you feel more hopeful and connected.

By making a purchase from Guideposts, you join our community in touching millions of lives, inspiring them to believe that all things are possible through faith, hope, and prayer. Your continued support allows us to provide uplifting resources to those in need. Whether through our communities, websites, apps, or publications, we inspire our audiences, bring them together, and comfort, uplift, entertain, and guide them. Visit us at guideposts.org to learn more.

We would love to hear from you. Write us at Guideposts, P.O. Box 5815, Harlan, Iowa 51593 or call us at (800) 932-2145. Did you love *As Time Goes By?* Leave a review for this product on guideposts.org/shop. Your feedback helps others in our community find relevant products.

Find inspiration, find faith, find Guideposts.
Shop our best sellers and favorites at
guideposts.org/shop

**While you are waiting for the next fascinating story
in the *Whistle Stop Café Mysteries*, check out
some other Guideposts mystery series!**

SAVANNAH SECRETS

Welcome to Savannah, Georgia, a picture-perfect Southern city known for its manicured parks, moss-covered oaks, and antebellum architecture. Walk down one of the cobblestone streets, and you'll come upon Magnolia Investigations. It is here where two friends have joined forces to unravel some of Savannah's deepest secrets. Tag along as clues are exposed, red herrings discarded, and thrilling surprises revealed. Find inspiration in the special bond between Meredith Bellefontaine and Julia Foley. Cheer the friends on as they listen to their hearts and rely on their faith to solve each new case that comes their way.

The Hidden Gate
The Fallen Petal
Double Trouble
Whispering Bells
Where Time Stood Still
The Weight of Years
Willful Transgressions

Season's Meetings

Southern Fried Secrets

The Greatest of These

Patterns of Deception

The Waving Girl

Beneath a Dragon Moon

Garden Variety Crimes

Meant for Good

A Bone to Pick

Honeybees & Legacies

True Grits

Sapphire Secret

Jingle Bell Heist

Buried Secrets

A Puzzle of Pearls

Facing the Facts

Resurrecting Trouble

Forever and a Day

MYSTERIES OF
MARTHA'S VINEYARD

Priscilla Latham Grant has inherited a lighthouse! So with not much more than a strong will and a sore heart, the recent widow says goodbye to her lifelong Kansas home and heads to the quaint and historic island of Martha's Vineyard, Massachusetts. There, she comes face-to-face with adventures, which include her trusty canine friend, Jake, three delightful cousins she didn't know she had, and Gerald O'Bannon, a handsome Coast Guard captain—plus head-scratching mysteries that crop up with surprising regularity.

A Light in the Darkness
Like a Fish Out of Water
Adrift
Maiden of the Mist
Making Waves
Don't Rock the Boat
A Port in the Storm
Thicker Than Water
Swept Away
Bridge Over Troubled Waters
Smoke on the Water
Shifting Sands
Shark Bait

Seascape in Shadows
Storm Tide
Water Flows Uphill
Catch of the Day
Beyond the Sea
Wider Than an Ocean
Sheeps Passing in the Night
Sail Away Home
Waves of Doubt
Lifeline
Flotsam & Jetsam
Just Over the Horizon

MIRACLES & MYSTERIES OF MERCY HOSPITAL

Four talented women from very different walks of life witness the miracles happening around them at Mercy Hospital and soon become fast friends. Join Joy Atkins, Evelyn Perry, Anne Mabry, and Shirley Bashore as, together, they solve the puzzling mysteries that arise at this Charleston, South Carolina, historic hospital— rumored to be under the protection of a guardian angel. Come along as our quartet of faithful friends solve mysteries, stumble upon a few of the hospital's hidden and forgotten passageways, and discover historical treasures along the way! This fast-paced series is filled with inspiration, adventure, mystery, delightful humor, and loads of Southern charm!

Where Mercy Begins
Prescription for Mystery
Angels Watching Over Me
A Change of Art
Conscious Decisions
Surrounded by Mercy
Broken Bonds
Mercy's Healing
To Heal a Heart

A Cross to Bear

Merciful Secrecy

Sunken Hopes

Hair Today, Gone Tomorrow

Pain Relief

Redeemed by Mercy

A Genius Solution

A Hard Pill to Swallow

Ill at Ease

'Twas the Clue Before Christmas

Find more inspiring stories in these best-loved Guideposts fiction series!

Mysteries of Lancaster County

Follow the Classen sisters as they unravel clues and uncover hidden secrets in Mysteries of Lancaster County. As you get to know these women and their friends, you'll see how God brings each of them together for a fresh start in life.

Secrets of Wayfarers Inn

Retired schoolteachers find themselves owners of an old warehouse-turned-inn that is filled with hidden passages, buried secrets, and stunning surprises that will set them on a course to puzzling mysteries from the Underground Railroad.

Tearoom Mysteries Series

Mix one stately Victorian home, a charming lakeside town in Maine, and two adventurous cousins with a passion for tea and hospitality. Add a large scoop of intriguing mystery, and sprinkle generously with faith, family, and friends, and you have the recipe for *Tearoom Mysteries*.

Ordinary Women of the Bible

Richly imagined stories—based on facts from the Bible—have all the plot twists and suspense of a great mystery, while bringing you fascinating insights on what it was like to be a woman living in the ancient world.

To learn more about these books, visit Guideposts.org/Shop

THE SON OF GOD

THE SON OF GOD

Book Two of GOD'S HAND IN HISTORY

BY

MARY WILSON

Illustrated by Vera Louise Drysdale

OUR SUNDAY VISITOR, INC.
HUNTINGTON, INDIANA 46750

ISBN: 0–87973–696–8
Library of Congress Catalog Card Number: 77–81931

Published in the U.S.A. by
Our Sunday Visitor, Inc.
Noll Plaza
Huntington, Indiana 46750

CONTENTS

The Next Stage in History

IN this book, the second part of 'God's Hand in History', we take up the story at the place in the world's history where quite a lot of people, many unknown to each other, have started to understand that there is a great moral law. 'Moral' means the right way to live, the right way to behave to each other.

For instance, complete and absolute honesty is the same wherever you find it. An honest man, whether he comes from Asia or Europe or Africa or Australia, will not steal, will speak the truth, does not cheat and is trustworthy. When such a man meets another such man they understand each other, and can work together to give a right way of life to the world.

The people in the first part of this book, although some of them lived hundreds of years and thousands of miles apart, shared many of the same moral ideas.

Buddha, Zoroaster, Confucius and others all felt that the most important thing in life is to put other people before oneself, and to be clean and upright in all things. It had come clear to them that just as Nature works by certain laws—in the way that the sun shines and the plants grow—so there are laws, moral laws, about human nature and human society which follow a pattern too.

Through fifteen hundred years of history God had taught the Jewish people something more. This was that a whole nation is meant to live straight, and that a nation which does so will find His Plan. On the other hand a disobedient nation can take a wrong road in just the same way as a disobedient man, and with the same results.

However, it is one thing to have a moral law, which tells you what is the right thing to do. It is another thing to have power to do it, or even to want to do it.

The world needed to see that there is a Power which puts adventure back into goodness, so that it becomes a battle to win, not just a bore.

It would see this through God's Power alive in a man.

Some Person was needed who was stronger than death, who had no fear, who loved everybody, and who could bear all the pain and suffering in the world, someone whom everyone could see and know, someone who would do everything so differently that the whole world would want to be like him.

The New Man who would make people new.

Everything was going to be new, and yet everything good and lasting from the past was going to be part of the new world too.

The Waiting World

THE world was waiting for something new.

What sort of a world was it, and what had been happening in it? The kingdom of the Jews had come and gone. Great empires had come and gone too. The Jews themselves had scattered into many lands, taking their Jewish faith with them, and forming little Jewish colonies wherever they went.

Between the years 356 and 323 B.C. the Greek king Alexander, now known to us as Alexander the Great, rose to power in an astonishingly short space of time. In fifteen years his armies swept over and conquered all the lands between Greece and India, and from there back to Egypt, which he thought would create a unified world.

His Empire was a landmark in the history of that time, for though it did not long survive him as an empire, it lived on in a different way, leaving behind it the legacy of the Greek language. This became a link between the people of the Mediterranean lands, as it enabled them to exchange ideas and understand each other, and this played an important part in the history of the next several hundred years. The scattered groups of Jews also spoke Greek, and the records that they made of all that happened in those days are written in Greek.

Meanwhile Judæa, the country the Jews had come from, had been fought over by one great nation after another, until about a hundred years after the time of Alexander, it had become a Syrian colony under a king called Antiochus. The Antiochus family did their best to dishonour and kill the Jews' great idea of one God. The Jews were tortured and oppressed, and false gods were set up in the temple, but a brave Jewish family called the Maccabees rose against the Syrians. They rallied the country, recaptured Jerusalem and brought the people back to their true faith.

Unfortunately the freedom fought for by the Maccabees did not last long. Later rulers fought against each other. The country became divided, and civil war started which went on for a hundred years. This opened the way for another set of conquerors, the Romans, and in 63 B.C. they took Jerusalem under their famous general Pompey.

So the next part of the story takes place in what we should call an occupied country, or a colonial territory. The Roman Empire covered most of the lands round the Mediterranean, and was steadily spreading its power eastward into what we now call the Middle East. It stood for order and peace, and many people felt they were protected by what was called the Pax Romana or Roman peace. The Roman authorities found that it helped them to keep order when they had the good will of some of the conquered people. So in 40 B.C. the Emperor Augustus appointed a man called Herod, who was partly Jewish, to be king in Judæa, the southern province of Palestine.

Among the first Jews to work with this occupying power was a group of priests called the Sadducees. They were ready to be friendly in return for being allowed to keep their position as priests.

Against them arose an opposition party called the Pharisees, whose aim at first was to stop the Jews from working with the Romans. Pharisee means separate, and they to tried bring the Jews back to a pure faith, entirely separated from the Romans.

The Pharisees thought it meant keeping apart from all the other nations too so that the Jewish faith would not be weakened by outside ideas. They made a great point of sticking exactly to the laws which Moses had laid down, and many more which had grown out of them— until they finally knew so much about what to do and what not to do that they felt that they were better than anyone else. That is why today self-righteous people are called Pharisees.

As well as the Pharisees and the Sadducees there were the ordinary people of the country. Some were revolutionaries, working ceaselessly against the Romans. Others were rather hopelessly accepting the situation. But all of them were living for the day when God would send the Special Person, or Messiah, He had promised, and who they thought would finally turn out the Romans and give them back their kingdom.

They did not realise that something far bigger was going to happen.

Zacharias the Priest

ABOUT sixty years after the Romans had started to govern Judaea, a priest called Zacharias was standing before the altar in the Temple.

Zacharias was descended from Aaron the brother of Moses. Another of his ancestors was Eli who was High Priest when Samuel was a boy, and another was the prophet Jeremiah.

There were twenty-four groups of priests who were descended from two of Aaron's sons. They took it in turns to serve in the Temple for one week every six months, but there were so many priests in each group, or 'course' as they are called in the Bible, that no one man could hope to serve more than once in his lifetime. Some never had the chance at all.

Each group took two services a day, one at sunrise and one at sunset, and each time the priests drew lots to see who should go into the Holy Place. This was the part of the Temple nearest to the Holy of Holies, where no one went except the High Priest once a year.

One day in October in a certain year, Zacharias drew the lot which showed that he was the one chosen to go into the Holy Place. It was the great moment of his life. It had not come before and it would not come again.

The people stood in the great court outside. They could not go in, but Zacharias called them to prayer. Then he washed his hands and face before them in a special bowl, and walked up the wide steps alone, knowing that he carried the prayers of the whole nation with him. As he disappeared through the curtains and stood before the altar he could hear the crowds outside murmuring their prayers. He lit some sweet-smelling spice or incense, and clouds of scented smoke went up from it, just like the prayers of the people going up to God.

They were the prayers of a nation that longed to be free, and to have the king they believed God had promised them. Zacharias, standing there alone, represented them before God. Perhaps he thought of God's calling to His people for the last fifteen hundred years, of how often

they had turned away and how often men had been sent to call them back.

His own ancestors had been among these holy men. One of them, Jeremiah, had been called by God to warn the people of what would happen to them if they turned away from Him, but they had not listened. Jeremiah poured out his heart and life in answer to this call, but had to see his people lose everything because they did not listen.

Perhaps he thought of the great priest Zadok who lived in the time of King David, and from whose family the High Priests were drawn. Now they were called the Sadducees, which is another way of saying Zadokites. Zadok, or Sadouq, means faithful, honest, trustworthy, just and kind, but as we have seen, the Sadducees had gradually lost many of these qualities, and the strictness of the Pharisees had not made up for the loss.

So Zacharias must have stood there praying that God's high calling for his people would be fulfilled. In front of him was the altar, on his right the great seven-branched candlestick, and to his left God's table on which stood the dedicated bread.

He was surrounded by all that had come down to his people from the past, and he himself was a link in the chain which led to the future.

Zacharias and the Angel

AT this time Zacharias was already an old man and he had been married for many years to a woman named Elisabeth. She, like her husband, came from the family of Aaron who had been called long ago with his brother Moses to take the children of Israel out of Egypt.

Although their families went so far back into the past, they had no children of their own, and this was a grief to them, as it did not look as if they were going to have any descendants to play a part in the future. They had often prayed for a child, but now they were both old, and it did not seem likely that they would ever have one.

Suddenly as Zacharias stood praying he saw an angel standing by the altar on which the incense was burning. For a moment he was afraid and wondered what this meant, but the angel said, 'Fear not, Zacharias, for I have come to tell you that your wife Elisabeth is going to have a son. You must call him John.'

Then the angel said that this child John was going to turn the hearts of the people back to God. The child, he said, would be filled with God's Spirit. He would turn the hearts of fathers towards their children and turn those who are disobedient to the wisdom of good men. He would go ahead of the Lord with the same spirit and power as the prophet Elijah.

Zacharias said, 'But I am old, and my wife is old too. How do I know that this is true?'

The angel replied, 'My name is Gabriel, and I have been sent from God to tell you this, but because you have not believed me you will not be able to speak from now until the time that the child is born.'

Then the angel left him and Zacharias was alone again. He spent a long time thinking about this message. He waited so long that the people in the courtyard began to wonder what was the matter, and when he finally came out they crowded round to ask what had happened, but Zacharias could not speak.

He was dumb, just as the angel had said he would be.

God's Call to Mary

LIVING in the same country there was a young woman called Mary, who was Elisabeth's cousin, and she was soon to be married to a man called Joseph.

A few months after the angel had been to Zacharias he came to Mary and said, 'Hail, Mary', which was a way of greeting people. He told her that God loved her, and had especially chosen her, and that He would send her a child whose name was to be Jesus.

This child, the angel said, was not going to be just her child, but was God's own Son, whom God Himself was sending into the world for Mary and Joseph to look after.

The name Jesus was a very special name, and meant Saviour—

someone who would save people from sin and evil and open the way for a fresh part of God's plan for the world.

Many men had been sent to tell the people of Israel about God, but though they were often wise and upright like Moses, Daniel and others, they were ordinary human beings.

This was something new.

God had never before sent His own Son into the world, who would have His own Spirit, and yet would live in an ordinary family.

Mary found this was more than she could understand, so she asked how such a thing could happen.

The angel answered that God's Spirit would move in her and His Power would come upon her, and that the Holy Child which was to be born would be called the Son of God. 'Your cousin Elisabeth,' he said, 'who is an old woman now, is also going to have a child.'

'I am the handmaiden of the Lord,' said Mary. 'Let God do whatever seems right to Him.'

She did not argue.

She said 'yes' at once to God.

When the angel had gone, Mary was left quite alone thinking about what he had said, and what he had told her about Elisabeth. She decided she would go to see her cousin and stay with her for a while.

As soon as Elisabeth saw her coming she knew what had happened without being told, so Mary did not have to explain why she had come. Elisabeth knew that Mary was going to be the mother of God's Son.

She welcomed her and said, 'Blessed is she that believed, for the things which God has told her will come true.' And she took Mary in to live with her and Zacharias for three months.

At the end of that time Mary went home, and soon afterwards Elisabeth's son John was born.

John

ALL this time Zacharias had not been able to speak, and when his son was born he was still dumb and could not answer friends and relations who came to ask what the child was to be called.

They all thought that he should be called Zacharias after his father, but Elisabeth said, 'No, he is to be called John.'

The friends and relations were quite put out. 'None of your family have ever been called by that name,' they said. 'He must be called Zacharias after his father,' and they tried to find out from Zacharias whether he agreed.

He, however, knew that this was the child God had sent and that he must be called by the name God had chosen. He asked for a writing tablet on which he wrote, 'His name is John'.

And immediately he was able to speak again.

Now John, though he was not God's own Son like Jesus, was a chosen child, and one of the things the angel had told Zacharias was that he was to be very specially brought up. He was to live a hardy and obedient life, because he was going to 'make ready a people prepared for the Lord'. He was to prepare the hearts of the people for the new kind of life that Jesus was about to bring them.

In old pictures you often see John and Jesus as boys playing together. John is generally dressed in animals' skins to show that his parents had obeyed the angel by bringing him up to be content with simple things and not to demand anything for himself.

As he grew older he spent more and more time alone in the wilderness, or barren country outside Jerusalem, thinking over all that God was calling him to do, so that he would be ready when the time came.

The Birth of Jesus

MARY went back to her own home in the village of Nazareth, and she would probably have been glad if her baby could have been born there. It was winter, and very cold, just the sort of weather when it would have been more comfortable to stay at home.

At this same time, however, the Roman Emperor, Caesar Augustus, sent out an order for a list to be made of all the families living in the lands over which he ruled. Each head of a family had to go back to the town where he had been born, and be counted with his wife and children.

Although Joseph was living in Nazareth, in the northern province, Galilee, he had been born in Bethlehem, in the southern province, Judæa. So when the order came he and Mary had to set out in the cold winter weather, and go to Bethlehem.

Bethlehem was called the City of David, and Joseph and Mary were both David's direct descendants. David was descended from Abraham so that Jesus was sent into the family chosen by God many hundreds of years earlier. Joseph knew this and was grateful that he had been chosen to look after God's Son, and be a father to Him on earth.

There was nothing outwardly special about him though, as he and Mary started off for Bethlehem together with many other people who were all going for the same reason.

Bethlehem was so full that there was no room anywhere. Mary and Joseph went from place to place trying to find somewhere to stay, until in the end the innkeeper, seeing how tired they were, offered them his stable for the night. There was no room in the inn itself.

They went in thankfully, and lay down in the straw among all the cattle and donkeys that were there already.

There Mary's child was born.

That same night some shepherds were out on the hills guarding their sheep, when suddenly out of the darkness an angel came to them. The darkness vanished, and all around them was a glorious light.

Though it was an amazing and wonderful sight, they were terror-struck. They knew it was not of this world, but the angel reassured them.

'Fear not,' he said, 'for I bring you good tidings of great joy, which shall be for all people.'

Now the shepherds were neither rich nor clever, but they knew how to listen, and as they listened they heard the news which the angel had brought.

'Unto you is born this day in the city of David, a Saviour who is Christ the Lord. And this shall be a sign unto you. You shall find the babe wrapped in swaddling clothes, lying in a manger.'

As he finished speaking, suddenly the sky was filled with angels and the voices of angels, singing and praising God.

'Glory be to God in the highest,' they sang, 'and on earth peace and goodwill to men.'

Then the light faded, and the angels disappeared. The shepherds were again alone on the hillside, and they knew that they must find out what this was all about. They decided to go at once and hurried off to Bethlehem where they found Mary and Joseph with the baby, who was lying in a manger as the angel had said. It was all true, and they told everyone they met what they had heard that night about this child, and who He was. Then they went back into the night again, full of gratitude, and praising God for what He had shown them. They left people wondering at the news they brought.

Mary was also wondering as she saw all those who came to see her and the baby. She said nothing, but she thought a lot about what this was going to mean for the world.

Some, like the shepherds, would be grateful. Would others welcome Him too?

The Wise Men

AT the time when Jesus was born, a new bright star appeared in the sky for everyone to see. Few people bothered to find out what it meant, but there lived in a neighbouring country Wise Men who studied a great deal, and who knew all about the stars.

When a brand new one appeared, these men began to wonder what it was. They knew all that had been written about God sending someone who would be a great king or leader, and they felt sure this was the sign that He had come.

Taking offerings of gold and precious stones, they went westward, following the star. It led them to Jerusalem where they asked for the king of the Jews, saying that they had seen His star and had come to worship Him.

The king of the Jews at that time was Herod, who had been appointed by the Romans. When he heard that another king had been born he was troubled and began to wonder if this new king would take his place. All the other leaders were troubled too.

Among Herod's counsellors were certain Jewish priests who advised him about their laws and customs. They knew all that had been written about the people of Israel and God's plan for them, so

19

Herod called them together and asked if they knew where this new king was. He pretended to be eager to see Him.

The priests replied that He must certainly be in Bethlehem, because one of the old prophets called Micah had been told by God that Bethlehem would be the place where He would one day be born.

On hearing this Herod called the Wise Men and told them to go to Bethlehem and then to let him know exactly where the child was, so that he could go and worship Him. What he really meant was that he would have Him killed. The Wise Men did not realise this at first, so they promised to bring back word, and set off.

The star went on shining in the sky, and they followed the way it showed them, until they too found Mary and Joseph and Jesus.

The humble shepherds had been to see Jesus and now so had the Wise Men. They knelt down and gave their presents to Jesus, and then they started to go back and tell Herod where He was.

But God warned them in a dream not to go to Herod. So they changed their plans and went home another way.

How Jesus and His Parents had to Escape

HEROD waited impatiently for the Wise Men to come back, and when he realised that they had outwitted him he was furious. He was convinced that they wanted to make Jesus king instead of him, so he ordered his soldiers to kill all the boys in Bethlehem who were less than two years old, in the hope that the new king would be among them.

God again sent a warning. This time He spoke to Joseph in a dream. He said, 'Take the young child and His mother and go to Egypt, because Herod is looking for Him to kill Him. Stay there until I let you know that you can come back.'

Joseph quickly woke Mary and they took Jesus and wrapped Him up warmly. Then they went through the night and on for several days until they came to Egypt.

There they lived till Herod died, when Joseph dreamed that an angel stood beside him one night and told him that they could go home. So they packed their things and started off, but when they reached their own country of Judæa they heard that Herod's son

Archelaus was now king in his father's place. This made Joseph afraid to stay long in the southern province. God also warned him in another dream that it would not be safe, so Joseph took his family quickly on to the northern province, Galilee, and to his own town of Nazareth.

There they settled down to live simply with the other families of that town, and we know almost nothing of what Jesus did when He was a boy. Joseph was a carpenter and, as far as we know, Jesus was brought up to be a carpenter too.

There is a picture in one of the big galleries in London which shows Him as a boy with Joseph in the carpenter's shop, and His mother is standing looking on. She and Joseph loved Him deeply and He loved them. As He grew up He became strong in spirit. He was full of wisdom, and the grace of God was on Him.

The Things God Says Come True

JESUS came into a world like ours where men were looking for power and freedom for themselves and their countries.

Rome had built a great empire, and though her soldiers kept the peace in the colonial countries and stopped them from fighting each other, it was a peace kept from on top. It was not the peace of free people working together under God.

Many of the Jews kept the rules or commandments that Moses had given and went to the synagogue. No doubt they took their children and gave money too, but for many it had become more of a custom or a duty than anything to do with obeying God in the deepest places of their hearts. They felt that the priests could keep in touch with God for them. It was a very different idea from the earlier one, of a whole people chosen by God and belonging to Him.

On the other hand there were still among the Jews men and women who had kept God's Plan for His people in their hearts. They never lost the feeling that they were chosen to show the world God's love and care, and to show too, how much better His way is than ours.

When Elisabeth's son John was born, and Jesus too, God spoke to some of these men and women about what His Plan meant.

Jesus' own mother has left us the thoughts she had from God. So has John's father. And so has a very old man called Simeon who felt he had been waiting to die till Jesus should be born into the world.

All these people put God's Plan first. It was a bigger plan than just for them or their country. It was for the whole world. They had learned the secret of waiting and watching for what God was going to do, and not being so busy with their own affairs, nor so soft and selfish that His quiet voice was drowned or crowded out.

All through history it is through people who have been quiet enough and humble enough and trusting enough to listen in this way that God has been able to work.

Here are some of the thoughts God gave Mary as she was thinking about Jesus:

'My soul praises the Lord, and my spirit has rejoiced in God my Saviour. For He has looked with favour on the lowliness of His handmaiden. Why, from now on all the generations will called me blessed! For the powerful one has done great things for me, and Holy is His Name. And His mercy from one generation to another is on those who fear Him.

'He has done a mighty deed with His arm. He has scattered those who took pride in all that their hearts imagined, and He has uplifted the lowly. The hungry He has filled with good things, and the rich He has sent away empty. He has come to the aid of Israel His servant, remembering His mercy (as He said He would to our fathers) towards Abraham and his offspring for ever!'

And these are the words of Zacharias, the father of John:

'Blessed be the Lord the God of Israel, for He has graciously visited and brought deliverance to His people. He has caused to arise for us a Lord of Salvation, in the family of His servant David, in accordance with what He said through the mouths of His holy prophets down the ages, to save us from our foes and from the hands of all those who hate us, to deal mercifully with our fathers, and to remember His holy promises, the oaths which He swore to Abraham our father, that we, rescued from our enemies' hands, should be granted to serve Him without fear in holiness and right living before His face all our days.'

Then he speaks to his own little son:

'And you, my child, shall be called a prophet of the Highest. For you shall march before the face of the Lord, to make ready His ways, to bring a knowledge of salvation to His people through the forgiveness of their sins, by reason of our God's tender mercies which are seen in His causing the Sunrise to come upon us, to enlighten those who are straying in darkness and the shadow of death and to guide our feet into the way of peace.'

And here is the song which Simeon, the old, old man, sang after God had allowed him to see the child Jesus:

'Now let Thy servant go, Lord, according to Thy word, in peace. For these eyes of mine have seen Thy salvation, which Thou hast prepared for all people to see, a light to illumine the nations, and the glory of Thy people Israel.'

And to Mary, Jesus' mother, the old man said:

'This child is destined to make many in Israel fall and many rise again, to be a sign to be attacked—indeed your own heart will be pierced with pain—for the purpose that the thoughts of many hearts may be revealed!'

24

Jesus the Boy

EVERY year Joseph and Mary went to Jerusalem in a large party with all their friends and relations to celebrate the Passover, which was the anniversary of the time when the people of Israel had escaped from Egypt.

In the year that Jesus was twelve, they went as usual to the celebrations and He went with them. As it was such a big party it was hard to stick together, and Jesus did not stay with His parents all the time. Sometimes He would be with one group of friends, sometimes with another, and sometimes He went off on His own to find things out for Himself.

They spent several days in Jerusalem and when it was time to go back to Nazareth, Mary and Joseph looked round for Jesus to take Him home. They did not see Him as they were starting but supposed He was probably with another group and did not think much about it. To go from Jerusalem to Nazareth on foot or on horseback took several days. All through the first day Mary and Joseph kept thinking that Jesus would reappear and tell them what He had been doing, but when they stopped for the night there was still no sign of Him.

They began to feel anxious. Everyone was camping in different groups, and they went from one to another to see if Jesus was in one of them, but He was nowhere to be found. Mary and Joseph, who by now were quite worried, turned back to Jerusalem by themselves to look for Him.

The morning after they arrived they went to the Temple. They reached it tired and fearful, and whom should they see but their young son sitting with all the wisest men of Jerusalem, talking and asking questions, and answering them too.

His mother and Joseph were astonished, but they were also rather cross. Mary ran forward and asked Jesus what He meant by being so thoughtless.

'My son, why have you done this to us?' she asked. 'Your father and I have been looking so anxiously for you.'

Jesus seemed to think it was surprising that they should be worried. He knew by now what His work was to be and whose child He was, so perhaps He thought it was as clear to them as it was to Him.

He had come to the Temple because it was the house of His Father, God, and He wanted to talk about His Father with men who had thought about and studied God's promises for many years. So He said to Mary and Joseph, 'Why did you look for Me? Did you not know that I have to be about My Father's business?'

They could not understand what He meant.

He went home with them and was obedient to them until the time came for Him to go out into the world to do what He had been sent to do.

His mother thought of what He had said, and kept it in her heart as she watched Him growing up and gaining all the time in wisdom and understanding.

John the Baptist
and Jesus

WHILE Jesus was growing up, John was growing up too. As he grew older he lived more and more simply, mostly in the desert by himself. He knew that God had something special for him to do, and he spent his time preparing himself for it.

At last God spoke to him in the wilderness, and said that the time had come to go to the people of Israel and tell them to be ready for what Jesus was soon coming to give them.

We know nothing about those early years of either John or Jesus, but I sometimes wonder if they did not occasionally meet and talk to each other about what God was calling them to do.

John knew who Jesus was, and he knew that he had a special work to do for Him. The prophet Isaiah had said that someone would come from the wilderness saying, 'Prepare the way of the Lord. Make His paths straight,' and John knew that he himself was that person.

Wherever he went he called people together saying, 'Repent, for the Kingdom of Heaven is at hand.' The Kingdom of Heaven would be a new world ruled by God, and to repent means not just to be sorry, but also to change one's ways. So the only way to be part of God's world was to be sorry enough to change.

When they asked what to do, John told them many simple things, such as not to be greedy and keep things for themselves.

'If you have two coats,' he said, 'give one to someone who has none,' and 'If you have enough to eat, share it with those who need it.'

Some of the tax-gatherers came to John too. To them he said, 'You must not take more money from people than you are really supposed to take.' Nobody liked these tax-gatherers. They worked for the Romans and collected money from the Jewish people to give to the Roman government. So John told them to be honest.

He told the soldiers not to be rough or brutal. As they were often on guard at the Customs they had many opportunities for stealing or taking bribes. So he told them to be content with their wages.

John made it clear that everyone had to choose between right and wrong, including the king. The king did not much like this. He was a son of the king who had tried to kill Jesus as a baby many years before, and his name was Herod Antipas. He wished he could get rid of this man who kept saying, 'Change your ways', but did not dare to because John had so many followers.

John was so wise in all that he told people that they began to wonder if he were the man God had said He would send to help and lead them. But John told them he was not. He told them that he had only come ahead of someone far more important to prepare the way.

'I can baptise you with water,' he said, 'but one mightier than I will come and baptise you with the Holy Spirit.'

Baptism was a sign that sin was washed away, so that people could make a new start. They went down into the water, and came out ready to live in a new way. They came in crowds, as people always come to a man who speaks honestly and without fear.

They kept saying to John, 'Who are you? Are you Elijah come back again?'

And John said, 'No, I am a voice crying in the wilderness "Make straight the way of the Lord", as the prophet Isaiah said. Someone is coming after me whose shoes I am not good enough to untie.'

Everyone was puzzled, and they were just wondering who they were waiting for, when Jesus Himself came down to the River Jordan, where John was baptising.

John saw Him coming and said, 'Look, here He is. This is the Lamb of God who takes away the sins of the world. This is the One I was telling you about.'

Jesus was a man by now. For thirty years He had been quietly living at home, working with Joseph and listening to all that God was saying to Him, until He knew that the time had come for Him to leave home and go out into the world.

The first thing He did was to go and find John and say to him, 'Will you baptise Me too?'

John could not understand this at all. He had been telling everyone that Someone very important was coming. It did not seem to be the right way round for him to baptise Jesus, and he said so.

He said, 'I need you to baptise me. Why do you come to me?'

Jesus replied, 'Let it be so now,' and because Jesus asked him, John did it even though he did not understand.

So Jesus went down to the water in front of all the people, and John baptised Him.

As He came out of the water again, the Spirit of God hovered round Him like a white dove, and God spoke and said, 'This is My beloved Son, in whom I am well pleased.'

The Temptation of Jesus

THERE are two great forces in the world, good and evil. These clash with each other all the time. We all feel that fight going on in ourselves every day. Sometimes we let the good win, sometimes the evil.

Jesus went through all these battles, every one that we have to fight in our hearts. That is why He understands us. From the beginning of His life to the end, He won the battle every time.

His first great battle came soon after John baptised Him. God His Father must have let it happen in this way to help us and to show how much stronger Jesus is than the devil.

Jesus felt the Spirit of God working in Him, and He went out by Himself into the desert to fight this battle and find God's way of winning it.

It was natural that the spirit of evil should try and persuade Jesus to do what he wanted. He hoped to stop Him from bringing the answer to everybody in the world, and he tried to make him set about it in the wrong way by suggesting that He could impress people by getting quick and easy results.

The devil still does everything he can to stop God's Plan from working out. He cleverly persuades people that they should do what he wants instead of what God wants. In that way he gets many people into his power. He starts when we are young and goes right on till we are old. His aim is always to make evil ideas and actions seem reasonable and attractive.

One of the first places he attacks is people's thoughts because no one does anything, good or bad, without having thought about it first.

Jesus spent a long time in the desert, He prayed and thought without eating anything for nearly six weeks, and He was hungry. So His first battle was to fight everything in Himself that said 'I want'. You know how it is when you feel hungry or tired or uncomfortable. Nothing else seems to matter except getting some food, or some rest or something to make life easier. It is a hard thing to put what God wants in front of all these feelings.

The devil often plays on our feelings. And he put before Jesus the idea that as He was God's Son He could make things easier for Himself. It was dry and rocky in the desert, and there was no food. 'If you are God's Son,' he said, 'just give an order and see if these stones will turn into bread.'

Jesus knew that He was God's Son, and He knew too that food was not the most important thing in the world anyway. So although He was still hungry, He did not let 'I want' win. He said firmly, 'Man shall not live by bread alone but by every word that comes to him from God Himself.' He knew in His heart that when He needed food God would give it to Him. So He refused to think about whether He could turn stones into bread.

But the devil did not give up. He tried to tempt Jesus in another way.

'Now,' he said, 'suppose you were on the roof of the Temple, it would be interesting to jump off and see whether God would save you. It says in the Psalms that He will send angels to hold you in their hands and stop you from hurting yourself.'

But Jesus said, 'Thou shalt not tempt the Lord thy God,' which to me means not trying to get God to do things for the wrong reasons. God had told Him, when He was baptised, that He loved Him, and there was no need to try and prove it in a showy sort of way.

By this the devil saw that Jesus was certain of God's love, and could not be made to doubt it or test it. God's love does not change even when things seem most difficult.

The tempter tried something else.

This time Jesus was tempted to think of getting power for Himself. He heard a voice which said. 'If you are the Son of God, you should be a great and powerful king. It would be quite easy for you to be king of all the countries in the world, and if you will only worship me, I will help you.'

It sounds wonderful to be king of the whole world and be very powerful and even do a lot of good things with the power, but when people want power for themselves, the devil gets into them, and they become ruled by him rather than by God.

Jesus knew He had not come into the world to get things for Himself. He was part of God, and He had come to do what God said, and to teach other people how to do it too.

So He simply said, 'Get thee behind Me, Satan,' and refused to let these cunning suggestions take root in His heart. This time the devil saw that it was no use trying any more, so he went away.

Then when Jesus was feeling worn out and hungry God His Father sent angels to feed Him and look after Him.

No one was there when Jesus went through all this. He must have told His friends about it afterwards, so that they could tell us and help us not to be fooled by the devil either.

It helps us to understand the battle that goes on all the time between good and evil and how to win it.

Jesus did not try to fight the devil alone. He simply turned to God His Father and His promises, for God's help is always there whether we feel like asking for it or not. The story of the temptation is the story of choice—God's way or man's way.

Jesus did not just say 'no' to the devil. He chose God's way in place of every clever suggestion the devil made, and so was able to offer the power of choice to the whole world.

The New Kind of Person

THE next step in the unfolding plan of God after Jesus had come was the way He actually lived here in the world.

Many of the prophets had talked about what we now call moral standards. A standard is something absolute, otherwise it would not be a standard at all. There is an absolute standard of weight for a pound, otherwise it would not be a pound. There are also absolute

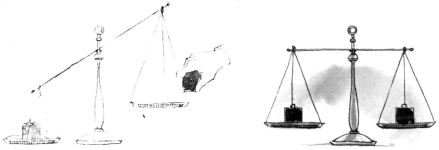

standards, given by God, of what is right, or moral. The prophet Amos pictured them as a plumb-line, showing whether a wall is standing straight or crooked. Moses gave them in the Ten Commandments.

Jesus showed them in His own life. Absolute honesty, purity, unselfishness and love were alive in Him.

Jesus was the New Kind of Person, and He showed the way for each one of us to be the new kind of person too.

The stories called the Gospels, or Good News, tell us how He lived and what He did. They paint a picture for us in words, telling us what He did and said, through talks and stories. By telling us just how to do it, He brought to life the next great part of God's Plan, which was to make this new kind of life a gift from God that everyone everywhere could have if he chose.

One of the most important talks that Jesus gave is called the Sermon on the Mount. Many people had followed Him to hear what He had to say, and He spoke to them from a hilltop so that they could see and hear Him better.

First He talked of the kind of people whom God's blessing can reach most readily.

He said, 'Blessed are the needy in spirit, for theirs is the Kingdom of Heaven.' He said, too, that God can reach those who are sad and comfort them. He can also reach those who are humble enough to know that they need Him. Many people think that they can manage all right by themselves, and then they miss all that God wants to give them.

Then Jesus said that God would bless everyone who was really longing to do what was right. He called it hungering and thirsting after righteousness. One could be hungry and thirsty for God's way, He said, and God would satisfy that kind of hunger as well as the other.

Then He said another very important thing, which was, 'Blessed are the pure in heart for they shall see God.' You know how a window has to be clean to let the sun through, and people's hearts have to be clean to let God through. To be absolutely pure means to be clean right through, and no one who keeps bitter or dirty thoughts in his or her heart, or hangs on to dirty habits, can ever know God.

Another lot of people He spoke of were those who were ready to be merciful and forgive others, even those who had hurt them. They would be forgiven by God for what they had done wrong themselves.

Jesus ended the part about blessings (known as the Beatitudes), by saying that those who are persecuted or attacked for the sake of what is right are also blessed by God.

'Blessed are you,' He said, 'when men shall revile you and persecute you and say all manner of evil against you falsely for My sake.'

Then in case anyone thought that it sounded rather discouraging, He said 'Rejoice and be exceeding glad.' It was all part of the battle and always would be. It had happened to the prophets and it would happen to them. He wants us to be like salt, giving taste and interest to everyone we mix with. Tasteless salt is good for nothing except to be thrown away.

These were new ideas, and though some accepted them, others rumbled inside. Moses, for instance, had allowed divorce. Jesus was against it. Nor was revenge part of God's way. Moses had said 'You must not kill', but Jesus said that to lose your temper, or call other people fools, was just as bad. Even if someone has a grudge against you, He said, you can be the one to go and make friends.

The old idea was to love your friends and hate your enemies. 'But I say to you,' said Jesus, 'that you should love your enemies and pray for them. You are all God's children, and He makes the sun rise on good and bad alike. Besides, it is easy enough to like those who like you. It isn't difficult to speak to those who speak to you. Even tax-gatherers manage that.'

He showed them how different God's ideas are from ours. People collect money and belongings, and give their hearts to them, and these things come to mean more to them than God does. Then if the things get lost or stolen, or rusty or moth-eaten, they feel they have nothing left.

'God is your Father,' He said. 'He can look after you. You don't have to fret and worry about whether you're going to have enough to live on. Look for God and you will find all that you need.'

In all this, He told them, the place to start is with yourself. He gave the example of a man trying to get a speck of dust out of another man's eye, when all the time he had an enormous plank in his own.

'You will see more clearly to get the speck out of your brother's eye,' He said, 'when you have been honest about the plank in your own.'

Then He set them the highest possible standard, which was to be perfect as God is perfect.

Everybody listened to Him in astonishment. He spoke with such certainty, unlike the scribes who read the laws in the synagogue each week but never managed to make them come to life and show men how to live.

The Men who Followed Jesus

THE story of Jesus' life and all the things He did were written down by different people after He died.

Four men wrote the stories of the life of Jesus which are called the Gospels. They were called Matthew, Mark, Luke and John. I have put some of the stories into this book, and you can look the rest up for yourselves.

They are about the battle that goes on in people's hearts and the fight for a new world.

*　　*　　*

On the day that John the Baptist had met Jesus by the River Jordan he had said to his followers, 'Look, there is the Lamb of God.'

To the Jewish people a lamb meant something very precious that was given to God as a sacrifice, and though most of the men with John probably had no idea what he meant, two of them at least realised that this was no ordinary man who had appeared among them.

One of these men was called Andrew, and he had a brother called Simon. When Andrew heard what John the Baptist had said he ran quickly to find his brother and took him to Jesus, saying, 'We have found the Special Person whom God has sent.'

As soon as Jesus saw Simon He knew that he was someone whom God had called and He said, 'You must be called Peter now because Peter means a rock.'

A rock is something firm and unshakable, and Peter was not at all a rock-like person at that time. He often said and did quite foolish things, but Jesus knew how different he was going to become.

'Where do you live, Master?' asked the brothers. Jesus answered, 'Come and see,' and they both went and stayed all day talking to Him.

Peter and Andrew came from a town called Bethsaida up in the northern part of the country. It was in the province of Galilee by a great lake. The town of Nazareth where Jesus' own family lived was there too, and He chose Galilee as the place to begin His work.

So the next day Jesus and His friends set off together for the north, and as they started they met a man called Philip who also came from Bethsaida.

Jesus said to him, 'Follow Me,' and Philip joined the party.

These men are called saints now, and in pictures they often have haloes round their heads, though when they were alive they looked no different from anyone else.

Peter and Andrew were fishermen. They may not have realised when they started to walk back to their home town with Jesus that they were going to alter their plans as a result of meeting Him, but actually it was a turning-point in their lives.

They were the first men whom Jesus called and who answered that call and decided to become His friends.

They did not know that they were going to spend the rest of their lives with Him as they set off that morning towards Galilee, passing on the way through a country called Samaria.

The Woman who Pretended

THE people who lived in Samaria were called Samaritans. They did not like the Jews, and the Jews did not like them either. This was because many centuries before the people of the Northern Kingdom of Israel had been taken prisoner by the Assyrians. The Assyrians had sent other people to live there who were not real Jews, and the land was renamed Samaria.

Although this had happened many centuries ago, the Jews, who lived in the southern part of the country, never forgot.

Jesus and His friends had a long way to go to get to Samaria, and as they were walking along the hot and dusty road they came to a well. It was the middle of the day and Jesus sat down beside it to rest, while the others went to the town to buy food. It was a very old well, which hundreds of years earlier, Jacob had given to his son Joseph, and it was still called Jacob's Well. It is there to this day.

After a while a Samaritan woman came for some water, and Jesus asked her for a drink. This surprised her because she could tell that He was a Jew by the way He dressed and talked, and the Jews never spoke to the Samaritans if they could help it.

So she said, 'How is it that you who are a Jew are asking for a drink from me—a Samaritan?'

Jesus answered, 'If you had known who it is that is asking you for a drink, you would have asked Him for one, and He would have given you living water.'

This both interested and puzzled the woman, because she saw that He had no bucket or rope with Him, so she said, 'You have nothing to pull the water out of the well. Where are you going to get this living water from? Are you greater than our ancestor Jacob who gave us the well?'

But Jesus was not talking about ordinary water. He could read people and see into their hearts, and He knew that this woman had so far spent her life in the wrong way. In fact all her neighbours must have known it too, and decided not to speak to her. Otherwise she would have come for water in the evening when it was cool, which was the usual time for women to come to the well together. She was left out and disapproved of, and was not used to being spoken to in a friendly way by anyone.

Jesus did not disapprove of her, but He wanted to give her a new clean life, instead of the dirty old way she had been living. So He spoke to her in a way that would make her curious. He said, 'Anyone who drinks from this well will be thirsty again, but the water I give will be a spring of life that lasts for ever.'

This time the woman was really interested. Like most of us she wanted to know of a way of saving work, and she said, 'Please, sir, give me some of this water so that I need never be thirsty any more, nor have to come here to get water.'

But Jesus was not trying to save her trouble, but to help her to face the truth about herself. The living water He spoke of was the new kind of life He was going to give her, and because He knew the truth about her He went straight to the point.

Before she could have the new life, she had to be honest about the old one, and Jesus helped her to speak the truth.

Without saying any more about the water, He said, 'Go and bring your husband here.'

'But I have no husband,' replied the woman.

He said, 'You are right to say "I have no husband," for you have had five husbands, and the man you are with now is not your husband. You were speaking the truth about that.'

He did not try to make her like Him. He just said the thing that needed to be said. She might have gone off in a huff, but He risked it, and she stayed. She could not leave someone who understood her so well, even if it was uncomfortable.

However, she was not quite ready to stop pretending, so she tried to change the subject. She did her best to start a discussion about whether it was better to worship God in Samaria or in Jerusalem, but Jesus told her that where people pray is not the point.

The point, He said, was to pray to God with a truthful spirit.

This was another chance for her to look into her own heart, but she still did not want to, so she changed the subject again.

She remembered all the stories she had heard about the Special Person the Jews were waiting for, so she moved on to something she thought had not yet happened, and said 'I know that the Messiah is coming whom they call Christ. He will explain everything to us when He comes.'

She may have thought that would be the end of the conversation, but Jesus said, 'I am the Messiah.' And she knew that it was true.

There was no getting away from it. She was face to face with the seemingly far-away Person who could explain everything. He knew exactly what she was like, but understood her and wanted her to be different.

Just then the men who had gone to get the food came back again. They were amazed to find Jesus talking to a Samaritan woman but did not like to ask any questions.

By then she had so much to think about that she left and went back to the town, even forgetting the water-jar she had come there to fill. There she said to the men she knew, for she had no women friends, 'Come and see a man who

has told me all the things that I have ever done. Can he be the Christ?'

When they heard this they poured out of the town to see, and found Jesus and His friends still sitting by the well. They begged Him to stay and tell them more, so He stayed for another two days. Some of them believed straight away what the woman told them. Others said to her, 'Now we believe, not just because of what you said, but because we have heard and seen Him ourselves, and we know that this is the Christ who has come to save the world.'

Jesus said to His friends, 'There are so many people in the world who need help, and so few to help them. It is like a field of ripe corn ready to be cut and brought into the barn, but there are not enough workmen to do it. We must pray for more workmen.'

At the end of two days He went on to Galilee with Peter and James and John.

*   *   *

One of the things that He had said earlier was that only the pure in heart could see God. Once the woman had let Jesus show her all the uncleanness that was in her heart, He was able to wash it away, and then she knew who He was and could help other people to recognise Him too.

Besides meaning clean, purity means to be whole or complete. When you see a jar labelled 'Pure Honey' it means that there is nothing less good added to it to alter the taste, or make it anything that it ought not to be. A pure heart has nothing in it that would stop a person from knowing God.

In Galilee

JESUS went to many of the towns and villages in Galilee, and one place that He went to was Nazareth, where He had been brought up. On the Sabbath Day He went into the synagogue and was handed the book of Isaiah so that He could read aloud to the people.

He opened the book at the place where the prophet had written that someone was coming sent specially by God who would bring hope to the poor, who would comfort the broken-hearted, who would set bound people free, and give sight to the blind. This Person would show men that God is ready to receive them and to heal their illnesses of body and heart, and give them a new way of living. Then He shut the book and sat down. Everyone's eyes were fixed on Him.

'This is happening today,' said Jesus, and He told them how Isaiah's words were coming true.

Now for many years the Jewish people had heard of this Special Person, or Messiah, who would come. It was always going to happen one day, but not here and now. Anyway, they thought, when this Person did come He was going to be a great king who would drive out the Romans, and be quite easy to recognise. So when their neighbour, the carpenter's son, got up in the synagogue and said He was the Person God had sent, they simply did not believe it.

They said, 'Nonsense. This is only Joseph's son. We have known him ever since he was a child, and we know all his family.'

Jesus said, 'A prophet never seems to be understood in his own family and with his own relations and friends. It was just the same in Elijah's time. There were a lot of widows in Israel at the time of the famine but none of them helped Elijah. The one who did was a poor woman from another country.'

This made the people of Nazareth so angry that they took hold of Jesus and pulled Him out of the synagogue. They meant to throw Him down the hill on which the town was built, but He passed through the midst of them and went on His way.

Jesus was hardly able to heal anyone in Nazareth because so few people trusted Him, and He went on to another town called Capernaum. This was where Peter and Andrew had their fishing business because it was at the side of a large lake, which was known as the Sea of Galilee.

Again Jesus went straight to the synagogue with his friends and began to talk to the people.

It was quite different from what had happened in Nazareth. Everybody listened. Nobody tried to throw Jesus out of the town, and when He had finished talking in the synagogue Peter took Him to his own home for supper.

When they came there, Peter found that his wife's mother, who lived with them, was ill. You can imagine that this was a blow to them, because it was not so easy to have a lot of extra people to supper when they had someone ill in bed. It must have been rather inconvenient. However, they told Jesus what had happened. Instead of saying that He would not bother them, and would go somewhere else, He went and took the old lady's hand and helped her to get up. Immediately the fever left her, and she came and helped to get the supper.

The news of this went all round the town and after sunset when it was cooler, all those who had anyone ill in their family brought them to Peter's house and they all stood round the door and Jesus healed them. The whole town gathered to see what He was doing.

He went away quietly for a time, very early in the morning, and listened to God His Father, so that He would know what to do next.

He needed His Father's help most when things seemed to be going successfully.

Everyone was very enthusiastic about Him, so His disciples were surprised to hear that they were going to leave a place where they seemed to have made a good impression and go on to another town.

The Nobleman's Son and Jairus' Daughter

TWO of the people Jesus healed when He was in Galilee were a boy and a girl.

He had been away across the lake, and when He came back to Capernaum, He was met by a man who was a leader in the town. This man was rich, with many servants, but he was heavy-hearted because his son whom he loved was ill, so ill that nobody thought he could recover. The father was quite certain that there was one Person who could cure the boy, so when he heard Jesus had arrived he went and begged Him to come to his house and heal his son.

'Please come,' he said, 'before my child dies.'

Jesus answered, 'Go home, your son is alive.'

This meant having faith, because what the father had asked was that Jesus should come back with him, and actually be with the boy and heal him. It took quite a lot of believing to trust that Jesus had only to say that the child was well for it to happen.

The father might have argued, and said the illness was so serious that Jesus must come Himself. After all he was a very important man and most people obeyed him.

He was also a believing man though, and he believed enough to know that anything Jesus said was true. So he went home. It was a little way off and he did not arrive till next day. As he came near to his home his servants met him. As soon as they saw him they said, 'Your son is alive.'

'When did he begin to get better?' asked the father.

'Yesterday,' they said, 'at one o'clock.'

And the father knew that was the moment when Jesus had said, 'Your son is alive.'

This made all his servants believe Jesus too.

A little later the chief man in the synagogue at Capernaum, whose name was Jairus, came to find Jesus. He knelt before Him and said,

'Please come to my house and cure my daughter. She is dying, and she is my only child.'

So Jesus went with Jairus, but it was difficult to go fast. There were so many people all trying to see Him or speak to Him. It must have been hard not to be impatient, especially as after a while a messenger arrived from the father's house, saying, 'Your daughter is dead, so there is no point in bothering Jesus about her.'

But when Jesus heard the message all He said was, 'Do not be afraid. Go on believing and she will be all right.'

So the father went on believing.

When they reached the house many people were there crying because the child had died. Jesus paid no attention to them and went in. He would not let any of them come with Him, but took Peter and James and John and the little girl's parents.

Up in the room there were more people weeping, and He turned them out too saying, 'Stop crying. She is not dead, she is fast asleep.'

They laughed at Him, but they had to go.

Then Jesus went and took the child's hand and said, 'Little girl, wake up.' Immediately she opened her eyes and got up, and Jesus told her parents to give her something to eat.

The Men
Jesus Called

PEOPLE pressed to hear
Jesus, and great crowds
followed Him. They did not just
come for comfort. They came as people always will, to someone with
new ideas. Jesus upset all the old ideas and has been upsetting them
ever since, so that those who are stodgy and comfortable fight Him,
as well as those who are simply crooked.

One day by the side of the lake of Galilee the crowd was so great
that He got swallowed up in it, and He looked around for something to stand on. His eye fell on two boats drawn up on the shore.
One of them belonged to Peter, who had just come back from an
unsuccessful night's fishing, and Jesus asked Peter if He could speak
from it. Peter pushed it out a little way from the shore and Jesus
climbed into it. Then He spoke to that great gathering with strength
and certainty so that everyone could hear. There were no microphones
in those days, but He never seems to have had any difficulty over
making Himself heard.

Peter and his brother Andrew were friends of His already, and had
been around with Him, but as they listened this time, they knew that
here was someone they would like to follow all their lives.

When Jesus had finished speaking, He turned to Peter and said,
'Let down your nets now, and catch some fish.'

45

'We've been trying all night,' Peter answered, 'and have caught nothing. All the same, if you say so we will try again.'

He and Andrew tried again and this time the nets came in so full that they broke, which made them call to some friends who worked from a near-by boat, to come and help them.

These were two other brothers called James and John, and they brought their boat over and gave a hand to pull in the heavy catch. There were so many fish that both the boats overflowed and began to sink. Peter was frightened. This was something beyond his understanding. He may have wondered if the sinking boats were meant as some sort of punishment for his past, and he was frightened. Something was happening that was bigger than he could understand.

He fell on his knees and said, 'Please leave me, for I am a sinful man.'

But Jesus said, 'Fear not, from now on you shall be fishers of men.' That is to say, they would catch people for God. This was a sign that God had called them and wanted them.

They brought the boats ashore, and Jesus said, 'Follow me.' So they left their boats and all they were doing and went with Him. Then Jesus asked James and John to come too, and they went with Peter and Andrew, leaving their boats and nets with their father Zebedee.

Sometimes people find it hard to understand why anyone should leave what he is doing if Jesus calls him, especially in the world today when everyone is so busy doing things and making things. But Jesus still goes on calling people, because He needs men and women and children today who put God's Plan before their own.

When He called Peter and Andrew and James and John it meant that they had to give up their own plans for their lives, and take on God's plan for the world. Many people think they can do what God wants in their own way, but God's Plan means obeying, and that nearly always means doing things differently.

It means not doing things that are wrong, but there are also things that are good in themselves, yet not God's plan for us. There was nothing wrong about Peter and his friends being fishermen. It was just that Jesus had different plan for them.

Soon after this Jesus met a man called Matthew. He was one of the tax-gatherers, whom nobody particularly liked. But when Jesus saw him sitting counting the money he had collected He loved him, and said to him too, 'Follow Me.'

So Matthew, who was also known as Levi, left his money and went with Jesus.

Like Peter, the first thing he thought of was to take Jesus home to his own house to give him a meal. Matthew's house was not at all like Peter's. He must have been quite a rich man, and he gave a great feast for all his friends to meet Jesus. Most of his friends were tax-gatherers or publicans like himself, so of course those were the people he invited.

As you may remember, these publicans worked for the Romans, which was one of the reasons why the Jewish people did not like them. There was one lot of Jews in particular who refused to have anything to do with them. These were the Pharisees. They were the people who were so strict about doing exactly what Moses said on the outside, but not so particular about doing it inside. When they heard that Jesus had gone to a party with Matthew and all his publican friends, they thought it was quite wrong for someone who was supposed to be good to go and have supper with a lot of people whom they had labelled bad.

Some of them went and grumbled to Peter and the others about it. They were not brave enough to go and tell Jesus Himself. Jesus got to hear of it, and He said He had not come to change people who thought they were all right but people who knew they were wrong. He left the Pharisees to think that out further for themselves.

Another thing that Jesus said was that those who are well do not

47

need a doctor, but those who are ill do. Matthew and his friends knew that they had done a lot that was wrong and that they needed Jesus to help them. The Pharisees were so sure they were right that they did not need Jesus. In the same way the people who think they are right in any age and country always fight against Jesus.

The Twelve Apostles

IT was hard for the Pharisees to accept that people were looking more to Jesus than to them. Up till then they had said what should be done, and indeed many of the things they did were right, like washing their hands before meals, and keeping one day specially for God in the week. But they had come to put these and other things before the needs of people, and before God Himself.

They called the seventh day of the week the Sabbath, and on that day no one was supposed to work. Once Jesus and His friends were walking through a cornfield on the Sabbath, and as they were hungry they picked some ears of corn and ate the grains. According to the law, picking corn counted as work, and no one was supposed to work on the Sabbath. So the Pharisees, who had seen this happening, said to Jesus, 'Look, your disciples are breaking the law.'

But Jesus replied that the Son of Man, which was what He often called Himself, was the Lord of the Sabbath too, and that the important thing was to obey God on that day.

From that time the Pharisees tried to set traps for Him to see if He would say or do anything for which He could be arrested. One day they were in the synagogue on the Sabbath and there was a man there with a withered hand. Possibly he had been brought there on purpose, because we are told that the Pharisees all watched to see what Jesus would do.

He knew very well what they were thinking, and was saddened and angered by the hardness of their hearts, but He said openly to the man, 'Stand up.'

Then He looked round at everyone, and said, 'Tell me. Is it right to

48

do good on the Sabbath or to do evil, to save life or to kill?' He asked whether if any of them had a sheep that had fallen into a pit on the Sabbath, they would not pull it out.

No one would answer without giving himself away, and Jesus said to the man, 'Stretch out your hand.' So he stretched it out and it was healed.

At this the Pharisees got up and went out. They went to see the Herodians, the men who worked with the Romans and who were supposed to be the enemies of their country. They had never had anything to do with them before, but now they felt they needed Roman help to kill Jesus.

They were not going to be able to do this right away, because crowds followed Him wherever He went, but Jesus knew that people coming in crowds would not by itself build a new world.

It was clear too that there would have to be a group of men trained to carry on when He was taken from them, men who would be ready to give themselves wholly to God's Plan for the world, as He Himself had done.

So one evening He went away and prayed all through the night to see what to do next. He prayed to find men who would stay close enough to Him to learn all that He wanted to teach them, so that they could teach others.

When morning came He had decided on twelve men. Six of them we know already. Four were the fishermen brothers, Peter and Andrew, James and John. Philip and Matthew had joined them. The other six were called Bartholomew, Thomas, another James with his brother Judas, another Simon, and Judas Iscariot.

They were to be apostles or men specially sent, men who had left their own work and were to take on God's work for the rest of their lives.

From then onwards these were the men Jesus kept specially with Him, and all but one of them stayed with Him and later took what He had taught them to many other countries.

The ones we hear of most are the first six, especially the two pairs of brothers, but they were all different types of men. The second Simon was also called Zelotes, which means a Zealot or nationalist. He was one of the rebels who were against the Romans and were planning to drive them out of the country. Jesus took him to be part of a bigger revolution in which people would turn against what was wrong and make the world different.

How Jesus helped Simon
to be Honest about himself

NOT every Pharisee was against Jesus, and one, whose name was Simon, asked Him to have a meal in his house, and Jesus went. People got to hear of it, and knew where He was. One was a woman who had done many wrong things in her life. What she had heard about Jesus had made her sorry and want to be different. She knew she had been wrong, but she thought there might be one good thing she could do, and that would be something that would help Jesus.

She brought a box of precious sweet-smelling ointment and came to Simon's house with it. In those days and in that country people did not wear shoes and stockings, but went about in sandals or with bare feet, so their feet were often sore and dusty. This woman knelt down by Jesus and started rubbing His feet with the ointment to make them feel more comfortable. As she did it she was crying, so that her tears fell on Jesus' feet, and she wiped them off with her long black hair.

Jesus said nothing at first, nor did Simon, but in his heart the Pharisee was thinking to himself, 'If Jesus were really a great prophet and teacher, he would know that this is a bad woman. If He were really a good man He would not let a bad woman come near Him.'

Jesus saw his face and knew what he was thinking, and He said, 'Simon, I would like to tell you a story.'

'Please do, Master,' answered Simon.

'There were once two men who owed money to a third man,' said Jesus. 'One owed five hundred pence and the other owed fifty pence. When neither of them was able to pay, he forgave them both and said they need not pay. Which of these two men do you think would love him most?'

Simon thought, and then he said, 'I suppose the one who was forgiven most.'

'You are right,' said Jesus. 'Now you know that when I came to your house you gave me no water to wash my feet, but this woman has cried over them and washed them with her tears. She has given me ointment for them too, and in her own way has done much more for me than you did.'

This made Simon feel uncomfortable because washing was one of the things the Pharisees made a good deal of fuss about, and it was part of what made them feel they were always right. Yet he had not done it for Jesus.

Then Jesus said, 'I know this woman has done many wrong things, but she has a loving heart, and she is sorry, so the wrong things she has done are forgiven. People who know they have been forgiven are more loving than people who think they have never done wrong.'

Then He said to the woman, 'You are forgiven. Your faith has saved you. Go in peace.'

She went away with peace and joy in her heart, but the Pharisees who were there muttered angrily to each other, 'Who is this Jesus who forgives sins, as well as everything else He does?'

They found it hard to face that they too had sins to be forgiven.

The Battle in People's Hearts

IT is interesting to think more about why the Pharisees did not like Jesus. Why was it that not everybody was pleased to see someone who was honest and pure and loving and unselfish? Why did they not do all they could to help?

It is because of the battle in the world between God and the devil. You have heard about this battle all through this book, and the choice that people had to make in the olden days and have to make now. Adam and Eve chose wrongly.

The children of Israel kept making wrong choices, but Moses and the prophets kept bringing them back to making the right ones. The devil had attacked Jesus Himself and tried to get Him away from God's Plan. When he could not do that, he tried to stop the ordinary people from following Jesus.

He built up in their minds the thought of getting things for themselves. Jesus only talked of asking nothing for yourself.

The devil tries to make people go the easy way. Jesus asks them to go the hard way, so when Jesus came the battle became fiercer.

Selfish people began to see that if they followed Him they might not get what they wanted. Even some of the things that seemed good, like praying in the Temple, could be done for the wrong reasons.

When these people saw that they would have to change the way they lived, and do things in God's way and not their own, they decided to fight against Jesus. Instead of admitting where they were wrong, they decided that Jesus was wrong, because if He was right they would need to change.

They fought so hard, as you will see, that at one time it looked as if Jesus had lost the battle.

This battle is still going on, and these stories show how we can fight in it today. As you read them you can decide on which side you are going to be, because what went on in people's hearts then is just the same as what goes on now

52

How John the Baptist was put in Prison

WHILE Jesus was teaching, many people were also going out to listen to John and some of them began to wonder whether it was John or Jesus who was the Special Person.

So they decided to ask John. They said, 'Teacher, who is this man who was with you by the Jordan? He baptises people too.' Actually Jesus did not baptise people Himself. He let His disciples do it. What He did for people was something only He could do.

John knew this and he answered, 'You heard me tell you when I first came, that I was not the Special Person; that I was only preparing the way.'

'I am rather like somebody arranging a wedding,' he said. 'At a wedding the bridegroom's friend arranges for the bridegroom to marry the bride. He does not marry her himself. He just gets everything ready for his friend and is happy because his friend is happy. I am not the Christ, the Special Person. He must become more important in people's lives while I become less important.'

Soon after this King Herod put John in prison, and Jesus went north to Galilee so they did not meet again.

John was not afraid of anybody, not even of the King. He spoke out fearlessly against wickedness, and said strong words to the king, who had sent his own wife away and had stolen his brother's. This made Herod very angry, so he had John arrested and taken to prison. At least no one then could hear what he said.

John, who had done so much to tell people about Jesus and who had had crowds round him listening to what he had to say, was shut up alone in a castle.

Some of his friends were allowed to come and see him and talk to him, so he was able to ask them what was happening. Perhaps they told him the stories of all the different people Jesus had met, the fishermen, the Pharisees, the rich men and the poor ones.

Possibly John in his prison was a bit puzzled by what he heard. He lived a very strict life. Many people thought that he hardly even ate or drank enough to keep himself alive.

Jesus seemed to go everywhere. He met all sorts of people and went to meals with them and told them much more what they should do than what they should not.

John had told everyone that Jesus was the Christ, the Special Person.

Was he really?

He would like to be quite sure. So John asked his friends to take a message to Jesus saying, 'Are you the Person we were expecting, or must we still wait for someone else?'

The messengers left the prison and took the message to Jesus. When they came to the place where He was, they found Him healing the blind and the lame, and getting rid of evil spirits.

At first Jesus did not answer their question. He let the messengers sit and watch what He was doing. Then He turned to them and said, 'Go back and tell John what you have seen and heard. How blind men can see again and lame men can walk, and everyone is learning about the Kingdom of God.'

The messengers understood that it was only God's Son who could do all these things and they went back to let John know.

When they had gone Jesus said to the crowd that John was part of God's Plan. Everything he had said was true. People who believed John were more likely to believe Jesus. Those who did not believe John often did not believe Jesus either.

'In fact,' he said, 'you do not listen to what God has to say whoever says it. You have the laws of Moses, but you do not keep them. You think Elijah was a great man, but John is greater than Elijah and you pay no attention to him. John came and ate very little, so you say he is mad. I come and eat and drink an ordinary amount and you say I am greedy. You are like a lot of children who do not want to play a game because someone else has suggested it.'

How John Died

A LITTLE while later, it was King Herod's birthday and he invited many of the great men of the land to come to a feast in the castle where John was in prison. Herod had living with him in the castle the lady who had been married to his brother. Her name was Herodias and she really hated John. Herod, though, respected him. John had been brave enough to speak honestly to him, and Herod must have known he was right. But Herodias had been waiting for some time to see a way of getting rid of him.

It was on his birthday that she saw her opportunity. She had a daughter who danced very well and this girl went in after the feast and danced before all the guests. Herod, who had been drinking a lot of strong wines, was so pleased that he felt he must give her a present. So when she had finished he called her over to him and said, 'That was very well done. You did so well, that I will give you anything you ask for, even half my kingdom.'

The girl did not expect to be offered anything so big, and did not at all know what to ask for. She felt sure her mother would have a good idea, and ran out of the room to ask her.

This was just what Herodias had been waiting for. She said immediately, 'Ask to have John the Baptist's head cut off and brought in on a dish.'

The daughter could have refused. Nobody has to do wrong things because someone suggests it, even if the person is their mother. But this girl had been brought up by a bad mother, so perhaps she was used to doing wrong things.

She went back to Herod and asked for John the Baptist's head.

It was a terrible shock to Herod. He had never expected to be asked to do such a thing, and he knew it was wrong.

But he was not brave enough to say so. He had promised in front of all his friends to give the girl anything she asked for, and he was going to stick to it. He gave the order at once for soldiers to go to John's cell and cut off his head. Herod was never happy again. He felt everyone was against him, and that he had enemies who would stop him from being king.

A little later, when people brought him news of all that Jesus was doing and how He was preaching about the Kingdom of God, he became still more frightened.

He said, 'Surely I cut off John the Baptist's head. Has he come to life again? Or who is this?' He thought that the Kingdom of God that Jesus was speaking about might take the place of his kingdom.

So he too joined the men who wanted to kill Jesus.

The Man who was Determined to get in

JESUS went through many of the towns in Galilee, and everywhere people followed Him. One day after being away for a while He came back to Capernaum, and as soon as He arrived the word very quickly went round that He had come.

It is possible that He went to Peter's house, where He had been before. Perhaps He made His home there when He was in Capernaum, but it is certain that He was in someone's house because we are told that there was a tremendous crowd round it who could not get in. There was no room even to stand by the door.

Everyone who could had squeezed in, and the rest were standing about outside when up came four men carrying a sick friend on a stretcher.

They had heard that Jesus had come and thought this was the moment for their friend to be cured. He was unable to walk, so when they arrived and found there was absolutely no way of getting into the house through the door, they decided to try something else.

There was no hope of the sick man getting in alone. There was still less hope of four other men going in with him, but they were determined that he should get in somehow.

They looked about for some way of doing it. The only way they

could see was through the flat roof. Fortunately in that country roofs were not made of bricks or iron or concrete, but of something more like plaster, so they climbed up the walls and started clearing away enough of the roof to make a hole for the stretcher to come through.

It must have been quite surprising for the people inside to have the roof taken off the house they were sitting in, but even more surprising when they saw a stretcher with a man on it being lowered through the hole.

Jesus was not surprised. He was glad that the man and his friends were so determined. He knew they had faith.

The funny thing was, though, that Jesus said nothing to the man about his illness. All He said was, 'Your sins are forgiven.' He knew that the man was not just ill in his body, but that he was bothered about things he had done wrong.

As Jesus said this certain men who were there began to be angry. These men were called scribes and they had come specially from Jerusalem to see if they could find fault with the things Jesus said.

Moses had given the people of Israel the Ten Commandments, but since then a great many extra ones had been added and the scribes were supposed to see that they were all kept. They said nothing, but they thought to themselves, 'Who is this man who tells people their sins are forgiven? God is the only person who can do that.'

Though they did not say this aloud, Jesus knew what they were thinking and asked them, 'Why are you grumbling in your hearts? Do you think it is easier to say "Your sins are forgiven", or "Get up and walk"?'

The people who with their own eyes saw this lame man walk with the power that flowed out of Jesus might also believe that the same power could forgive sins and heal the heart. So Jesus said to the man on the stretcher, 'Get up. Pick up your bed and go home.'

Immediately the man got up, picked up the stretcher and pushed his way out of the crowd and went home.

After that there was nothing more the scribes could say, especially as everyone else thanked God and said it was the most wonderful thing they had ever seen.

No one could stop the crowds coming, but there were still many people who did not understand what Jesus was trying to do. Among these were His own relations. All they could see was that here was Jesus, whom they had known ever since He was a child, doing a lot of things that might get Him into trouble. The last time He had come home He had gone into the synagogue and said He had been specially sent by God and that had made trouble.

Now there were always crowds following Him about. His family wished He would come and live at home and behave like everyone else. One day they followed Him to Capernaum to try and see Him, but the house was so full of people that they could not get in. So they sent in a message saying they would like to speak to Him.

But Jesus had come to start a revolution. He had not come to stay at home and be just like everyone else. That would never have made any difference. He did not really belong to one family more than another. His revolution was to make the whole world into one family with God as the Father.

So when He got the message, He looked round at all the people who were with Him and said quietly, 'My family are all those who listen to God and do what He says.'

Talking and Listening to God

JESUS taught people how to pray.
He said that the name we are to call God is Father. He is Father of everyone in the world, and no one else anywhere had ever given Him that name before. Jesus said 'our' not 'my' all the way through the prayer He taught, which begins, 'Our Father which art in Heaven.' It goes on, 'Hallowed (or Holy) be Thy name.'

Next, Jesus said, pray for the whole world to obey God—'Thy kingdom come, Thy will be done in earth as it is in Heaven.' Then ask for everybody to have what they need each day—'Give us this day our daily bread'. Ask to forgive and also to be forgiven—'Forgive us our trespasses as we forgive them that trespass against us.'

Jesus ended by saying for all of us, 'Lead us not into temptation, but deliver us from evil'—God is stronger than evil—'For Thine is the kingdom, and the power and the glory for ever.'

Praying, He said, is like knocking on a door. You knock and God opens it. He is a Father who wants to give good things to His children, because He loves us more even than our own fathers and mothers do.

He will tell us what is right if we will only do it. If a child, Jesus said, asks his father for bread, will he give him a stone, or if he asks for some fish will his father give him a snake? Well, if your own fathers here treat you kindly, how much more will your Heavenly Father give you everything that is good for you?

'Anyone who listens to what I am saying,' said Jesus, 'and does what I tell him is like a wise man who built his house on a rock, and when it rained and the wind blew, the house stood firm because it was built upon a rock. Anyone who listens to Me and then does not do what I say is like a foolish man who built his house on the sand, and then when storms came and the winds blew it was washed away.' The difficulties came, and because the man did things the easy way rather than God's way, he and his house had no strength and the difficulties swept them away.

Jesus told them another story about listening. These stories are called parables. A parable is a story about something you know to make a picture of something you don't know and can't understand.

'There was once a sower,' He said, 'who went out sowing seeds. Some of the seed fell by the roadside and was trodden on, or eaten by birds. Some fell on stony ground, and though it sprouted up quickly, it soon withered away. There was so little earth, that the seeds could not grow roots. Some fell into thorn bushes, and the bushes stopped them from growing up. Some fell on good earth, and took root, and grew up, and became a plentiful crop of good corn.'

His friends were puzzled by the story and could not understand what Jesus was trying to tell them, so He explained it. He said, 'The seed is what God says. The different places are different kinds of people.

The ones by the wayside are people who just listen for a time, and then the devil comes along and tells them something else instead, and they listen to him.

'The ones on stony ground are people who like all the nice things that God says, but not the hard things. They do not have any proper roots, so when things get difficult they stop listening.

'The ones in the thorn bushes are those who listen to God for a while, but are so busy either doing things for themselves, or enjoying themselves, that they think they have no time. In the end all the things they do stop them from taking time to find out what God wants.

'The good ground is where people listen to God and then do what He says. Out of their lives grow the things that God really wants, and these things spread to tens and twenties and hundreds of other people.'

A Home where Jesus went

JESUS went to many homes. When He went to Peter's home, Peter's mother-in-law was cured of a fever. In Simon's home a woman who had done many wrong things came in. She went away completely different.

There was another home where Jesus went quite often. There are three stories about it in the Bible. Once after Jesus had been in Galilee for a while He went back to Jerusalem to go to one of the Feasts, and on the way He stayed at this home in Bethany. It belonged to a family of two sisters called Martha and Mary, and a brother called Lazarus.

The ones we hear of first are the two sisters. Some people think that Mary was the same woman who went to see Jesus in the Pharisee's house and washed His feet. Whether this was so or not, Mary was very different from her sister Martha.

Martha was a busy person, and one day Jesus came in at a time when the two sisters were alone at home. He sat down and started talking to them, but soon Martha began to worry. She felt she simply must cook the supper. So she bustled off and began getting everything ready, but Mary did not move.

She just sat listening to Jesus. After a while Martha became impatient because Mary was not coming to help. I rather think she was the elder sister who expected Mary to do what she said, and now Mary was paying no attention to her at all.

The more Martha thought about it the less pleased she became, and the more sorry for herself. How was she going to get her sister away from Jesus to come and help her? She spoke quite sharply to Jesus too for keeping Mary, even though He was the guest in their house. In fact she was not thinking of anyone but herself. It is funny how many people want to get Jesus to see things from their point of view.

'Lord,' she said, 'don't you mind that my sister has left me to do everything all by myself? Tell her to get up and help me.'

Jesus had come to show people what God was like, and to help them to learn to listen and obey.

He had not come to be told what to do by cross people who wanted their own way.

So he said kindly, 'Martha, Martha, you are anxious and troubled about many things. Only one thing is needed. Mary has chosen that good part which shall not be taken away from her.'

The Man who was not so Determined

ONE of the Feast Days in Jerusalem had come round, and Jesus went up from Galilee to celebrate it.

There was in the city a pool with five arches round it, and under these arches lay many sick people. They were blind or lame, many could not walk at all; and they sat or lay there all day.

Every so often the water in the pool moved as if someone were stirring it. It was said that an angel came down and touched it, and the first person who got into the water after this stirring was healed of his illness. One man had been lying by the pool for thirty-eight years, and had never managed to get into it. Unlike the man who came in through the roof he had no friends to put him in, nor did he have any plan for getting to the water. He just lay there.

He was still just lying there when Jesus came by and said to him, 'Do you want to get well again?'

The man was very sorry for himself, and started giving all the reasons why he could never get into the pool.

'Sir,' he said, 'I have nobody to put me into the pool when the water is stirred up. While I am trying to get there somebody else always steps into it before me.'

Jesus had rejoiced in the faith of the man who came in through the roof, but He was sorry for the limp man who did not have enough push to get well. He did not compare them, but He gave each one what was needed.

This man needed to be helped to do something for himself. He was not an unbelieving man. For thirty-eight years he had held on to the idea that he could be cured, even though during all that time he had never found a way of getting into the pool.

Jesus made him do something.

He said, 'Get up. Pick up your bed and walk.' And the little spark of faith in the man's heart came alive, and he got up and picked up his bed, as Jesus had told him to do, and walked out.

This happened on the Sabbath, and as he went out he met some

men who said, 'Do you not know it is the Sabbath? You should not be carrying a bed on that day.' They were not in the least interested in the fact that he had got well. He replied, 'It was the man who made me well who told me I should pick up my bed and walk.'

'Who told you to do that?' they asked. The man who had been healed did not know who Jesus was. He looked round, but could not see Him.

Later, however, he went to the Temple, and there Jesus saw him again. He said, 'Look, you are well now. Do not do wrong again or something worse may happen to you.'

So once more Jesus showed that He knew that illness and wrong living often go together. After this talk the man realised who had healed him, and he went back to the Jews who had asked him and said, 'The man who made me well was Jesus.'

This caused another uproar. First Jesus had healed on the Sabbath. Then he had made the man carry his bed. If He went on doing this kind of thing, all the careful rules that had been made about how to behave would be broken.

People had become used to living by rules. They even kept on making new ones, as if the ones they had already were not enough. They were so busy obeying all the rules that they had not time to listen to God's Voice speaking in their hearts.

Jesus only did what God told Him to do, and His answer to the Jews who attacked Him was, 'My Father has worked until now, and I work too.'

This only made them more determined than ever to find a way of killing Him, so Jesus went back to Galilee to go on training the twelve men God had given Him.

Food for the Body and the Spirit

BY this time more and more people wanted to know about the way of living that Jesus had brought, so He sent His twelve friends out in pairs to all the villages round about Galilee with power to master evil spirits and heal the sick. Later on He sent another seventy, to go ahead of Him to every town and village He would be coming to Himself.

To them also He gave power to do all that He did. He told them to go in faith, without money, and to live in the homes of those who would take them in.

'I send you out like lambs among wolves,' He said, and He told them to speak out fearlessly about the Kingdom of God, and to accept such food and drink as they were given. If no one would listen in one place they should go on to the next, but it would be a bad day, He said, for those who refused to listen.

When the twelve came back from visiting the villages, they were full of joy, and they told Jesus that they had been able to do all He had told them. He suggested that they should go to some quiet place to rest a while and to think, because there were so many people coming and going that there was no time even to eat. It seemed a good idea and they decided to slip away quietly in a ship to the other side of the lake.

It was no use. People saw them leaving. The word went round, and soon men, women and children from all the cities round about had flocked after Jesus and His friends, and had caught them up on the far side of the lake.

Jesus was so sorry for them that He could not send them away. They were like sheep without a shepherd.

It was many miles from shops or markets where they could get anything to eat.

He stood looking at them and said to Philip, who was standing by Him, 'Where shall we buy bread for all of them to eat?'

He said this to see what Philip would say, because He Himself already had a plan. But Philip was puzzled. He tried to work it

66

out. He said, 'Even if we had two hundred pennyworth of bread, it would only be enough for each person to have a very little.' One of the disciples said, 'I think we ought to send them all back to their homes where they can get some food for themselves.'

'Why don't you give them something to eat?' asked Jesus. Then Andrew said, 'There is a boy here who has five loaves and two small fishes, but what are they among so many?'

Jesus never did anything in a small way.

He said, 'Make all the people sit down.' So the disciples made everyone sit down on the grass in groups of about fifty. Then He asked the boy to bring the loaves and the fishes to Him. These He blessed and divided among the people. As He did so there was no longer a very little of each, but plenty for everyone.

He gave some first to His twelve friends and asked them to pass it round to everyone, and they all had enough. In fact there was more than enough, for when the meal was over there was still a lot of food left over and lying on the ground.

Jesus told them to go and tidy it all up, so that nothing should be wasted, and they found they were able to fill twelve baskets with bread and fish that the people had not eaten.

When the people saw what Jesus had done, they said among themselves, 'This must be the prophet who is to come into the world,' and they would have carried Him off and tried to make Him king by force. Knowing this, Jesus went away by Himself so that even His disciples could not find Him and they had to go home across the lake without Him.

They were rowing back through the night when Jesus, walking on

67

the water, caught them up. At first they were terrified, but Jesus called to them saying, 'Do not fear,' and told them who He was.

At this Peter jumped out of the boat and ran to meet Him. He did not think about himself, and as long as he kept his whole heart and mind on reaching Jesus he was all right. Suddenly he realised he had nothing solid to stand on and immediately he began to sink.

Then Jesus put His hand out and saved him, and took him back to the boat.

Next morning the crowds, finding that Jesus and His friends had all disappeared, set out after them with tremendous determination, and were soon all around Him again.

'How did you get here?' they asked.

This time Jesus did not give them the answers they wanted. They were not looking for God's way, and He knew it. 'It is not Me you want,' He said. 'It is loaves of bread like those I gave you yesterday. You ate them and were filled, but I have not come just to give you bread which only lasts for a day or two.'

Jesus said this because He knew that many of them were following Him not for what they could learn and give, but for what they could get for themselves.

Then they tried to argue with Him about how Moses had given the people manna in the old days, but Jesus said that was not what He was talking about.

He was talking of the food that feeds people's spirits, which is faith and trust.

'I am the bread of life,' He said, 'and if you believe that God has sent Me it will give you life. But even though you have seen Me you still do not believe Me.'

Then they all started muttering to each other that this was only the son of Joseph and Mary, and what did He mean by saying He had been sent by God.

'Don't whisper among yourselves,' said Jesus. 'Just believe that to have faith in Me gives people life.'

But the bread was the only thing they understood or wanted. They did not face the fact that there are many people who have all that they need for their bodies, but still have hungry and dissatisfied hearts.

Because they would not let Jesus satisfy the hunger in their hearts they turned away and stopped following Him.

'Do you want to leave too?' said Jesus to His twelve chosen friends.

And Peter answered, 'To whom should we go?'

The Outside and the Inside

SOON after this the Pharisees again found fault with Jesus. They said, 'Why do you and your friends go against what we have been taught about the washing of hands before meals?'

Jesus answered, 'Why do you go against what you have been taught by God? Isaiah was quite right when he said that people honour God with their lips, but their hearts are far from Him. You make a lot of rules about washing the outside of pots and cups, but you disobey God in order to obey your own rules and customs. You wash the outside of things, but leave the inside dirty.

'You are like graves with nice white stones over them, but inside there is nothing but bones and rottenness.

'You like to look good outside, but really it is all pretence. You think it is important what people eat, but it is not what you put into your mouth that harms you. It is what comes out of your heart. Evil thoughts, murder, thieving, lying, pride and much else all come from inside you.

'These are the kind of things that make people dirty, not just eating before they have washed their hands.'

The Pharisees did not like being talked to like this, and complained to the disciples, who said to Jesus, 'You know the Pharisees are offended by what you said.'

'Yes,' He replied, 'but we must plant God's thoughts in the world. All that is not planted by Him must be pulled up and thrown away.'

However, there were some Pharisees who did want to have Jesus as a friend, though many of them did not dare to say so openly for fear of being unpopular or laughed at.

One of these was a man called Nicodemus, and he came to see Jesus by night when nobody could see him.

'Master,' he said, 'We know that you are a teacher sent by God, because no one could do what you do unless God was with him.'

This was all very well, but it did not cost Nicodemus anything to come and say it in the middle of the night, and Jesus said to him, 'I

tell you truly that unless a man is born again, he cannot be part of God's kingdom.'

'What does He mean?' thought Nicodemus. 'How can a man be born again? He can't possibly become a baby for a second time.'

Then Jesus told him that it was his whole spirit and nature which had to become different. It was not a matter of having a new body, but a new spirit from God. God's Spirit is like the wind. It blows where it pleases. You cannot tell where it is coming from or where it is going; nor do people know where He will take them, or what He will make them able to do.

Nicodemus said that he still did not see how that could happen, and Jesus said, 'How can you be a teacher in Israel, and not know these things?'

As Nicodemus was a Pharisee he was also a teacher and he must have begun to realise that with all his learning he really knew very little about God's way of working.

He was one of the rulers. He was probably rich and successful, and did not want to run any risks by standing for something which might make him unpopular.

But Jesus had not come to make a few people rich or popular or successful. He had come to bring new life to the whole world, and to help men to fight the battle of right against wrong.

He said to Nicodemus, 'God so loved the world that He gave His only Son, so that whoever believes in Him should have life that lasts for ever. He sent Him that the world should be saved.'

'But,' He said, 'some people like darkness better than light because those who have done wrong hate the light which shows them up.'

This must have made Nicodemus think, because he had come to Jesus in the dark. He was not thinking about the world, but only about himself. He had been ready to come at night and say, 'I know you come from God, and are doing wonderful things,' but was not ready to stand with Jesus and face all that He had to face if what was wrong in the world was to be put right.

Jesus showed him that this was not good enough, and that he would have to start all over again, because all his ideas about what was right were wrong. It was not possible to help Jesus in a quiet kind of way without anyone knowing too much about it.

What Nicodemus decided that night we do not know, but we do know that later on he did become brave enough to let it be known that he was a friend of Jesus.

Peter realises Who Jesus is

JESUS always took care to strengthen the faith of His disciples when they were confused by people who would not believe Him or listen to Him.

He knew just when they needed help, and when they were going to find it hard to go on believing.

So He took them north to a place called Caesarea Philippi far from Jerusalem and His enemies. As they went He talked to them and said, 'Who do people say that I am?'

They replied, 'Some say that you are John the Baptist. Others say that you are Elijah or Jeremiah, or one of the old prophets who has come to life again.'

'But you yourselves,' said Jesus, 'who do you say that I am?'

Immediately Peter said, 'You are the Christ, the Son of God.'

71

'You are blessed, Peter,' said Jesus. 'You have not learnt this from other people but from My Father who is in Heaven. Your name Peter means a rock, and on this rock I will build My Church.'

Then He began to tell them something of what was going to happen to Him. He said He would have to go to Jerusalem and suffer. The rulers and the chief priests would turn against Him and He would be killed, but in three days He would come to life again.

When Peter heard this he was shocked. He called Jesus away privately and said, 'How can You say such things? That must never happen to You.'

He and the other disciples were still clinging to the idea that Jesus was going to be a great king, who would rule instead of the Romans.

Then Jesus said something unexpected to Peter. He had just called him the rock on which He meant to build, but when Peter said, 'This can never happen to You,' Jesus replied, 'Get behind me, Satan. These thoughts of yours are man's not God's.'

He spoke to Peter as if he actually were the devil and called him by the devil's name. It was not a mistake. Trying to get people away from the Cross, or the hard way, is what the devil does, and anyone who is soft or tries to make someone else soft is playing the devil's game.

Peter was saying what Satan wanted him to say and trying to prevent Jesus from facing the hard things that were the next part of God's Plan for Him.

'Anyone who wants to follow Me,' said Jesus, 'must forget about himself every day. If you try to keep things for yourself you will only lose them. You only learn to live by giving everything for Me.'

Then He said, 'Every man must learn to carry his own cross every day.'

Jesus spoke of the Cross because He knew that He would be put to death on a cross, and that the cross for everyone is when a person's own will is crossed out, and God's will wins.

He knew that people might have everything in the world that they thought they wanted, and yet not be satisfied, but He told them that some of them would see the beginning of a new world before they died.

Jesus with Moses and Elijah

AFTER He had said these things to His friends they all went on together for about a week. Jesus told them many things about Himself, but He had one special thing He wanted them to understand which most of them had not understood.

This was about life going on for ever. Moses and the old prophets had not said much about this.

Moses had taught the Law. Elijah and many of the other prophets had told the people of Israel about how they were called and chosen by God. Some had the idea that God would punish people who did wrong. All had spoken of listening and obeying.

Jesus did much more. He came and showed people how to live, so that for ever afterwards they would know. He showed them how to die too, and best of all He showed them what happened next.

One day, about a week after He had been so stern with Peter, Jesus gave him a very special chance to know more about Him. He took not only Peter but James and John up on to a high mountain. It was a long way up, and Peter and his friends were very tired by the time they got there.

Jesus went off a little way and started praying but the three men with Him were so sleepy they could barely keep their eyes open. They were almost asleep, when suddenly an amazingly bright light jerked them awake.

They looked round to see where the light was coming from and found that it was all round Jesus. Instead of His ordinary clothes He was dressed in something white and shining. He had two other men with Him, and was talking with them. They were all bright and shining too, and there was a glory round them such as is never seen on earth. Somehow Peter and the others knew that these two men were Moses and Elijah.

Moses and Elijah who had left the earth many hundreds of years before were there in front of them talking to Jesus, and so they could not be dead. They were alive somewhere else.

73

Peter, James and John knelt there for a long time looking and listening. Just as they were three friends, so there in the brightness were also three friends, talking. They talked of how Jesus would go to Jerusalem soon, and how He would die there. But He was not going to have His life taken away by others. He was going to give it Himself and would still go on living. His real glory was in Heaven where Moses and Elijah were.

Somehow it joined up all that had happened in the past with what was happening then and what was going to happen later.

Moses and Elijah, whom everyone thought of as being dead, were very much alive and part of the Plan.

It was glorious, but Peter found he was fearful at the strangeness and unexpectedness of it all. Yet he wished that he could go on looking for ever.

He tried to think of a way of keeping the bright figures there, and he started talking, hardly knowing what he said.

'Please, Master,' he begged, 'may we stay here? Could we build three little huts in this place, one for you, one for Moses, and one for Elijah?'

But as he was speaking God's voice came to him and his friends, saying, 'This is My much loved Son. Hear Him.'

They hid their faces in the ground. When they looked up Moses and Elijah had gone again, and Jesus was standing by them helping them and touching them.

'Do not be afraid,' He said, 'Get up.' He helped them to their feet and they saw He was still the same person that they knew and loved. He had let them into a great secret, because He knew they were going to need strength and courage in the days ahead.

As they walked down the hill again they talked to Jesus about what had happened and asked many questions. He asked them not to tell other people what they had seen till after He had died and risen again. It had been given specially to them and perhaps not everyone would understand it. It had been a way of letting them know and understand more about Him.

Jesus and Children

IN the days that followed Jesus tried to tell more of His friends what was going to happen to Him, but they found it hard to understand. They were still sure He was going to be a great king, and one day when they were all out together jealousy came up between them. They began to quarrel about which of them would be greatest in the new kingdom.

Jesus knew what they were doing and when they reached the house where they were staying that night He called them together.

'What were you all quarrelling about on the way here?' He asked.

They must have felt rather silly and did not like to answer, but just then a little child came in. Some people think the house was Peter's and maybe it was Peter's child. Anyway, when Jesus saw him, He called him over. The little boy came to Him, and all the disciples stood round wondering.

Jesus understood children, and they always came to Him. He took the child in His arms and said, 'You must all change and become like children who have everything to learn.

'Anyone who welcomes a child like this for My sake is welcoming Me. And the person who welcomes Me, welcomes not only Me, but the One who sent Me. It is the humblest among you who is really the greatest.'

He told them that it was a terrible thing for any grown-up person to teach a child to do wrong.

'Do not look down on children either,' He said. 'God thinks so much of them that He has special angels looking after each of them who are in touch with Him all the time.'

Then Jesus talked of the sort of thing that God thinks important, like finding one lost sheep out of a whole flock. There may be ninety-nine who are all at home and safe, but the one God thinks of specially is the one that has been lost.

So then the disciples began to see that it is not the people who want to be the most important who really are the most important.

75

The people who count are the ones who care for others, no matter who the others are.

It was a difficult lesson for them to learn, though, and they do not seem to have understood it fully, as you will see.

A little later they were in a village where many people came out to welcome Jesus. Among them were mothers with babies in their arms.

They wanted Jesus to bless the babies, but the disciples said Jesus was much too important a person to be bothered with a lot of children, and their mothers must take them away.

When Jesus saw what His friends were doing He was quite cross with them.

He said, 'Let the children come to Me. They all belong to God's Kingdom, but people who stop them coming do not belong to it.'

What Happened at the Harvest Festival

JESUS had been in Galilee for some time, and did not come to Jerusalem because the Jews there were trying to find a way of killing Him. In the autumn the time for the Feast of Tabernacles came round. It was what we might call the Harvest Festival, when the custom was for everyone to go up to Jerusalem for the Feast.

His family came to Him and said something like this, 'Go up to Jerusalem and let people see what you're doing. You must not stay tucked away here doing things in secret. If you can do so many wonderful things why not go and show yourself to the world?'

They still had a faint hope, perhaps, that He was going to be a success in some way that would give them credit, but actually they did not believe in Him at all. You remember He had not been able to do much in Nazareth earlier on, because everybody there, including His own relations, had been so unbelieving.

It was hard for them to accept the fact that He had not come into the world to do them credit, or to be run by them. He had come to put God first in everything, and wanted them and everyone else to do the same.

They tried hard to persuade Him to go, but Jesus knew that they did not mean to help Him in what He had to do. So He said to them, 'You go up to the Feast. I am not coming yet, for My time has not fully come.'

When they saw that He had made up His mind, they went without Him, but after they had gone He followed quietly by Himself.

By then the Jews who had expected Him to arrive with His family were all wondering where He was. There was a lot of talk going on about Him too. Some said He was a good man. Others said that He was deceiving people. They all thought and felt many things, but were afraid to speak openly in case the enemies of Jesus should attack them also.

Half-way through the Feast Jesus came Himself, and went straight into the Temple and taught. The people were amazed to hear Him speak and teach so clearly. They said 'This man has not had much schooling. How does He come to know so much?'

So Jesus said, 'I have been sent by God. I am telling you what God says, not what I know Myself. Any man who does what God says will come to understand Him.'

Then He said, 'Moses gave you the Law, but none of you keeps it. Why are you trying to kill Me?'

This made people wonder all the more. Some said, 'Nonsense, who is trying to kill you?' Others said, 'He speaks very boldly. Do the rulers know that He really is the Christ?'

Many others said, 'If Christ did come could He do anything more than this man?'

It was hard to believe that the Person they had waited for all these years was going to look like one of themselves. If He had appeared from nowhere with a flash of lightning it would have been more interesting and easier to believe.

Jesus came to show ordinary people how to do things that were not ordinary. He wanted to make everything so new that no one would think it extraordinary to be full of God's Spirit. When the Pharisees heard what was going on they sent guards to arrest Him. He knew that the time was not far off when He would be taken, and He said, 'I shall only be with you for a little while, and then I shall go back to Him who sent Me. You will look for Me but you will not find Me, because you cannot come where I am going.'

'Whatever can He mean,' asked the Jews, 'saying that He is going where we cannot find Him, and that we cannot go there too?' And they began to argue among themselves.

Some said, 'This really is the Prophet.' Others said, 'This is the Christ.' But some said, 'Oh no, prophets never come from Galilee.' 'Surely,' they said, 'the old prophets all said that the Christ was coming from Bethlehem?'

They had evidently not heard that Jesus had actually been born in Bethlehem, which all goes to show that many people often talk of things they know very little about.

The arguments became quite fierce. Some thought that Jesus should be arrested. Some thought not. In the end the officers went back to the Pharisees without Him, because they were not at all sure in their own minds that He ought to be arrested.

'Why have you not brought Him?' asked the Pharisees angrily.

'No man ever spoke as this man does,' answered the officers.

This enraged the Pharisees.

'Has He fooled you too?' they asked. 'Have any of the rulers or the Pharisees ever believed a word He says?'

Then Nicodemus, the half-brave Pharisee, who had been to see Jesus by night, said, 'Surely by our law we do not judge a man without hearing what he has to say about what he is doing.'

But they laughed at him and said, 'Do you come from Galilee too? Look round and see if any prophets have ever come out of Galilee.'

Nicodemus said nothing more, but he began to be more certain in his heart about who Jesus really was.

Jesus explains about Unselfishness

JESUS wanted His friends to be able to remember the things He said, and so He often told them stories which would stick in their minds. He noticed everything that was going on and tried to help His friends to learn from everything they saw.

Once He went to a meal with one of the Pharisees, and He saw that each guest, as he came in, tried to get the best place he could find.

So Jesus said to them, 'Don't try and get the best seat at a party. It might happen that someone more important than you will come in afterwards. Then the man who is giving the party will ask you to give him your place, and you will feel ashamed and have to go to a less good one. It is better to come and sit quietly in one of the less good seats. Then your host may well say, "Do come to a better one".'

The men at this dinner probably felt they were extremely important people, and each one was trying to show that he ought to be in a better seat than all the others. In those days people were much the same as they are now. They would invite some important friend to dinner hoping to be invited back.

Jesus said to them, 'Don't only ask people to your feasts who can ask you back. You should ask people who cannot do anything for you in return. God will reward you in Heaven.'

This made one of the guests say, 'What a wonderful thing it would be to go to a feast in Heaven.'

Jesus must have known that many of them were so busy on their own affairs they would not have time to go to Heaven even if they were asked.

So He told this story.

There was a certain man, He said, who planned a great party and invited many people. When it was ready he sent his servant to tell the guests that it was time to come. But when the message came everyone began to make excuses for not coming.

One had just bought some land and had to go and look at it that day. Another was too busy on his farm. He had just bought some oxen and wanted to try them out on pulling his plough. A third sent a message that he had just been married, and could not possibly leave his wife. Each one thought that what he had himself was more important than what God could give him.

So the Giver of the Feast said, 'Very well, if the people I specially invited will not come, I shall ask everyone else. Go out and invite people in from the street. The others have lost their chance.'

Jesus knew how hard it was for people to put God's Plan before their own, and as He travelled about the country He met many people and talked to them about how to put God first.

Some wanted to come with Him. Others wanted to have things the easy way.

Once He met a rich young man who asked how he could be part of God's Plan and put it first in his life. Jesus said, 'Keep the commandments of Moses; live cleanly; do not steal, lie, or kill. Honour your father and mother.'

'But I have done all that,' said the young man.

Jesus loved him and said, 'There is still something missing. Sell your possessions, give away your money, and follow me.'

The young man felt he was not ready to be as unselfish as all that, and he went sadly away. He would have liked to have come with Jesus, but he did not want to come enough to part with all the beautiful things he had.

Jesus then spoke to His friends about money. He told them that it will be hard for a man who relies on his riches to become part of God's Kingdom. 'As hard,' He said, 'as for a camel to go through the eye of a needle.'

His friends were all dismayed.

'Who then can be saved?' they asked.

Jesus replied, 'The things which are impossible with men are possible with God.'

'Well, we have left everything and followed You,' said Peter. Then Jesus told them something that the rich young man had not waited to hear.

'Anyone,' He said, 'who has left his home and family for the sake of God's Kingdom will have much more given to him in this world, and will live for ever in the next.'

'Finding God's Plan,' He said, 'is like buying a very valuable pearl. It costs you all you have, in fact you have to give your whole life and all you have to get it, and then you find it is a much bigger treasure than anything you have ever had.'

Another time a man tried to trick Jesus into telling him how to live so that he would have eternal life.

'Well,' said Jesus, 'what does the law say? What do you make of what it says?'

The man answered, 'It says love God with all your heart and soul and strength and mind, and love your neighbour as yourself.'

'That's quite right,' said Jesus. 'Do that and you will live.'

This was a bit uncomfortable, and the man tried to make out that he did not understand.

'Who is my neighbour?' he asked.

Jesus did not answer the question directly, but He told him a story. This may well have been as they were going up the road from Jericho. It was a wild and deserted road where robbers often stopped people, so the story Jesus told was about a man who was travelling from Jerusalem to Jericho, and on the way he was attacked by robbers. They took all his money and escaped, leaving him lying by the road-side half dead.

83

He had been lying there for some time when a priest from the Temple came down the road. He saw the wounded man, but he was too busy to stop. He crossed over to the other side of the road, pretending he had not seen him.

The next person to come was also one of the Jewish people. He belonged to the Levite tribe who served in the Temple and were supposed to set a good example, but he did the same as the priest.

Then there came a Samaritan down the road. Now you remember that the Jews never did anything for the Samaritans, nor the Samaritans for the Jews. They did not really think of themselves as neighbours at all.

When this Samaritan saw the unfortunate traveller lying there, he did not bother about who he was, or how busy he was himself. He got off his donkey, and bandaged the man where he was hurt. Then he lifted him on to the donkey, and took him to an inn. There the Samaritan asked the innkeeper to look after him, and left some money to help to pay for anything that might be needed. He said, 'Please look after this man, and use this money. I will call back later and give you more if you need it.'

'Now,' said Jesus, 'who do you think was a neighbour to the man who was attacked by the robbers?'

'I think it was the one who showed mercy,' replied the man who had asked the question about what a neighbour was.

'That is quite right,' said Jesus. 'You go and do the same.'

The Story of the Boy who ran away

ANOTHER story Jesus told His friends was one to show what God's love really means, how love means living for other people, not just feeling that you like them. He told them first that He Himself had come to live His life for other people, like a good shepherd who looks after his sheep and knows them all. If one gets lost he goes looking till he finds it.

Then He told them about God's love for people too, and how God is like a father who never stops loving His children even if they do wrong. He told them a story to show what God is like.

He said that there was once a man who had two sons, and the younger son said to his father, 'Please, Father, give me my share of our family fortune and let me do what I like with it.'

So his father gave him his share and let him go. The young man liked having a lot of money, and he decided to go travelling. He found his way to a country a long way off, where he went to the bad, and spent all his money in worthless and evil ways. He did no work. Then one day he found he had no money left. On top of that things were going badly in the country to which he had gone. There was a famine, and people were hungry. The young man had no money and no food, but he managed to get a poorly paid job looking after pigs. As he watched them grubbing up roots and nuts he was so hungry that he would have been glad to have eaten the same things himself. And nobody gave him anything.

After a while he came to himself and began to realise just how wrong he had been.

'Why,' he thought, 'even my father's servants are better off than I am. I will go home and tell my father I am sorry. I will tell him that I don't deserve to be his son any more, and I will ask him if I may be one of his servants.'

So he made his way home.

All this time his father had been watching and waiting for him.

He saw him coming when he was still a long way off, and went running
to meet him, and kissed him.

Then the son said all he had thought of saying about being sorry
and asking to be made one of the servants, and that he was quite
ready for any punishment the father might want to give him.

But his father did not want to punish him. He only wanted him to
come back and be sorry, and be willing to start again. He gave him new
clothes and had a wonderful meal prepared and gave a party for him.

All this time the elder son had stayed at home. He had served his
father and had not run away or done anything wrong, and the day
his younger brother came back he was out in the fields working. As he
came near home he heard music and sounds of a party coming from
the house, so he called one of the servants and asked what was happening. The servant told him that his brother had come back, and that
was why there was such excitement.

Then the elder brother felt jealous. He went to his father and
said, 'Why are you giving this party for my brother when he has
behaved so badly? Why can't I have a party too?' And he refused to
go in.

'My son,' said his father, 'you are with me all the time, and everything I have is yours, but your brother has been away for years. He
was lost and now he is found again. It is almost as if he had been dead
and had come alive again.'

Jesus did not put into the story what the elder brother thought.
Perhaps it was because there are so many elder brothers, and sisters,
in the world, and they just have to decide for themselves what they
think about this story. It is one of the great stories of God's love for
all kinds of brothers, and all kinds of people.

Lazarus Falls Ill and Dies

ONCE in the winter Jesus was walking in the Temple in what was called Solomon's Porch. Some of the Jews came up to Him and said, 'If You really are the Christ, You must tell us plainly.'

So Jesus answered, 'I have told you and you do not believe Me. My sheep hear My voice and listen to Me and follow Me. You are not My sheep because you do not listen to Me. My Father gave My sheep to Me and no one can take them from Me, because I and My Father are one.'

It was just as Jesus said. The people did not believe Him. They took up stones to throw at Him. 'For which of My good works do you stone Me?' He asked.

They said, 'How can You say You are God when You are only a man?'

Jesus said, 'I am the Son of God, and My Father is in Me, and I am in Him.'

At this the Jews were angrier than ever and tried to take Him prisoner, but Jesus escaped and went away over the River Jordan to where He had first met John the Baptist. Though some people were angry, many others believed what He said, and He stayed by the Jordan for a while talking to them. He was there when a message came to Him from the sisters Martha and Mary at Bethany, saying that their brother Lazarus was ill.

There are no stories about Lazarus' friendship with Jesus, but we can tell from what is written that Jesus knew all the family well, and loved them. Martha was a managing sort of person, but she loved her brother. So when one day he fell gravely ill, she cared tenderly for him.

Both she and Mary did everything they could for him, but soon they saw that there was only one person who could help, and that was Jesus. So they sent a message saying, 'Please come. Our brother Lazarus whom You love, is ill.'

You would have thought that when Jesus heard this He would

drop everything He was doing and go at once to His friends who needed Him so badly. Instead of this He waited for two days. Martha and Mary and Lazarus wanted Him, but Jesus had to make sure that it was part of God's Plan for Him to go.

Bethany was very near Jerusalem. The rulers and the Pharisees were turning more and more against Him, and the next time He went anywhere near them would be the last.

It was important that the big battle of the Cross should happen at the moment God intended. So Jesus waited. He told His friends that Lazarus's illness would all be used to show the greatness of God's Power.

After two days He said, 'Let us go to him now.'

Then His friends were afraid. They knew how the crowds had tried to stone Him, and they felt it was much too dangerous. They begged Him not to go.

'No,' said Jesus, 'the night is coming now. I must work while there is still light.'

Then He said, 'Lazarus has gone to sleep, but I shall go and wake him up.'

His friends thought that if Lazarus were really asleep, he would be getting better and there was no point in running into danger simply to wake him.

Jesus knew very well, though, that Lazarus had died and so when He saw they were hoping he was still alive He told them what had happened.

'Lazarus is dead,' Jesus said. 'But I am glad it has happened because it will help to make your faith stronger. Anyway, let us go to him now.'

Then when His friends saw He meant to go back to the stones and the danger, one of them, Thomas, said, 'Very well, we will go and die with Him.' And though they did not understand it all, they went.

Jesus brings Lazarus back to Life

ALL this time Martha and Mary had been at home waiting and hoping that Jesus would get there in time to save their brother's life, but by the time He arrived Lazarus had been dead for four days.

As Bethany was only about two miles from Jerusalem, many of the

Jews who lived in the city had come out to see Martha and Mary, and tell them how sorry they were that Lazarus had died.

Martha felt desperate. She was still a busy, bustling sort of person, and when she heard that Jesus had reached the edge of the village she hurried to meet Him, and in her grief reproved Him for not having arrived in time. The moment she saw Him she said, 'Lord, if only You had been here, my brother would not have died.' Then she added, 'But I know that even now God will give You anything You ask.'

'Your brother will come to life again,' answered Jesus quietly.

'I know he will come alive at the end of the world,' replied Martha.

'Do you believe that I can give life to anyone who trusts and believes Me?' He asked.

This must have made Martha think what she did believe, because she answered very simply, 'Yes, I do believe that you are Christ the Son of God.'

Then she went home much more quietly and found Mary.

Mary was still sitting at home. There was nothing she could do by rushing about, so she waited for Jesus to come, or to have some word from Him. When Martha arrived she whispered to Mary, 'Jesus has come and He wants you.'

When Mary heard this she got up quickly and found Jesus still sitting where Martha had left Him, and when she saw Him even she could not help saying, 'Oh, Master, if only You had been here my brother would not have died.' She wept as she said this, and her friends who had followed her from the house wept too.

Jesus groaned in His spirit and was troubled, and said, 'Where have you put him?'

They said, 'Come and see,' and Mary led the way to a cave with a stone in front of it, which was where the body of Lazarus had been laid.

As they stood there, Jesus wept too.

Then some of the Jews said, 'See how He loved him!' Others said, 'If He can give back sight to the blind, why did this man not stop Lazarus from dying?'

Then still very much troubled in His heart Jesus moved up to the cave and said, 'Move the stone away.'

'Oh no,' said Martha, still impatient and unable to understand. 'You cannot do that. He has been dead for four days.'

'Did I not tell you,' said Jesus, 'that if you would only believe and have faith you would see the glory of God?'

89

So they rolled the stone aside.

Jesus stood in front of the cave and spoke to God saying, 'Father, I thank You for hearing Me, but I am thanking You for the sake of all these people, so that they may believe that You really did send Me.'

Then he called loudly 'Lazarus. Come out!'

Immediately the man who had been dead came out. He was wrapped in the white cloth that had been put round him when he was laid in the tomb, so it was not very easy to walk.

'Take those off him,' said Jesus, 'and let him move freely.'

This made many of the Jews who were there believe and trust Jesus, but others went straight back to the Pharisees to tell them what had happened.

The Pharisees immediately called a meeting to decide what to do. They said, 'This man certainly does very wonderful things. If He goes on like this everyone will follow Him, and not us. What shall we do then? It will upset everything. The Romans will think we cannot keep order and will take our power away from us.'

'Perhaps,' said Caiaphas the High Priest, 'it would be better for one man to die for the whole nation, rather than having trouble come upon the whole nation.'

From that moment the Pharisees and the chief priests decided that Jesus must die.

They gave an order for anyone who knew where He was to tell them, so that they could arrest Him. But Jesus knew it still was not quite the time for this to happen, so He went away again with His disciples to a place called Ephraim on the edge of the desert.

Jesus' Last Journey

JESUS stayed a while in Ephraim, until He knew the time had come to start back towards Jerusalem.

He knew that He would die, and come to life again and so would be able to be with His friends for ever, which was better than being king of a little kingdom for a short time.

In spite of all He had told them, His friends could not understand this. They still thought He was going to be an earthly king, and when Jesus said they were all going to Jerusalem they thought the time had come for this to happen.

He walked along in front of them with determination in His heart, and they followed wondering.

As they went along the road they were met by James and John and their mother. They were two of Jesus' first friends and had left their fishing with Simon and Andrew to go with Him. Their mother was the wife of the old fisherman, Zebedee, and she was another of those who thought Jesus was going to have power and greatness on earth. So when she saw Him, she said, 'Please, may I ask You something?'

'What is it?' asked Jesus.

'When You become king,' said the mother of James and John, 'may my two sons sit one on Your right side and the other on Your left?'

Jesus asked them if they were able to bear all the suffering He Himself would bear.

'Yes,' said James and John, 'we are able.'

'My suffering and sacrifice,' Jesus said, 'you shall indeed share, but it is not for Me to decide what place people shall have in the kingdom of God My Father. That is for My Father to decide.'

When the other ten disciples heard what James and John had asked for, they were indignant. Perhaps they wished they had thought of it themselves, or maybe they knew it was wrong. Jesus called them to Him, and said, 'You know that kings are people who give orders to others. But that is not what you are meant to do. You are meant to

serve and care for everyone. Whoever wants to come first will end
by coming last. I myself came to serve people, and you must do
the same.'

As He and His friends came closer to Jerusalem they passed
through Jericho. Everyone heard of their coming and ran out to
meet them, and there were crowds along the streets, waiting to
see Jesus.

One of the men who was eager to see Him was a tax-gatherer called
Zacchaeus. He was one of the men who had made people pay more
taxes than they should and had kept what was over for himself.
All the same, he wanted to see Jesus. Unfortunately he arrived late,
and by the time he had made his way to where Jesus was he found himself right at the back of the crowd. Being a very small man he could
not see over people's heads, so he climbed up a tree and waited for
Jesus to come by.

He did not think he would be particularly noticed, but when Jesus came to the tree, He stopped. Then He looked up into the tree and said, 'Come down, Zacchaeus. You must be quick because I want to come and stay at your house.'

Imagine how pleased Zacchaeus was. He scrambled down, ran home, and ordered a meal to be prepared. Then when Jesus and His friends arrived, he gave them a great welcome.

The rest of the crowd grumbled and said Jesus had gone off again with a bad man, but Zacchaeus, when Jesus came into his house, decided that he was going to put right all that he had done wrong. He said to Jesus, 'I will give half what I have to the poor, and if I have wrongly taken anything from anyone I will give them back four times as much.'

Jesus rejoiced when He heard this. He said, 'I have come to look for people who were lost and save them.' He also said, 'This day is salvation come to this house.' Salvation means being saved from evil, like greed and selfishness. Jesus never thought people were too bad to change, and He does not think it now.

The Man who Betrayed Jesus

ALL this time there was one man who was very uneasy about what was going to happen next. He was one of the twelve men whom Jesus had specially chosen to be with Him, and his name was Judas Iscariot.

Judas was the man who looked after the money which was given to Jesus to buy food and other things. Today we might call him the treasurer, or the accountant.

No one knows what went on in his mind, but we can guess. He, like the others, had hoped that in the end something grand and great would happen, and that he would be part of it. He must have seen before they did that the power and kingdom of Jesus were not coming in the way they had all expected.

Instead of being on the winning side he might find himself on the side that seemed to have lost, and many dark thoughts started to go round in his mind.

After Lazarus had come back to life, the Pharisees and chief priests were really worried. They felt it was time not only to kill

Jesus, but to get rid of Lazarus too. As long as Lazarus was alive he was a living proof of the power of Jesus.

So these priests and others began looking round for someone who would help them to catch Jesus at a time when He was alone, and did not have people near who would protect Him. Judas knew all this, and as he turned everything over in his mind, he listened to the thought, 'Why don't you help them to catch Jesus?'

It happened that on the last night before they reached Jerusalem, Jesus and His friends, including Judas, stopped for supper at Bethany where Martha, Mary and Lazarus lived.

Probably the others did not realise exactly what Jesus was going to face when he reached Jerusalem, but I think Mary knew. She knew she might not be able to do much more for Him, so during supper she went and fetched a pound of sweet-smelling and very expensive ointment called spikenard. She poured this over His feet till the whole house was filled with the scent of the ointment. Then she wiped His feet with her hair.

When Judas saw what she was doing he was not pleased at all. There was a dark cloud in his heart as there always is in the hearts of those who are thinking of doing something which they know to be wrong, and all he said was, 'What a waste of good ointment. That jar is worth a lot of money. We might have sold it and given the money to the poor.'

This was not because he loved poor people, but because he loved money, and he was a thief. Quite likely if he had had the ointment he would have sold it and kept the money and not given it to the poor at all.

Some of Jesus' other friends wondered when they saw what Mary was doing, but Jesus said, 'Why do you murmur? Let her alone. You will always have poor people with you but you will not have Me. She will always be remembered because of what she has done tonight.'

Jesus looked sadly at Judas because He knew he was going to make the wrong choice in order to get something for himself. Judas like everybody else had to decide for himself what he was going to do, and choose between God and the devil.

Into
Jerusalem

THE next morning Jesus went on towards Jerusalem. As this was the place where many powerful people were waiting to kill Him, you might have thought He would try to go in quietly without anyone noticing Him, but He did nothing of the sort. He went into the city in such a way that everyone was bound to know He had come.

He told two of His friends to go and fetch a donkey which they would find tied by a certain house. This donkey had never been ridden by anyone, and if the owner asked them why they wanted it they were to say, 'The Master needs it.' The owner would then let them have it.

This happened just as Jesus had said. They found the donkey, gave the message to the man it belonged to and brought it back with them. Then they all put their coats on its back to make it comfortable to sit on, and started off with Jesus riding.

Most people, by the way, do not try riding on a donkey that has never been ridden. The donkey would kick them off, but this one did not.

As they went, people who had come up to Jerusalem for the Feast saw them coming, and ran to welcome Jesus, shouting and cheering. They waved palm branches and strewed others on the ground. Five hundred years earlier Zechariah the prophet had said that a King would come riding into Jerusalem on a young donkey, and here it was happening. The people welcomed Him by shouting 'Hosanna', the cheer they would give to the King God had chosen.

The disciples must have thought that Jesus was mistaken in saying that things would go so badly. Surely after this great welcome people would never let Him be killed. They did not realise that it is quite easy to stand and cheer somebody whom you like, but not so easy to fight for that person when things get difficult.

Even in the middle of it all, when they were on the top of the last hill going down to Jerusalem, Jesus stopped and looked at the city sadly. 'Oh, Jerusalem,' He said, 'if only you had known where real peace comes from,' and He wept at the thought of all the people turning away from what God wanted to give them.

'The time is coming,' He said, 'when you, Jerusalem, will be pulled down. Not one stone will be left standing upon another, because you did not understand that God was visiting you.'

This came true not many years later, when the Roman Emperor Titus utterly destroyed the whole city.

Then Jesus went straight on to Jerusalem and into the Temple.

Everyone was asking who He was, and people told their friends, 'It is Jesus, the prophet from Nazareth.' He spent the day in the Temple teaching, and went back to Bethany in the evening. He was with many friends all the time, so the chief priests could not take Him prisoner. He never ran away, but followed God's Plan step by step.

At this point Judas went to where the chief priests were having a meeting in the High Priest's palace. They were trying to find an excuse for having Jesus arrested, and just as they were talking about it, Judas, one of Jesus' own friends, came in and offered to help.

He said to the priests and the officers of the Temple, 'How much money will you give me, if I get Him into your hands?'

96

The chief priests eagerly accepted his offer, and promised to give him thirty pieces of silver if he would keep a look out for some moment when Jesus was alone away from the crowds, and come and let them know. After this, all Judas had to do was to wait for the right moment.

In the Temple

JESUS cannot have been pleased with what He saw in the Temple, and the next day He came to put it right.

Many people had begun to use the Temple almost like a shop. Animals and birds, chiefly doves, were sacrificed there, and instead of bringing a sheep or dove with them, it was often easier for people to buy them at the Temple. So a market had been set up with people selling various kinds of animals, and there were tables where money could be changed, all of which made the people in charge of the Temple richer.

Jesus was really angry when He found this happening. He drove away the money-changers with a whip, and scattered the coins on the floor. Then He said to the

sellers of sheep and doves, 'Take these away and do not turn My Father's house into a market. It is meant to be a house of prayer, and you have made it a den of thieves.'

This made His enemies more determined than ever to get rid of Him. He was upsetting the whole way they lived, all the things they were used to, and customs that had been going on for a long time. They did not want to be upset and have to live differently. They also saw that if they no longer sold doves and lambs in the Temple, they would lose money. It was Jesus who was causing all the trouble, they felt, so Jesus must go.

Jesus knew what they were thinking, so another day when He was again in the Temple He told them a story.

He knew the Pharisees were trying to trap Him, and He wanted to show them that He knew what they were doing. He also wanted to show His own friends what was going to happen.

'There was once a man,' He said, 'who had a vineyard, which he let out to gardeners. One day he sent a servant to the gardeners with a message asking for some of the fruit from the vineyard. But the gardeners only beat the servant and sent him back empty-handed. . . .

'The owner then sent another servant, but the workmen beat and ill-treated him too.

'A third servant came who was also wounded and thrown out.

'In the end the master thought to himself, "I will send my much-loved son. Perhaps they will listen to him and respect him."

'So he sent his son, but when the workmen saw him coming they said to themselves, "Here is the master's son. If we kill him, we shall be masters."

'When the son came, they did not listen to the messages he brought from his father, but they killed him.'

'What do you think,' asked Jesus, 'that the owner of the vineyard will do to these men? He will destroy them and take the vineyard away and give it to others.'

The Pharisees knew that Jesus was speaking about them. They hated what He said about everything being taken away from them because of the wickedness in their hearts, but it happened later all the same.

From that time they hired spies who would pretend to be honest men, but were really paid to listen for anything that Jesus said which could be twisted into an excuse to arrest Him.

For instance, one of the scribes later came up to Him and said, 'Can You tell me which is the great commandment that Moses taught?'

Jesus replied, 'The great commandment is that you should love God with all your heart, and with all your soul, and with all your mind, and with all your strength.' This was exactly what Moses had taught. Moses had also been given other commandments which tell people what to do and what not to do. Jesus said. 'You can put all those other rules into one sentence, and that is, "You must love your neighbour as yourself". On these two commandments hang all the Law and the Prophets.'

The man who had asked the question knew that this was true, and he began to change. He said, 'I see that loving God and other people is much more important than sacrificing animals.'

So Jesus said, 'You are not far from the Kingdom of God now,' and the man went away thinking deeply.

Jesus spent quite a lot of time in the Temple that week.

Later on He was sitting watching people putting money in the collecting box outside. The rich men came and gave large sums of money, but as Jesus and His friends watched, a very poor woman came who put in two pieces of money worth practically nothing; less than what it costs to buy the cheapest kind of postage stamp today.

Jesus did not feel her gift was worth nothing. He said, 'You know that poor woman has really given much more than all those rich men. Those two little coins were the last two she had, but the rich men had more at home. She was really much more unselfish than they were.'

Jesus Washes the Feet of His Friends

JESUS had come into Jerusalem on Sunday and for three days He spent the time mostly in the Temple giving people all He could, talking to them and healing them.

Then on Thursday He said to His friends that the time was soon coming when He was going to leave them, and that He would like to have supper with them all together first.

It was again the time of the Feast of the Passover, when Jewish families were accustomed to offer a sacrifice of a lamb that was absolutely perfect. This was in memory of the first Passover. At that time the eldest child in every Egyptian family had died, but God had passed over and spared the Israelites. Each family had sacrified a lamb instead.

Jesus did not kill a lamb. He did not need to because He was going to give Himself and He wanted to explain to His friends about it.

He told them to make arrangements for a special Passover supper in the home of a friend. They got it ready in an upstairs room in his house just for Jesus and the twelve of them. All twelve came because Judas was still trying to behave as if he were a friend.

During supper Jesus got up. He took off his robe and tied a towel round His waist. Then He poured water into a basin and began to wash His friends' feet. This was really a servant's work, and they were all horrified to see Jesus doing it.

When it came to Peter's turn, Peter said, 'Lord, You shall never wash my feet.'

But Jesus said, 'Unless I wash you, you can have no part in what I am doing.' Peter was still a man who quickly said all that he was feeling. He often spoke without taking much time to think, so when Jesus said this to him, he changed his mind and answered, 'Then please wash not only my feet, but my hands and my head as well.' One moment he did not want Jesus to do anything for him. The next he wanted Him to do more than He had offered.

When Jesus had washed His friends' feet, He put on His robe

again and sat down. He explained that He had been showing them once more that He had not come to be a great king and get power for Himself. He had come to give everything, even His life, so that men might find God's Plan. Part of that Plan was that people should learn to serve each other in the simplest and humblest ways.

He said to them, 'If I then, your Lord and Master, have washed your feet, you ought to wash one another's feet.'

He Talks to Them After Supper

DURING supper Jesus told His friends that even though He was going away they were not going to lose Him. He would come back and be with them till the end of the world, and with everyone who believed in Him.

There must have been something very special about meals with Jesus.

There was the time when He fed all the five thousand people sitting on the grass. There was the dinner with Simon the Pharisee when He forgave the woman who was sorry. Then there was the dinner at Matthew's house with all the tax-gatherers, the time too with the family at Bethany, and the meal when Zacchaeus' whole life was changed.

They all seem to show that Jesus felt that these times with Him were meant not only to feed people's bodies, but also to give them something new in their hearts as well.

The last supper which Jesus had with His friends has fed the hearts of people ever since.

While they were eating Jesus took bread and broke it into pieces and gave some to each one. He said to them that just as He had broken the bread to feed their bodies so His Body would be broken to feed their hearts and spirits.

Then He took a cup of wine and told them all to drink some of it. He said that as they drank this red wine, they were to think of it as the new promise of His blood pouring into them, and giving new life to them. They were to drink it together in remembrance of Him, and it represented the sacrifice of His very life's blood for them.

As Judas listened to Jesus, talking like this, he understood that any last hope he might have had that Jesus was going to be a success was gone.

He saw clearly that Jesus was not going to become a king in the way he had hoped, but was expecting to die soon.

Judas thought of the money the chief priests had offered him, and he knew that the moment had come to change sides.

Jesus knew exactly what was going on in his mind and He said to them all, 'One of you is going to betray Me.'

Everybody said, 'Is it I? Is it I?' Even Judas joined in and said, 'Master. Is it I?'

Jesus said, 'The one to whom I give this piece of bread is the one who will do it,' and He handed the piece to Judas. The others saw Him do it but they did not really believe it could be one of them. Jesus did not give Judas away. He just said, 'What you are going to do, do quickly.' Then Judas shut the door of his heart, and locked it. He made the wrong decision, and went out into the night.

His friends still did not see what was happening. They thought that as Judas had charge of the money, Jesus was suggesting that he should go and do some shopping for the Feast.

After Judas had gone Jesus told the others many more things about how much He loved them and how much God loved them.

'If you love Me,' He said, 'you will do what I say, and you need never be worried or afraid. I am going to prepare a place for you. You know where I am going and you know the way there.'

Then Thomas, who always found things difficult to believe and was always wanting to have everything explained, said, 'But we don't know where You are going, so how can we know the way?'

'You know Me, though,' answered Jesus, 'and I am the way. I am the way to life, and knowing Me means knowing My Father.'

Philip, who was good at working things out in his head, said, 'Show us the Father, then we shall be certain.'

'Oh, Philip,' said Jesus, 'do you mean to say I have been with you all this time and you still do not know who I am? Why do you say "Show us the Father"? If you have seen Me you have seen Him. We are the same. If you do what I say I shall be real to you.'

We can picture them all sitting round trying to understand, and after a while the other Judas (not the bad one) asked, 'How can You be real to us and not to other people?' Jesus answered, 'When a person really loves Me he does what I tell him. Then My Father and I can come into that person's heart and make Our home there. People who do not love Us do not keep to what We say.'

'You will not actually see Me much longer,' He said, 'but after I have gone, My Father will send the Holy Spirit who will teach you everything and remind you of all that I have told you.'

Peter said to Him, 'Lord, where are You going?'

'I am going,' said Jesus, 'where you cannot follow Me now, though you will follow Me later.'

'Lord, why can't I follow You now?' said Peter. 'I would lay down my life for You.'

Jesus answered, 'Would you really lay down your life for Me? I tell you, before the cock crows tomorrow morning you will have said three times that you do not know Me.'

Once more Jesus knew Peter better than Peter knew himself, as you will see.

Then Jesus prayed to His Father for the men who were with Him. He asked specially that they might love each other, and be at one with each other, and with Him.

'I in them,' He said, 'and Thou in Me, that they may be made perfect in one, and that the world may know that Thou hast sent Me, and hast loved them as Thou has loved Me.'

He also said this in another way, by saying, 'I am the Vine, and you are the branches,' and that if the branches stayed on the vine, they would bear fruit—that is, new life for other people would come from them.

The Night in the Garden

THE Garden of Gethsemane was a place where Jesus and His friends had often been, and Jesus knew that it was the place where Judas would bring the men who were to take Him prisoner.

In spite of all that He knew was coming He had spent the evening giving faith and courage to His friends, and by the time they reached the Garden it was late at night.

He went on a little way taking only Peter and James and John, who were the same three who had come up the mountain with Him the time He spoke with Moses and Elijah.

He said to them, 'My soul is very sorrowful, even unto death. Wait here, and watch with Me.'

Then He went a little way off by Himself and prayed.

It had been a long day, and everyone was tired. They were very unhappy too. At last they had realised that Jesus was going away and that He was to suffer in a way they did not yet understand.

They were so unhappy that they could not bear to face it and they went to sleep to try and escape from it all.

So Jesus was left alone, and He knew He had one more decision to face.

It was the middle of the night. Very few people knew where He was. He had friends with Him who would certainly have helped Him to escape had He asked them. He flung Himself down on the ground and prayed to God. He saw what lay ahead as the cup of suffering that He must drink.

'Dear Father,' He said, 'all things are possible to You. Take away this cup from Me. All the same, let it be not what I want, but what You want.'

God's answer to this prayer was not to say that things would be easier, but to send His Spirit to make Jesus strong.

Yet as He prayed the sweat rolled down His face and fell like drops of blood on to the ground.

He went back to Peter and the others, and found them still asleep, so He woke Peter and said, 'Could you not watch with Me just for an hour. You need to pray for strength too. Your spirits indeed are willing, but your flesh is weak.'

Peter and the others were soon going to know how true this was, but even so they could not keep awake. When Jesus went away to pray again by Himself they fell asleep once more.

After a while Jesus came and woke them all a second time, but still they could not stay awake.

When Jesus came back the third time, Judas and a gang of men were just coming into the Garden, so Jesus again woke His friends.

'Are you still asleep?' He said. 'Look, the moment has come for Me to be taken prisoner by evil men. Rise up, and let us go. The man who has given Me away is here.'

Peter, James and John sprang to their feet, but there was little they could do. In front of them was a crowd of men armed with sticks and swords, headed by Judas.

In desperation Peter, who had a sword, drew it and cut off the right ear of the High Priest's servant. Jesus said, 'Let Me do this much.' And He touched the man's ear and healed it.

Many of these men whom the High Priest had sent to take Jesus had never seen Him before. So Judas had said to them, 'The man whom I shall kiss is the one you must take,' and as soon as he saw Jesus, he walked up just as if he were really His friend, and kissed Him.

Immediately the men with swords came up and took hold of Jesus. It was a great many people to send out against one unarmed man, and Jesus looked round at them as if He were almost amused at all this fuss over taking Him prisoner.

'So you have come after Me with swords and sticks as if I were a robber,' He said. 'I was with you day after day in the Temple, yet you never laid a finger on Me. But this is all in the Plan. This is your time, and for the moment you have the power of the Dark Spirit.'

When His friends heard this they forgot all that He had told them. All of them, even Peter, ran away into the darkness and escaped, hoping that no one would recognise them.

So Jesus was left alone with the men who had taken Him prisoner.

Jesus is taken to the High Priest

THE men with Judas tied Jesus' hands and took Him away to the house of Annas, who was one of the chief priests, and the father-in-law of Caiaphas, the High Priest. It was Caiaphas who had said earlier that perhaps one man ought to die for the whole nation.

Peter, who had not after all run very far away, followed a little way off with John, to see what was going to happen.

It happened that John knew the High Priest, and had been in his house before. When the whole group of men went in with Jesus, John went in too, but Peter waited outside.

John spoke to the maid who had opened the door, and asked if he might bring in his friend. When she said he might, Peter came up from where he had been waiting, and as soon as the light fell on his face, the maid said, 'Aren't you one of His disciples?'

'No,' said Peter shortly, 'I am not,' and he went in and stood by a fire which was burning in the courtyard where many of the servants and soldiers were warming themselves, for it was night and very cold. So Peter warmed himself too, and said nothing.

Meanwhile Jesus was standing at the other end of the courtyard in front of the chief priests and the scribes and the elders. They had a crowd of people round them, and were trying to get some of them to tell lies about Jesus, and say He had broken their law. At first nobody would, but presently two men came forward who said, 'We heard this fellow say that he would pull down the Temple and rebuild it in three days.'

'Now,' said the High Priest, 'what have You to say to that? Do you hear what these men say?'

Jesus said nothing. He had once spoken of Himself as a temple that was going to be destroyed and would be rebuilt in three days, but He had been talking of how He would die and come to life again. He knew no one would either believe or understand Him if He explained this, so He did not try.

The High Priest then said to Him, 'Are You the Son of God?'

Jesus replied, 'I am, and one day you will see Me sitting by God in power.'

'You see,' said the High Priest, 'He has said it Himself. Nobody is allowed to say he is the Son of God. We do not need to hear from anyone else.'

They said it was blasphemy, which means dishonouring God, and in the Jewish law the punishment for blasphemy was death.

Then they laughed at Jesus and hit Him and made fun of Him. Even the servants joined in. But Peter still sat warming himself by the fire and saying nothing.

After a while one of the servants came to him and said, 'Surely you were also with Jesus of Nazareth,' and Peter answered angrily, 'I don't know what you're talking about.'

Another man came up soon afterwards and said, 'I am sure you are one of them. I can tell you come from Galilee by the way you talk.'

By now Peter was frightened and it made him speak even more angrily. He said furiously, 'I tell you I do not know this man of whom you speak.'

Almost as he spoke the cock crowed. Jesus from the other end of the courtyard turned and looked at Peter, and Peter remembered.

He remembered how he had said he would never leave Jesus, and how Jesus had replied, 'Before the cock crows you will have said three times that you do not know Me.'

He saw that even he had turned against Jesus because other people had turned against Him, and that he had done something that he knew Jesus would never do to him.

It hit him right in the middle of his heart and he went away and cried. He must have felt very ashamed. Yet afterwards he honestly told his friends he had done it, so that it would help others not to do the same.

When morning came the High Priest and his friends took Jesus to the Roman Governor because they had no power to order that anyone should be put to death. The Romans were the only people who could give the order, so they had to try and make the Governor believe that Jesus had broken the law.

They all arrived outside the House of the Governor, whose name was Pontius Pilate. They did not go in, because there was a Jewish rule about not going into a Roman building during the Feast time. It was supposed to make them unclean, and they liked the idea that they

were behaving correctly themselves even while they were handing over one of their fellow-countrymen to the Roman ruler, hoping He would be put to death.

Because of this Pilate came out to them and asked what was the matter.

They replied that Jesus was pretending to be a king, and wanted to turn the real king off the throne and disobey the Romans.

'Are you the King of the Jews?' Pilate asked Jesus.

'You say so,' replied Jesus.

'Do You hear what all these people say about You?' asked Pilate, but Jesus did not answer.

Herod sends Jesus back to Pilate

PONTIUS PILATE did not believe half the things the chief priests were saying. He was pretty certain they were only doing it because they were jealous. On the other hand he was not a brave man, and he did not want to get into trouble for deciding the wrong thing. However, after a while he came to the conclusion that Jesus had done nothing wrong and said so.

By this time the chief priests were beginning to be afraid he would let Jesus go, and said, 'But He is causing trouble all the way from here to Galilee.' As soon as Pilate heard the word Galilee, it gave him an idea. 'Is this man a Galilean?' he asked.

When they said He was, Pilate thought he saw a way out of having to make the decision.

Herod was the ruler of Galilee, and he happened to be in Jerusalem at that moment. So Pilate sent Jesus over to Herod hoping that he would decide. Herod was pleased when he heard he was going to see Jesus. He had heard a great deal about Him, and hoped that He would do some interesting miracles. However, when Jesus arrived, though Herod asked Him many questions, He said nothing.

All the chief priests and others had come too and were talking loudly about all the things Jesus was supposed to have done. Still Jesus said nothing.

Herod could not force Him to speak. So he did what mean and spiteful people often do. He tried to take it out of Jesus by hurting Him and making fun of Him.

He dressed Him up in a purple robe to make Him look like a king, and then laughed at Him and sent Him back to Pilate. But he decided nothing, nor did he say Jesus had done wrong. The only thing that happened was that Pilate and Herod, who had long been enemies, became friends.

Pilate now knew he would have to make up his own mind, and he was still afraid to do it.

His wife had sent a message to him warning him not to hurt Jesus because He was a good man.

So he called the people together again and said, 'You told me this man had been stirring up trouble, but I cannot find that He has done anything wrong, and neither can Herod. He has certainly done nothing to deserve being put to death. I will therefore have Him beaten and let Him go.'

Then Pilate brought Him out to the people and said, 'Here He is. I want you to know that I find no wrong in Him.'

By now the devil was really in charge of the priests. They had collected a crowd, and worked them up against Jesus.

When they saw Jesus they all shouted, 'Crucify Him, crucify Him.'

'Then you must do it yourselves,' said Pilate. 'I can find no fault in Him.'

Again everyone shouted, 'We have a law that says He ought to die because He says He is the Son of God.'

This frightened Pilate still more, and he went back to Jesus and said, 'Tell me, who are You? Where do You come from?'

But Jesus did not answer.

Pilate felt dreadful. He said, 'Why don't You answer? Don't You know that I have the power to crucify You, and I have the power to let You go?'

'You have no power over Me at all,' replied Jesus. 'You could have no power over Me now unless God was giving it.'

Pilate went back again to the people. He tried to think of a way out. It was the time of the Passover when it was the custom of the Governor to let one prisoner free, and there was in the prison a man called Barabbas, who had been arrested for murder, robbery and rebellion.

So Pilate said to the priests and all the people, 'Which prisoner would you like to have set free? You can have Jesus or Barabbas.'

The priests, however, were determined to get rid of Jesus, so they and all their friends shouted 'We want Barabbas.' They shouted so fiercely that Pilate gave in.

He made one more attempt to release Jesus, but they replied, 'If you let this man go you are not Caesar's friend. Anybody who says He is a king is no friend of Caesar's.'

That finished it for Pilate. If someone were to send in a report that he was against Caesar, he would lose his job.

He gave up. He felt there was nothing more he could do. He said to the priests and their friends, 'I am innocent of the blood of this good man. If you kill Him it is your fault, not mine.'

'We and our children accept that,' they replied.

Then he sent for a basin of water and washed his hands in front of everyone, meaning to say, 'If you shed the blood of Jesus it will not be on my hands.'

He felt after that he was not responsible.

There is still a saying today, 'I wash my hands of it,' and people sometimes use it without really thinking what it means and who was the first person to say it.

The Cross

PILATE had washed his hands, but he gave orders all the same that the Jews should have their way. He set Barabbas free, and ordered Jesus to be handed over to the Roman soldiers to be cruelly beaten and crucified.

The soldiers took Jesus, who was still wearing the purple robe, and because it was like a king's robe they wove a crown to go with it, made of thorns. They put it on His head and made mock of Him.

Then they took away the purple robe, and gave Jesus back His own clothes, and took Him away to nail Him on to the Cross.

This was the moment which Jesus knew must come, but He was ready for it. Though His enemies had decided to kill His body, they could not kill the real Him. They could only hurt Him.

They thought that if they killed Jesus it would be the end of Him. Really it was the beginning of something new.

It was the custom for those about to be crucified to carry their own crosses to the place where they were to die, but after all that He had gone through Jesus was not able to carry His. There was an African called Simon of Cyrene standing in the crowd, and the soldiers made him carry the Cross for Jesus. Two thieves were also taken out to be crucified with Him.

The Cross is like a big 'I' with a line drawn through it.

The big 'I' is all the 'I want' in our hearts. Jesus let this be crossed out in Him. He had chosen what God wanted.

What brought Him to the Cross was the sin or 'I want' in all the different people who wanted their own way more than God's. The men like Nicodemus who were afraid to come into the open, the people who wanted to be important, the ones who cheered when things went well and ran away when things got difficult, the ones who pretended to be good but were not.

In fact all the people who are just like us.

What Jesus did was somehow to let our sins kill Him so that they do not need to kill us.

As He went along the road with the soldiers, many men and women followed Him in tears, but Jesus said to them, 'Do not weep for Me but for yourselves and for your children.'

The people of Jerusalem had turned away from God's way, and He knew that nothing could go right for them after that.

Outside the city Jesus and the soldiers came to a little hill called Calvary, and there they nailed Him to the Cross. They drove nails through His hands and His feet, and they put the two thieves on crosses, one on either side of Him.

Through it all Jesus never stopped loving them.

When they had done Jesus said, 'Father, forgive them, for they do not know what they are doing.'

One of the thieves said to Him, 'If You are really the Son of God, why don't You save Yourself and us?'

But the other replied, 'You and I have both done wrong and are being punished for it. This man has done nothing wrong.' Then he said to Jesus, 'Please remember me when You come to Your Kingdom.'

Jesus said to him, 'I promise you that you shall be in Heaven with Me today.'

Then He saw His mother and His aunt standing at the foot of the Cross, and with them was Mary Magdalene who had put the ointment on His feet, and cried because she had done so much that was wrong.

His friend John was standing by His mother, and Jesus said to him, 'This is your mother now.' And to His mother He said, 'This is your son.' So from that moment John took her to his own home and looked after her.

After that Jesus was very heavy-hearted for a time.

He said aloud the words which begin what we know as the twenty-second Psalm. It starts with, 'My God, my God, why have you forsaken me', but further on it says, 'All the ends of the world shall remember and turn to the Lord'.

For three hours everything went dark, though it was the middle of the day.

At the end of that time He said to God, 'Please, Father, take My spirit now,' and God took the spirit of Jesus to be with Him.

116

After He had died one of the soldiers took a spear and thrust it into His side, and made another great wound there.

When the Roman captain, whose soldiers had put Jesus on the Cross, saw Him die he said, 'Truly this Man was the Son of God.' Something went through the hearts of all the people who were looking on, so that they went home deeply troubled.

*   *   *

In the evening His mother and His friends came and took the Body of Jesus down from the Cross.

A rich man called Joseph of Arimathea, who had followed Jesus secretly, went to Pilate and asked if he might bury Him in the tomb he had bought to have ready for himself. Even Nicodemus, who had also been afraid to stand openly for Jesus when He was alive, took courage. He came and helped the friends of Jesus to take His body down from the Cross and wrap it in clean linen.

They laid Him in the tomb, and after rolling a great stone across the front of it, went away, still not believing that they would see Him again.

Easter Morning

E ASTER shows us for certain that Jesus is stronger than sin. On that spring morning two days after the Crucifixion, some women went sorrowfully to the tomb. One of them was Mary Magdalene. They took with them some sweet-smelling spices to put with the Body of Jesus, which they thought they would find lying there. As they went they wondered how they were going to roll away the great stone which blocked the entrance to the tomb.

To their surprise, they found it was already rolled away and the tomb was empty. The Body of Jesus was gone, and they saw a shining angel who said to them, 'Do not be afraid. I know you are looking for Jesus. He is not here. He has risen from the dead, as He said He would. Come and see where He was lying, and then go quickly and tell His disciples. He has already gone ahead into Galilee.'

So the women ran back quickly to tell the men, who found it very difficult to believe.

Peter and John set off at once, running together, but John ran faster than Peter and arrived first. He stooped and looked inside and saw the linen cloths that had been wrapped round Jesus lying there. But he did not go in himself.

Peter came straight after him and went right in. He saw the cloths lying there too. The one which had been round Jesus' head was folded neatly and lying a little way from the others.

Then John went in too, and when he saw the empty tomb, his heart told him that Jesus was alive. So he and Peter went home.

By this time Mary Magdalene had come back and was standing just outside the tomb crying. As she cried she looked in and saw two angels sitting there, one at the head and the other at the foot of the place where Jesus had been lying.

'Why are you crying?' they asked her.

'Because they have taken away my Lord,' she said, 'and I don't know where they have put Him.' She turned away, and as she did so there was Jesus standing by her, but she did not see who it was.

He too said to her, 'Why are you crying? Who are you looking for?'

Thinking He was the gardener, Mary said, 'Oh, Sir, if you have taken Him please tell me where you have put Him and I will take Him away.'

Jesus said to her, 'Mary,' and she knew who He was.

'Master,' she cried joyfully, but He would not let her touch Him. 'I have not yet gone to My Father,' He said. 'Go and tell My brothers that I am soon going to My Father and your Father, to My God and your God.'

At this Mary ran quickly to the disciples, and told them how she had seen Him and what He had said to her.

The other women who had gone to give the angel's message to the disciples, also met Jesus. He stood before them in the path and said, 'Peace be with you.'

Then He said, 'Do not be afraid. Tell My brothers to go to Galilee and they shall see Me there.'

Meanwhile the terrified sentries had run away into the city and told what had happened to the chief priests who realised that their plan had gone wrong. So they and the other Jewish leaders met to decide what to do. It made things dangerous for them if Jesus was really still alive. After talking it over among themselves they called the soldiers and gave them a large sum of money.

They said to them, 'This is the story you must tell. You must say that the disciples of Jesus came after dark and stole Him away while you were asleep. If this story reaches the Governor, and you get into trouble for being asleep, we will put it right with him, and see that you are not punished.'

The soldiers took the money and did what they were told. The story was spread about and some people still believe it.

But Jesus was alive all the time.

Jesus is Alive

THAT same evening two of Jesus' friends started off to walk to a village called Emmaus, about seven miles from Jerusalem. One of them may have been Jesus' uncle by marriage. He was a man called Cleophas, whose wife had stood by the Cross with the mother of Jesus.

As they walked they talked earnestly about all that had happened, so much so that Jesus came up and joined them without their noticing. Something at first stopped them from recognising Him.

Then He spoke to them.

'What are you talking about?' He asked them. 'And why are you so sad?'

'Are you a stranger,' said Cleophas, 'that you do not know all the things that have been happening here?'

'What things?' asked Jesus.

'About Jesus of Nazareth,' they replied. 'He was a great prophet. Have you not heard how our chief priests and rulers had Him crucified? We had been hoping that He was the One who was going to come and set us free.

'Yes,' they said, 'and what is more it is now three days since all this happened, and some of the women have given us a great shock. They went out very early to the tomb and came back saying that they could not find His Body, but that they had seen some angels who told them He was still alive. So we went straight off to the tomb ourselves, and found it was empty as the women had said. Of Him we saw nothing.'

Then Jesus spoke to them and said, 'O fools, how slow you are to believe all that the prophets have said? Should you not have expected Christ to suffer all these things and so to enter into His glory?'

And He began to tell them everything that Moses and the prophets had said about Him down the years.

They had nearly reached the village of Emmaus by this time, and

121

Jesus seemed to be thinking of going further, but they said to Him, 'Do stay with us. It is evening and the day will soon be over.'

So He went indoors with them and they all sat down together round the table for supper, but they still had not recognised Him.

When they had taken their places Jesus took the bread and blessed it. He broke it and passed it round. It was what they had seen Him do before. Quite suddenly they knew who He was, but even as they looked at Him and recognised Him, He vanished from their sight.

Deep in his heart each one had felt something stirring all the time that Jesus had been talking to them, and when He had gone they turned to each other and said, 'Didn't you feel it?' Neither of them had really dared to let himself believe it.

They did not wait a moment, but went back to Jerusalem as fast as they could go. They rushed in to the remaining disciples to tell them the news, only to find that Jesus had already been there too.

'The Lord is really alive,' said the eleven. 'Peter has seen Him now.'

That same evening they all met together. The doors were locked for fear of the Jews, but suddenly Jesus stood among them once more.

Only three nights before they had had supper with Him feeling that terrible things lay ahead, though they did not quite know what. All they could understand was that He was going away, and they thought that they would never see Him again.

Now that was all behind them, and Jesus was back with them again. He came and stood in the midst of them and said, 'Peace be with you. It is I. Don't be afraid.'

But afraid they were, thinking that they were seeing a ghost, so He showed them the marks the nails had made in His hands, saying, 'Why are you so troubled? See My hands and My feet. Touch Me and see. A ghost does not have flesh and bones as you can see that I have.' Then a great joy came into their hearts when they saw it was the Jesus they knew so well.

While some of them were still half doubting and half joyful, He said to them, 'Have you anything here to eat?' They had, and they gave Him some broiled fish and a honeycomb, which He took and ate with them.

Then He said, 'Just as My Father sent Me, so I am now going to send you,' and He breathed the Holy Spirit over them, and told them that they would have power to forgive people's sins, just as He Himself did.

This all happened on the very day on which Jesus had risen from the

dead, and though nearly all the disciples had gathered together, Thomas, for some reason, was not among them. The next time they met him they told him all about it and kept saying, 'We have seen the Lord.'

Thomas, however, was not a very believing person, and he was no different now from what he had always been. He said, 'Unless I see in His hands the mark of the nails, and the wound in His side, I will never believe.'

About a week later the disciples were once more together, and this time Thomas was with them. The doors were locked as before, but again Jesus came and stood in the midst of them and said, 'Peace be with you.'

He said to Thomas, 'Put your finger here. Look, here are My hands. Put your hand in the wound in My side. You must not doubt, but believe.'

At last Thomas was certain. He said, 'My Lord and my God.'

Jesus said to him, 'You believe because you have seen Me. Happy are the men who have never seen Me and yet believe.'

This is true of all of us today. We have not seen Jesus but we can trust what He says.

Breakfast with Jesus

SOON after this some of the disciples left Jerusalem and went home to Galilee where Jesus had said He would meet them.

Peter and Thomas, and a man called Nathaniel, were with James and John and two of the others, by the side of the Sea of Galilee. They were discouraged, and Peter had decided to go back to his old job. He said, 'I'm going fishing.'

'Very well,' said the others, 'we will go with you.' So they put out in the boat. It was evening, but though they fished all night they caught nothing. Just as the sun was coming up next morning Jesus came and stood by the side of the lake and called to them.

'Have you caught anything?' He asked. They could not see who He was and called back, 'No, we haven't.'

'Throw the net out on the right side of the boat,' said Jesus, 'and you will make a catch.' So they did, and when they tried to pull it in again they could not because it was so full of fish.

Something about this must have reminded them of the first time Jesus had helped them with their fishing, and John said to Peter, 'It's Jesus.'

As John said this, Peter, who still rushed into things ahead of everyone else, jumped into the water and swam to the shore. The others followed in the boat dragging the net after them. It was so heavy with fish that they were not strong enough to pull it into the boat.

When they landed Jesus had everything ready for them. A fire was burning on the beach and fish and bread were already cooking on it.

Jesus said to them, 'Bring Me some of the fish you have just caught.' And Peter pulled the net towards the shore. It had a hundred and fifty-three great fish in it, and though there were so many the net never broke.

'Come and have your breakfast,' Jesus said to them. All this time none of them dared ask Him who He was, even though they knew perfectly well, but they sat down with Him. Jesus took the bread and gave it to them, and gave them all fish as well.

When they had finished He said to Peter, 'Simon (which was his other name), do you love Me more than these?'

Peter was quite certain.

'Yes, Lord,' he replied. 'You know I love You.'

'Then feed My lambs,' said Jesus.

Jesus said again to Peter, 'Simon, do you love Me?'

Peter again replied, 'Yes, Lord, You know I love You.'

Jesus said, 'Then feed my sheep.'

Then Jesus asked him a third time, 'Simon, do you love Me?'

This hurt Peter's feelings. He could not think why Jesus kept on asking him the same question, and he said, 'Lord, You know everything. You must know that I love You.'

Peter had always had a way of saying things without thinking and this was a question he really did need to think out. He needed to know what loving Jesus actually meant. So Jesus said to him once more, 'Then feed my sheep.'

Peter felt sure that he loved Jesus, but the question was, did he love

Him enough to do all that Jesus had done for people? Was he ready to go through all that Jesus had gone through because of His care for people?

It was no good Peter just having a feeling that he loved Jesus. This was going to take more than feelings.

Jesus tried to show him something of what it was going to mean.

'When you were a young man,' He said, 'you dressed yourself and went where you liked. But when you are old you will stretch out your arms and others will dress you and take you where you don't want to go.'

This He said as a sign that in the end Peter would die in the same way as He Himself had died.

Peter thought about this for a moment, then he turned round and saw John.

'Yes,' he said, 'but what about him?'

'What is that to do with you?' said Jesus. 'You follow Me.'

The Friends of Jesus

THERE were so many things that Jesus said and did, that, as one of His friends said, if they were all written down, it would fill so many books there would not be room in the whole world for them.

Perhaps that is just as well. Enough is written down to make us want to know more, and the rest we have to get from Jesus speaking to us in our hearts today, as well as reading the stories of long ago.

Yet though all these stories happened hundreds of years ago, the people in them were just as we are today. They were jealous and fearful and greedy and untruthful, but all the ones who really wanted to find the way that Jesus came to show did find it. As people became different they saw life from a new angle, and things began to change around them.

These men and women became the new kind of people about whom Jesus had so often spoken. They put their lives, their homes, their jobs and their money into starting to build a new world.

When Jesus was with them as a Person He helped them and showed them how to start. After He died and came to life again, He spent another six weeks seeing many of them, but He told them that this would only be for a short time. He also told them that when He did go back to God He would send them a Helper, for it would not otherwise be possible for anyone to live as He had shown them. Jesus told His friends to go back to Jerusalem and wait for this Helper to come. Then God took Him up to Heaven before their eyes.

The next part of the story will tell how the Helper or the Holy Spirit came to a group of men and women who were ready for Him. Ever since then He has guided everyone who really wants to find what Jesus calls the Way, and they through Him have changed the course of history.

Today we stand at the point of decision. Dark clouds hang over the world, but we can still save our nations and the world if we are prepared to go the way that Jesus went and sacrifice our selfishness for their sake.

God has raised up people in every generation to fight the battle against greed and impurity, and we who decide to enlist are the next in line to take our place under Him in the eternal struggle of light against darkness.

Jesus made it clear that there can be no agreement between light and darkness—good and evil. He did not talk only about love and peace, but also about the people who are like vipers, ravening wolves and whitened sepulchres. He said there was no hope for them as they were. He said they would have to change in every way, and He was crucified by all those who chose impurity, dishonesty or power instead of Him.

When I was young I had no faith and nothing to give my life for, until I met people who showed me how to choose.

As I chose to reach towards honesty, purity, unselfishness and love in my own life, Jesus became real to me, as He can become real to everyone.

Anyone who lives these standards can give them to their country. Nowadays a big idea which you give your life for is called an ideology. In the tremendous struggle between good and evil that is going on in the world, no one is strong enough to fight on the right side without these absolute standards.

With them we can be fighters for a free world, and make our nations strong, or morally rearmed. In this way we can give our lives, however young we are, to bringing about 'the greatest revolution of all time whereby the Cross of Christ will transform the world'.

I am the way,
the truth and the life.